exploring

PHOTOSHOP CS

exploring

PHOTOSHOP CS

Annesa Hartman

THOMSON
★
DELMAR LEARNING™   Australia Canada Mexico Singapore Spain United Kingdom United States

THOMSON
DELMAR LEARNING

Exploring Photoshop CS

Annesa Hartman

Vice President, Technology and Trades, BSU
Alar Elken

Editorial Director
Sandy Clark

Senior Acquisitions Editor
James Gish

Development Editor
Jaimie Wetzel

Marketing Director
Dave Garza

Channel Manager
William Lawrensen

Marketing Coordinator
Mark Pierro

Production Director
Mary Ellen Black

Production Manager
Larry Main

Production Editor
Dawn Jacobson

Art/Design
Thomas Stover

Technology Project Manager
Kevin Smith

Editorial Assistant
Marissa Maiella

Cover Design
Steven Brower

Cover Image
Rooms, Oil on Canvas
© David Arsenault, courtesy
John I. Mickelbank

ISBN: 1-4018-4358-1

NOTICE TO THE READER

FOR MY MOTHER, CAROLYN

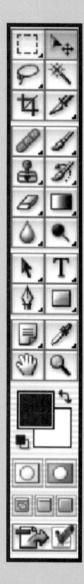

contents

CONTENTS

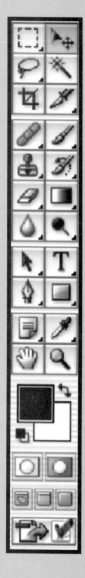

| preface |

preface

"The universe is full of magical things, patiently waiting for our wits to grow sharper."

Eden Phillpotts

INTENDED AUDIENCE

Quick, grab a seat. The show is about to begin, and it is full of a wonderfully mischievous cast of characters you don't want to miss. They call them "pixels," magical spirits brought to life by digital mayhem and transported by light. They are the muses of the digital artist, the star performers on the Photoshop stage, and the lead actors in this book, *Exploring Photoshop CS*.

Whether a new student to computer graphics, a computer arts educator, a professional visualizer, animator, designer, illustrator, photographer, or just plain curious dabbler, *Exploring Photoshop CS* has something for you. It offers a practical and straightforward introduction to the essentials of digital image creation, compositing, and photo retouching; comprehensive step-by-step lessons; easy reference to commonly used tools and features of the Photoshop program in general, and in this current version; and plenty of encouragement for artistic exploration.

EMERGING TRENDS

We have become a visually oriented society. Digital imagery is everywhere and impacts us in the smallest and greatest of ways. It's on the minute screens that await us at the gas pump, the ATM console at the grocery store, in the dashboard of a car, and on the back of an airline seat. Beckoning to us in wide-screen and billboard formats, it glows and moves, it informs and entices. And somewhere, somehow, and by somebody these digital images are conceptualized, designed, and developed.

Today's graphic designer clearly realizes that the world and its visual appetite are no longer flat. Digital imagery is going spatial, 3D, procedural, and participatory. And, to meet this trend the graphic artist must be capable of a continual shift of perspective, from the detail-oriented to the big-picture viewpoint.

When asking my designer friends what they saw in the crystal ball of digital imagery, it only confirmed the spatial path in which the graphic artist finds himself. With processor speeds and bandwidth improving, 3D, online environments, and virtual reality simulations will become a norm. Visuals will continue to be designed to fit on our traveling screens—the PDAs, cell phones, and in-dash car displays. Information will become more iconographic for Bluetooth and other multi-device connectivity systems. And more often, as seen now in classrooms and corporate boardrooms, imagery will be dynamically drawn and projected on digitally smart projection screens.

The capabilities of digital imaging have been vast and continue in this direction. Instead of "flat," however, think dimensional, meaning that visuals can become and be translated into modes once beyond our comprehension.

BACKGROUND OF THIS TEXT

"Any sufficiently advanced technology is indistinguishable from magic," expresses Arthur C. Clarke, author of *2001: A Space Odyssey* (1968) and astrophysicist. Aptly, Photoshop is an example of such a technology. For Photoshop, or any other currently used computer graphics software program for that matter, it is not uncommon to describe what it can do and how it is embraced by the user as anything but amazing, magical. Without lessening the impact Photoshop has made in the graphics and photographic industries, and the continual advancements occurring with each new version, this book is intended to demystify what ostensibly seems complicated but is really quite engaging and accessible. After all, as automated as the program can appear, it is still a product of the mortal mindset, which we can assume understands some method to the madness.

As is my book *Exploring Illustrator CS*, and in purpose all the books in Delmar Learning's Design Exploration series, the objective of this text is to be clear and no-nonsense in approach, never negating the practical, yet vastly experiential, aspects of the program. You could say it's the "Penn and Teller" of instruction. Yes, for the outside viewer it appears all magic (and we want to keep it that way!), but for the magician it really is just practiced tricks that can be easily explained and enacted.

TEXTBOOK ORGANIZATION

As you learn in the first chapter, Photoshop is a "must-know" program for the graphic artist, with the ability to retouch, blend, composite, layer, and add effects to photos and digital imagery, draw and paint, and save in different image formats for different purposes, such as for use on the Web, for print, or in other programs.

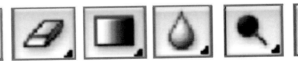

The way in which this book has been conceptualized and organized derives from the following intentions:

● Explore the questions that face today's Photoshop artist and provide some educated answers through the use of Adobe Photoshop's digital tools and features

● Offer process-oriented lessons developed from actual implementation in the classroom and production firms

● Develop an understanding of core concepts related to digital artwork and image creation through fundamental design principles and methods

● And, most importantly, open the door for continued, self-guided discovery

The textbook contains common features found in each of the Design Exploration books, but specifically I've presented this material so that each chapter builds upon itself, and the material is presented in a "need-to-know" basis. This eliminates the amount of information the reader must know to successfully complete a task. Each chapter also accommodates those who appreciate alternative methods of learning information, providing both textually and visually succinct explanations of important concepts, step-by-step experiences, or for those who prefer to wander around, final project files, samples, and a section for further exploration. The following is a brief rundown of what is learned in each chapter.

Chapter 1: A Discovery Tour

Right away, retouch a photo in Photoshop and discover the purpose of the Photoshop program.

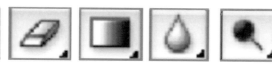

Chapter 2: The Staging Area

Take center stage and explore the workspace and navigational features of the program.

Chapter 3: Image Essentials

Get the "know-how" on bitmap and vector graphics, bit depth, resolution, and image formats.

Chapter 4: Selecting and Transforming

Using Photoshop's varied selection tools, and transform commands, you get up close and personal with selecting and transforming image pixels, the most fundamental of procedures in the Photoshop program.

Chapter 5: Working with Color

Uncover some fundamental concepts of color, such as how color is reproduced, color modes, and a hands-on study with color models. Additionally, get into some important aspects of color specifically related to Photoshop, such as tips for managing color in the program, channels, and using the color application tools.

Chapter 6: Image Correction

Presents fundamental techniques in the image-correction process, taking you step by step in adjusting tonal levels, retouching, and adding effects.

Chapter 7: Drawing and Painting

Get a thorough introduction to the drawing and painting tools and options in the program, advancing your creative possibilities to a whole new level.

Chapter 8: Masking

Practice techniques for hiding and revealing areas of an image while preserving the image's integrity. Includes practice with layer and vector masks, type masks, clipping masks, and quick masks.

Chapter 9: Compositing and the Design Process

Uncover the process and methods by which to composite, link, blend, merge, and organize graphical elements into more complex images or graphic layouts.

Chapter 10: Print Publishing

Learn about the different print processes and what it takes to prepare your digital images for print.

Chapter 11: Web Publishing

Get a quick tour of ImageReady. Learn about image optimization and what it takes to prepare your digital images for the Web.

FEATURES

The following list provides some of the salient features of the text:

- Learning goals are clearly stated at the beginning of each chapter.

- Written to meet the needs of design students and professionals for a visually oriented introduction to image composition and the functions and tools of Photoshop.

- Client projects involve tools and techniques a designer might encounter on the job to complete a project.

- Full-color insert provides photographic and artistic image examples achieved using Photoshop.

- "Exploring on Your Own" sections offer suggestions and sample lessons for further study of content covered in each chapter.

- "In Review" sections are provided at the end of each chapter to quiz a reader's understanding and retention of the material covered.

- A CD-ROM at the back of the book contains the support files to complete the book's exercises.

HOW TO USE THIS TEXT

The features discussed in the following sections are found in the book.

↗ Charting Your Course and Goals

The introduction and chapter objectives start off each chapter. They describe the competencies the reader should achieve upon understanding the chapter.

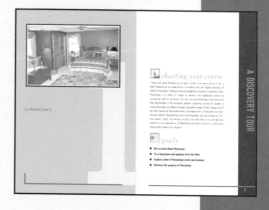

↗ Don't Go There

These boxes highlight common pitfalls and explain ways to avoid them.

! DON'T GO THERE — In the prior process, you will note that I had you create two swatches of the same color with varying alphas. This was purposeful. If you blend two different colors with two different alphas some pretty strange things can happen. Typically you end up with some haloing effects—where there are hints of one or the other color in the transparency. To avoid haloing, anytime you are creating a gradient that gradates Alpha, use the exact same RGB values in the two chips.

↗ In Review and Exploring on Your Own

Review questions are located at the end of each chapter and allow the reader to assess his or her understanding of the chapter. The section "Exploring on Your Own" contains exercises that reinforce chapter material through practical application.

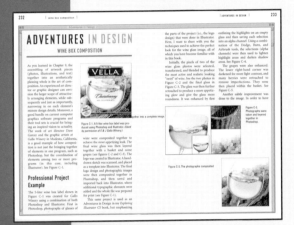

Adventures in Design

These spreads contain client assignments showing readers how to approach a design project using the tools and design concepts taught in the book.

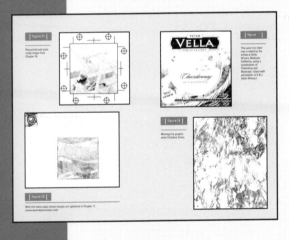

Color Insert

The color insert demonstrates work that can be achieved when working with Adobe Photoshop.

E.RESOURCE

This guide was developed to assist instructors in planning and implementing their instructional programs. It includes sample syllabi for using this book in either an 11- or 15-week semester. It also provides answers to the "In Review" questions, Powerpoint slides highlighting the main topics, and additional instructor resources. ISBN: 140184359X.

FILE SETUP

Located in the back of this book is a CD-ROM containing all files for completing the lessons in this book. These lesson files are compatible with Photoshop CS. For a trial version of Photoshop CS, visit *www.adobe.com/products/tryadobe.*

Before starting any of the lessons, create a folder on your local computer named My Lessons (or whatever name you prefer). From the CD, drag a copy of the lesson files to the folder. As you work on the lessons, open the lessons, assets, and sample files from this location. You can then also save your work in the same place.

ABOUT THE AUTHOR

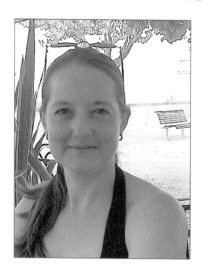

Annesa Hartman holds a Masters in Teaching with Internet Technologies, focusing her attention on instructional design for online technologies, web and graphic design concepts and programs. She is the Manager of Technology Learning Services at Landmark College, in Vermont, where she coordinates and instructs technology teaching and learning programs for the college's faculty, staff, and students. She also teaches computer graphic courses online, and is the author of two previous books, *Exploring Illustrator CS* and *Producing Interactive Television.* When she is not pushing pixels she is digging dirt in her garden or taking and teaching yoga and dance classes.

Formerly, Annesa was the director and Softimage instructor for Mesmer Animation Labs in Seattle, Washington (1994-1998) and was cofounder and consultant for Sway Design in New York City (2000-2002). Specializing in graphic art production, corporate training, online learning, and curriculum development, Annesa has spoken at many conferences and has developed and taught unique training programs for Accenture, Morgan Stanley Dean Witter, AOL/Moviefone, St. John's University (Queens, NY), Universidade Lusofona de Humanidades e Tecnologias (Lisbon, Portugal), and Macromedia. Annesa is a certified Photoshop instructor and was the subject matter expert and curriculum designer for Macromedia's "Design Techniques with Flash" course.

ACKNOWLEDGMENTS

It seems a dream that this book is finally finished. And not unlike any momentous task, it just wouldn't have happened without the help of my friends, colleagues, and students. Many, many thanks to all those who contributed content for the book's lessons, visual examples and Adventures in Design, including Max, Suzanne, and Mike Ruse, Geoff Burgess, Karen Kamenetzky, Bruce and Linda Lord, Terry Hartman, Joel Hagen, Christina Cross, Joe Summer-hays, Dave Garcez, Fred Smith, Gary Griest, Jeff Broome, Jeffrey Moring, Mike Hagelsieb, Wai Har Lee, Brian Sinclair, and Zolton Baize. Special thanks also goes to the ITS staff at Landmark College and to Terry and Charmaine for keeping my spirits up during the depths of the writing process. Much love as well to Peter Duggan, who willingly sacrificed his dance lessons to give me plenty of neck and shoulder rubs.

For their patient persistence (if there is such a thing), I also thank the staff at Delmar Learning. What a comfort to know that you are out there in full force promoting the Delmar Learning Design Exploration Series and making this experience worthwhile. Last, I would like to send a warm thank-you to my mother, Carolyn Murov, whose photographic talent supplied many of the images found in the pages of this book.

Delmar Learning and the author would also like to thank the following reviewer for his valuable suggestions and technical expertise:

JON MCFARLAND
Graphic Design and CAD Departments
Virginia Marti College of Art and Design
Lakewood, Ohio

QUESTIONS AND FEEDBACK

Thomson/Delmar Learning and the author welcome your questions and feedback. If you have suggestions you think others would benefit from, please let us know and we will try to include them in the next edition.

To send us your questions and/or feedback, you can contact the publisher at:

Thomson Delmar Learning
Executive Woods
5 Maxwell Drive
Clifton Park, NY 12065
Attn: Graphic Arts Team
800-998-7498

Or Annesa Hartman at:

Landmark College
Manager of Technology Learning Services
P.O. Box 820
River Road South
Putney, VT 05346
ahartman@landmark.edu

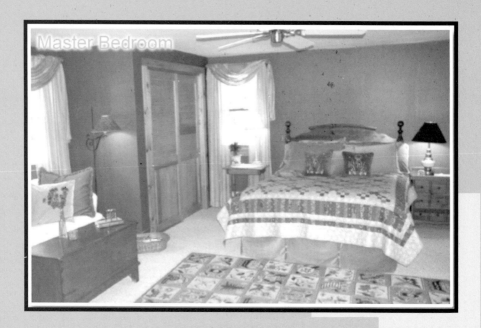
Master Bedroom

| a discovery tour |

charting your course

I hope you have brushed up on your "ta-da"s, because you're in for a Harry Houdini of an experience—a venture into the digital wizardry of Adobe Photoshop. If there's only one program to know as a graphic artist, Photoshop is it. And, if I begin to sound a bit highfalutin about its prospects, well, it's because I am. You can say Photoshop is the pinnacle (the Big Daddy) of all computer graphic programs, proven to handle in numerous ways just about any type of graphic image. In this chapter you'll get your hands-on Photoshop itself, and experience a first taste of its illusionary talents. Depending on your learning style, you can choose to "do" the lesson, "read" the lesson, or both. The trick here is to just get you started on the experience of Photoshop and then show you a little more about what makes it so magical.

 goals

- **Get excited about Photoshop**
- **Fix a bad photo and optimize it for the Web**
- **Explore some of Photoshop's tools and features**
- **Discover the purpose of Photoshop**

A MAGIC TOUR

No matter what kind of multimedia project you might be up against, Photoshop more often than not is going to play a pivotal role in the creation process. It will come to your rescue when the lighting for those wedding pictures was less than perfect, to remove the unwanted blemish on the bride's cheek, or superimpose the indisposed from the family portrait. Take for instance the photograph shown on the left in Figure 1-1, which was taken by a point-and-shoot camera, the film digitized on a CD, and then, much later, handed to me to put up on the Web. To tell you the truth, the photo quality was dreadful. However, with my bag full of tricks (Photoshop), a wave of my magic wand (a computer mouse), and $50 added to my client's invoice, I produced what looked much more like the real thing—a room in a fine country inn, not a room in a rundown shack. Okay, so maybe the differences in the two photos are not that extreme, but my point is that with a little magic, and about 15 minutes of your time, you can make a "ho-hum" image look "oh-wow," and download fast from the Web.

figure | 1-1 |

On the left is the original photo of a room in a country inn, and on the right is a 15-minute makeover version using Photoshop.

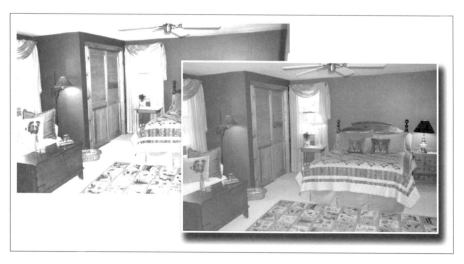

Lesson: The 15-Minute Photo Makeover

It is said that a magician never reveals her tricks, until now. In this lesson you'll learn how I fixed up the country inn photo (see Figure 1-1) and made it web ready. We won't get into too many specifics about the program just yet—there's plenty of that to come. However, you'll learn enough secrets to get the idea that Photoshop is not just hocus pocus.

Importing and Cropping the Photo

1. Open the Photoshop program. (A trial version is available for download at *www.adobe.com/products/tryadobe*. Install the program onto your hard drive.

2. Choose File > Open from the main menu, and on your local hard drive browse for the Exploring PhotoshopCS *lessons/ chap1_lessons/assets* folder. Open the file *masterbed.tif*.

   NOTE: As mentioned in the Preface, in order to save your work you must make a copy of the chapter lessons to your local hard drive, and select files from that location.

3. Press Shift-Tab on the keyboard to hide unnecessary window palettes (at least for the time being). Visible should be your imported image of *masterbed.tif*, the toolbox to the left of the interface, and the tool options bar and main menu located at the top. See Figure 1-2.

4. From the main menu at the top, choose View > Fit on Screen to enlarge the photo to your computer screen size.

5. Select Photoshop > Preferences > Units & Rulers (Mac), or Edit > Preferences > Units & Rulers (Windows), from the main menu.

figure | 1-2 |

The Photoshop interface (Mac).

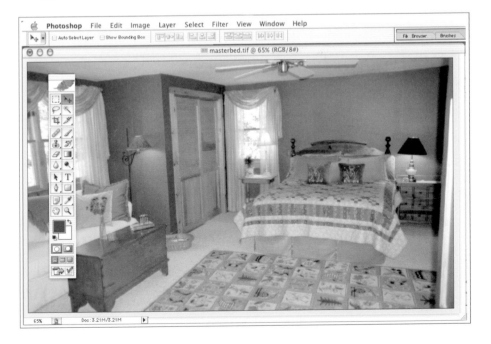

6. In the Preferences dialog box, set the Rulers units to "pixels" and click OK. See Figure 1-3.

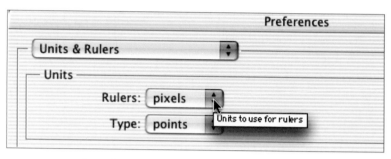

figure | 1-3

Setting the Ruler units to pixels.

7. Select the Crop tool in the toolbox. See Figure 1-4. With the Crop tool you can extract unnecessary or unflattering parts from an image.

8. In the tool's options bar type in the following parameters for the Crop tool (see Figure 1-5):

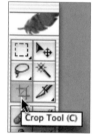

figure | 1-4

Selecting the Crop tool in the toolbox.

● *Width:* 550 pixels

● *Height:* 350 pixels

● *Resolution:* 72 pixels/inch

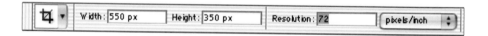

figure | 1-5

Entering parameters for the Crop tool in the options bar.

9. From the upper left corner of the image, click and drag down with the Crop tool to the lower right corner of the image. All of the image should be selected except for an unwanted section along the right edge of the image. See Figure 1-6.

10. Click once again on the Crop tool icon in the toolbox to bring up the Crop dialog box. See Figure 1-7. Select the Crop option to execute the crop. (Alternatively, you can double click on the image to execute the crop.)

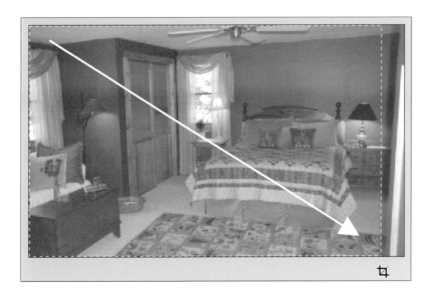

figure | 1-6 |

Cropping the image.

NOTE: Argh! What if you make a mistake? From the main menu select Window > History to open the History palette, if not already opened. Each step you perform in Photoshop is recorded in the History palette (up to 20 states by default). To go back a step, click on the state above the step you just made. For instance, from the Crop state click up to the Open state to revert the file. See Figure 1-8. You can also press Ctrl-Z (Windows) or Command-Z (Mac) to quickly undo the last step you performed.

11. Choose View > Actual Pixels to see the final cropped image.

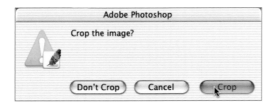

figure | 1-7 |

Executing the crop action.

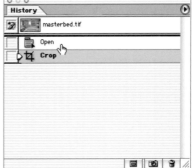

figure | 1-8 |

The History palette—a life saver!

12. Now, choose File > Save As. Make sure you are set to save in your *lessons* folder when the Save menu pops up. For Format choose Photoshop (top of the list). Your file name should read *masterbed.psd* (the native file format for Photoshop).

Fixing the Color

1. With some disgust, you've probably already noticed that the color of this image is not quite right—it's too red! Let's fix this in one easy step: choose Image > Adjustments > Auto Color. Ta-da!

2. Now, let's lighten the image a bit. Choose Image > Adjustments > Levels. The Levels histogram comes up. This determines the lights and darks (brightness and contrast) in an image. You'll learn more about levels in later chapters. Right now, just move the white arrow (the one on the right, lower side of the graph) in until you get 200 in the Input Levels box. Hit OK. See Figure 1-9.

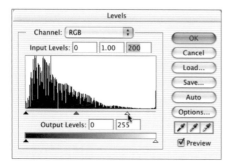

figure | 1-9 |

Adjusting the photograph's brightness and contrast using Levels.

NOTE: You may have noticed the Brightness/Contrast choice found under Image > Adjustments. I chose not to use this, as Levels gives me more control over my image.

Creating a Shadow and Border Effect

1. If not already open, choose Window > Layers to open the Layers palette. Layers organize information in Photoshop. Right now we only have one layer, which is our photo.

2. In the Layers palette, double click on the Background layer that contains the photo. The New Layer dialog box comes up. Type in the name *master bedroom* and hit OK. (This renames the Background layer and unlocks it for editing).

3. From the main menu, choose Image > Canvas Size. For Width, type in *590* (pixels), and for Height type in *390* (pixels). Select OK. This will increase each side of the canvas by 40 pixels. Hit OK. See Figure 1-10.

4. From the main menu choose Layer > Layer Style > Drop Shadow. Be sure Preview is selected, so that you can view the changes you make in the dialog box directly on the document. Enter the following parameters (see Figure 1-11):

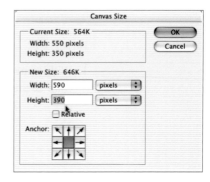

- *Angle:* 120 degrees

- *Distance:* 10 pixels

- *Spread:* 20 percent

- *Size:* 10 pixels

figure | 1-10

increase the canvas size.

5. Select OK.

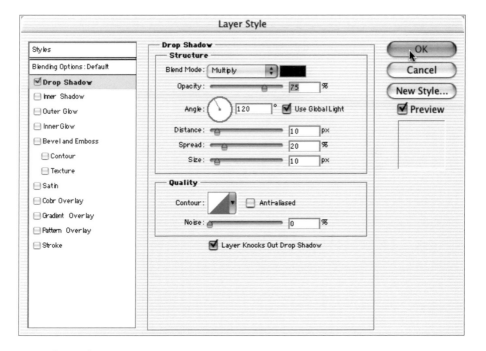

figure | 1-11

Create a drop shadow.

NOTE: In the Layers palette notice the small "f" icon next to the layer name. This indicates that there are effects (i.e., the drop shadow) on the image. To edit the effects simply double click on the "f" icon to open the Layer Style dialog box.

6. Now, let's select just the photo object, which can be a bit tricky. In the Layers palette, place the cursor over the layer name *(master bedroom)*. A pointer hand icon will appear. Choose Command (Mac) or Ctrl (Windows) on the keyboard and click down on the layer. The photo (the object in the selected layer) will be selected in the document. This is indicated by a series of moving dashed lines around the edge of the photo, also affectionately known as "marching ants." See Figure 1-12.

figure | 1-12

Marching ants indicate a selected area.

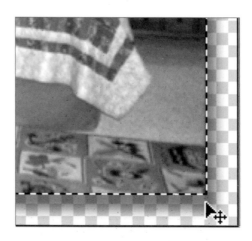

7. From the main menu, choose Edit > Stroke, and enter in the following parameters:

   ● *Width:* 4 pixels

   ● *Color:* Click on the color box to open the Color Picker and choose white

   ● *Location:* Center

8. Select OK.

9. Choose Select > Deselect to view the white border you just created around the photo.

10. Save your file.

NOTE: If you receive a Maximum Compatibility Photoshop Format option, keep the option selected to ensure compatibility of this file with future versions of Photoshop.

Creating a Title Effect

1. Select the Horizontal Type tool in the tool-box. See Figure 1-13.

2. In the options bar set the font type to Arial or Verdana, depending on what you have available on your computer. Set the font size to 24 points.

   For color, click the color box in the options toolbar (see Figure 1-14) to open the Color Picker.

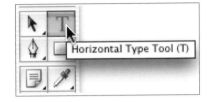

figure | 1-13

The Horizontal Type tool.

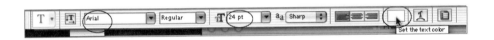

figure | 1-14

Change the font and font size, and set the text color.

3. Move the Color Picker dialog box to the right side of the screen so that you can see your image. With the Color Picker open, notice that your cursor changes to an eye-dropper when you move it over the photo area. See Figure 1-15.

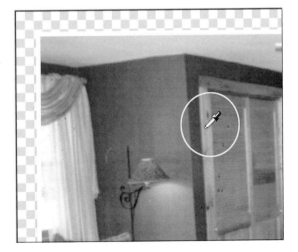

figure | 1-15

The Eyedropper tool takes a sampling of color from the photograph.

4. Move the Eyedropper tool over a light brown area of the closet door in the photo and click to take a sample of the color (see Figure 1-15). The color is recorded in the Color Picker. Select OK to close the Color Picker.

5. With the Horizontal Type tool, click in the upper left corner of the document. A blinking cursor will appear. Type in the words *Master Bedroom.*

6. Choose Layer > Layer Style > Outer Glow. Leave the default setting for the outer glow (unless you want to play on your own!) and hit OK. See Figure 1-16.

7. Select the Move tool in the toolbox (see Figure 1-17). Place the Move tool over the text and position it to your liking on the photograph.

8. Save your file. You're almost there.

figure | 1-16

The final, glowing title.

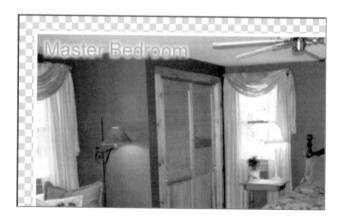

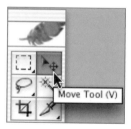

figure | 1-17

The Move tool.

Optimizing the Image for the Web

1. Okay, last detail. Let's prepare this photograph so that it can be used on the Web. We need to do two things: make it smaller in file size (compress it!), so that it will download quickly for those of us with slow Internet connections, and save it in the JPEG format, which is a file format the Web knows (you'll learn more about that in Chapter 11). For now, choose File > Save for Web.

2. The document opens up in a new window. Select the 2-Up option (see Figure 1-18). On the left side is your original image. On the right is the one you will compress for the Web. By having them side by side you can compare the quality of the web image with the original as you adjust the compression settings.

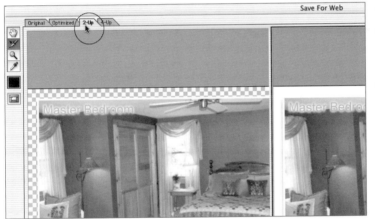

figure | 1-18

Select the 2-Up option in the Save For Web window.

3. In the Optimize panel, set the image quality to JPEG Low, found next to the word *Preset* (see Figure 1-19). Note how the quality of the image on the right deteriorates compared to the image on the left. Look closely at the title text in particular.

NOTE: If you are having difficulty seeing parts of an image, use the Hand tool found on the left side of the window to navigate the image view right, left, up, or down.

4. Now, set the quality to JPEG High. Much better. I know you are wondering why ever use the JPEG Low setting? Well, look at the box with numbers right below the two images. You will

note the lower the setting the smaller the number, allowing for a faster download (more to follow in Chapter 11).

5. Take a look at the estimated download time of the right-hand image at the bottom of the image's window. See Figure 1-20.

6. Click Save and save the *masterbed.jpg* file in your *lessons* folder. The image is now ready to be placed on a web page. See the completed image, shown in Figure 1-21.

7. Select File > Save to save the final Photoshop (*.psd*) file. You did it!

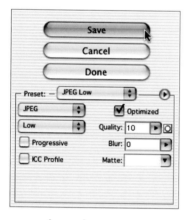

figure | 1-19

The Optimize panel properly prepares the image for web publication.

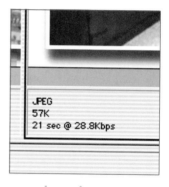

figure | 1-20

View the size and estimated download time of the web-formatted image.

figure | 1-21

The completed photograph—it's magic!

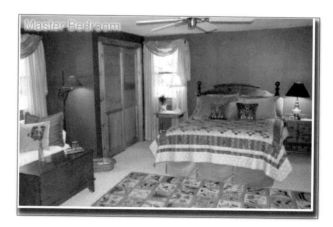

PHOTOSHOP—IN BRIEF

As you've probably surmised by its name, fixing up photos is the essence of what Photoshop can do; what it was originally intended to do, since its miraculous beginning in 1990 when Adobe first licensed the product. Now Photoshop and its immense toolset have grown to be a vital part of any magician's repertoire—something you'll begin to discover in the lessons of this book. No animator, illustrator, game developer, multimedia developer, or web designer could survive without the use of Photoshop in one form or another. It's got a way with working with one of the main ingredients of digital image construction—pixels. These are the tiny picture elements that when placed together in a grid make all the images we see on a computer screen. Chapter 3 gets into greater detail about pixels, among other important graphic essentials. For now, if I were to sum up what Photoshop does best in four simple bullet points, here's what you'd get:

- Manipulate photographs and other digital imagery to your heart's content, such as select, cut, paste, clone, colorize, compress, erase, transform, mask, and add special effects

- Composite, layer, and blend photographs and images

- Draw and paint

- Convert photographs and imagery into different formats for different purposes, such as use on the Web, to print, and to import into other programs

SUMMARY

Photoshop is the "must know" of all computer graphic software packages. For the successful graphic artist, it's as vital a prop as a deck of cards and a white rabbit to a magician. In this chapter you already discovered one of Photoshop's greatest and most used secrets: how it can fix a badly exposed photograph and make it web presentable. From here, there's only more magic to come.

in review

1. What does the keyboard command Shift-Tab do?

2. What's so great about the History palette?

3. In general, what are levels in Photoshop?

4. What are layers? How are they useful?

5. What are "marching ants"?

6. Name at least three uses for Photoshop.

↗ EXPLORING ON YOUR OWN

1. Visit the Photoshop area of the adobe site at: *www.adobe.com/ products/photoshop/main.html.*

2. The programmers of software packages such as Photoshop love to play tricks and hide fun, little surprises within the programs they create. These surprises are called "Easter eggs," and you can find them in Photoshop if you know where to look and what to do.

   Here's how to find the infamous magician Merlin. In Photoshop, go to Window > Layers (if not already open). Hold down Alt/Option on your keyboard, keep it held while you click on the small arrow in the upper right of the Layers window to open the layer options, and choose Palette Options in the drop-down menu. Merlin lives!

notes

_____
_____
_____
_____
_____
_____
_____
_____
_____
_____
_____
_____
_____
_____
_____
_____
_____
_____
_____
_____
_____
_____
_____
_____
_____
_____

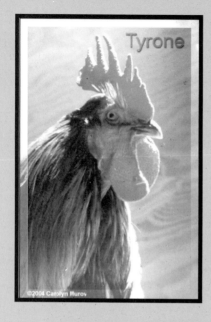
Tyrone

©2004 Carolyn Murov

| the staging area |

2

charting your course

If you were at a carnival, Chapter 1 would be the enticing gypsy beckoning you into the tent of digital enchantment. It was only a teaser, providing a small taste of what Photoshop has to offer. In this chapter you will pull back the curtain, step inside the tent, adjust your eyes to the darkness, and become a part of the performance rather than remaining a spectator. Here, you take center stage—where all the action happens—and explore the workspace and navigational features of the program.

 goals

● **Get comfortable with the Photoshop interface**

● **Set and delete preferences**

● **Navigate the workspace**

STAGING

Before producing your first Photoshop masterpiece, it helps to get acquainted with the program's interface, or work area, and set it up to your desired specifications. In theater, this process is called staging. First, you'll get familiar with such props as the document area, toolbox, options bar, palettes, and workspace. Then, you'll practice using the navigational tools of the program, avoiding any chance of getting lost among the bright lights of your virtual stage.

Lesson 1: Interface Highlights

Learn your way around in this lesson.

Identifying Props

1. Open the Photoshop program. Bypass the Welcome Screen (if one appears) and choose Close.

   NOTE: If a dialog box comes up asking if you would like to customize your color settings, choose No. See Figure 2-1.

figure | 2-1 |

Color Settings dialog box.

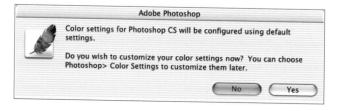

2. Choose File > New from main menu. Enter in the following information (see Figure 2-2):

   ● *Name,* type in: *myfile*

   ● *Preset Sizes,* choose: Default Photoshop Size

   ● *Color Mode,* choose: RGB Color, 8 bit

   ● *Background Contents,* choose: White

3. Depending on if you are a Macintosh or a Windows user, the Photoshop interface may look slightly different. The main props, however, are the same. Compare your open Photoshop interface with Figure 2-3, and note where the various parts of the program are located.

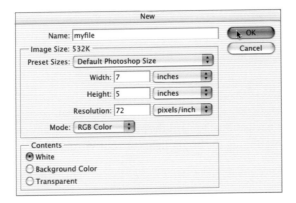

figure   2-2

New (document options) box.

figure   2-3

The Photoshop interface (Mac version).

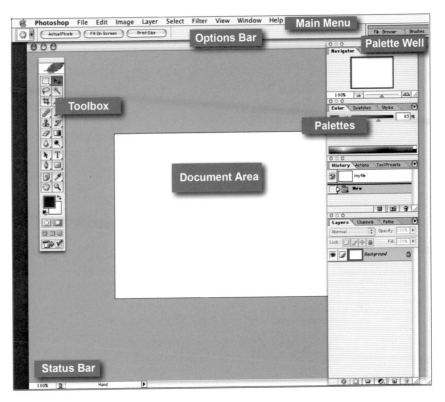

● *Document area:* When you created a new file in the step above you specified properties for a document area. This is the blank area in the center of the interface where you do all of your work (consider this your canvas or stage). At the top of the document area is a document title bar, which provides information about the document, such as its name, current magnification, color, and preview mode. It's not unlikely that you will have many document windows open at the same time, which is why it's good to look at the document title bars to know which is which. See Figure 2-4.

figure | 2-4 |
_____
The document title
bar shows specific
information about
an open document.

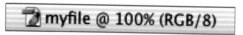

- *Main menu:* Along the top of the interface is the main menu, which contains all of the commands to perform certain tasks. The commands are categorized so that you can find them easily (so don't bother memorizing them all!). For example, if you want to open a palette window go to Window and a list of options will pop up. To make global adjustments to an image, go to Image. To edit stuff, go to Edit. You get the idea.

- *Toolbox:* Located by default to the left of the work area is the toolbox. This is where you choose the tools you need to select, edit, modify, and create your Photoshop masterpiece (see Figure 2-5). Tool icons with a black arrow in the corner contain hidden, related tools. With your cursor, click

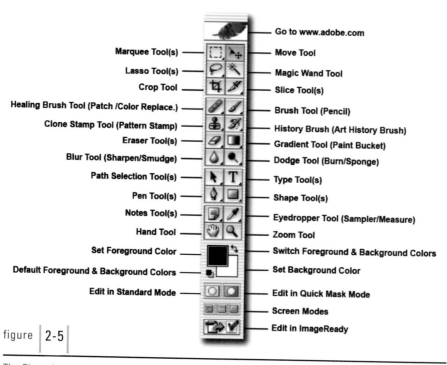

Go to www.adobe.com
Marquee Tool(s) — Move Tool
Lasso Tool(s) — Magic Wand Tool
Crop Tool — Slice Tool(s)
Healing Brush Tool (Patch /Color Replace.) — Brush Tool (Pencil)
Clone Stamp Tool (Pattern Stamp) — History Brush (Art History Brush)
Eraser Tool(s) — Gradient Tool (Paint Bucket)
Blur Tool (Sharpen/Smudge) — Dodge Tool (Burn/Sponge)
Path Selection Tool(s) — Type Tool(s)
Pen Tool(s) — Shape Tool(s)
Notes Tool(s) — Eyedropper Tool (Sampler/Measure)
Hand Tool — Zoom Tool
Set Foreground Color — Switch Foreground & Background Colors
Default Foreground & Background Colors — Set Background Color
Edit in Standard Mode — Edit in Quick Mask Mode
Screen Modes
Edit in ImageReady

figure | 2-5 |
_____
The Photoshop toolbox.

and hold down on a tool's icon to reveal the other tool choices (see Figure 2-6). You'll be using the toolbox a lot, so always keep it handy. You will learn about most of the tools in the next chapters of this book, but if you're the curious type and want to know what they do right now choose Help > Photoshop Help on the main menu. Select the section Looking at the Work Area, go to *Using the toolbox*, and review *Toolbox overview (1, 2, and 3)*.

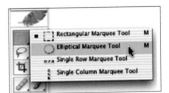

figure | 2-6

Reveal hidden tools in the toolbox.

- *Options bar:* Most of the tools selected in the toolbox have options. These are displayed in the options bar, located at the top of the work area, below the main menu. The options bar is context sensitive, which means that it displays different information depending on what tool is selected. Try it out: select some tools in the toolbox and watch the content change in the options bar with each new selection.

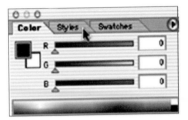

figure | 2-7

Palettes grouped by similar topic. Select a tab to bring a palette forward.

- *Palettes:* Palettes, usually located to the right of the work area, help you modify and monitor your images. By default, palettes are stacked together in like-minded groups, but you can also separate them by clicking on their title tabs and dragging them to another area of the workspace. Of course, you can redock any palette back into a group by dragging the separated palette's title bar over the desired palette group. See figures 2-7 and 2-8. Sometimes you might want your palettes out of the way, so that you can better see your workspace. You can hide your palettes by pressing Shift-Tab on the keyboard. To

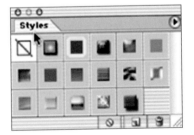

figure | 2-8

A palette can be separated from its group by clicking and dragging the title tab to a different area of the workspace.

bring them back, press Shift-Tab again. You can also close palettes by selecting the Close button in the upper left corner (Mac) or upper right corner (Windows) of any of the palette windows. To bring a palette back after you've closed it, go to Window on the main menu and select the palette name again.

● *Palette well:* As part of the options bar, there is a handy way to organize your favorite palettes called the palette well. The palette well is located to the right of the options bar, but is only available when using a screen resolution of at least 800 by 600 pixels (actually recommended is a setting of 1,024 by 768). Into the palette well you can drag the title tabs of any palette window and it stores them there in a convenient, tabbed list. One option available to the left of the palette well is the File Browser. It's a button located between the tabs and the options bar.

The File Browser allows you to quickly browse for a file on your local hard drive, and what's really cool is that it provides a visual thumbnail of the files for easy selection. Check it out! See Figure 2-9.

figure | 2-9

The really cool File Browser. Find a file quickly and visually!

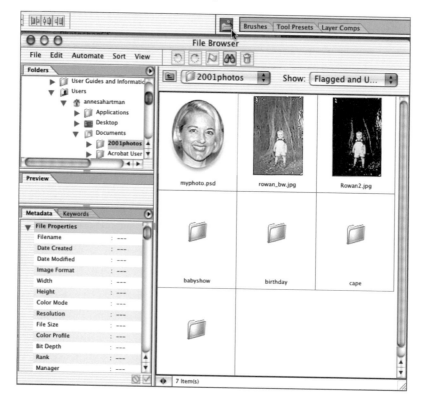

- *Status bar:* The status bar is located at the lower left edge of the Document window. It shows you info about a document's size and dimensions, the current tool being used and its magnification level, and other things. See Figure 2-10.

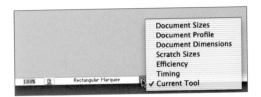

figure | **2-10**

The status bar options.

If you click on the narrow bar to the left of the status bar options list, a visual comes up showing you the document size if it were to be printed on an 8.5-x-11-inch sheet. See Figure 2-11. I find this visual to be incredibly useful before I print a document, because the document size you see on the screen is not necessarily the size it will be printed on paper. Photoshop can be pretty deceptive in this way. It has something to do with a thing called resolution, which you'll learn about in later chapters.

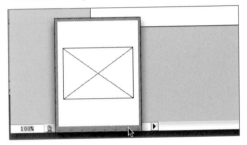

figure | **2-11**

Document size if printed on 8.5-x-11-inch sheet.

- *Context menus:* Hidden under the right-click option of your mouse if you're a Windows user, or when you Ctrl-click as a Macintosh user, you'll discover what are called context menus. Context menus are drop-down menus that give you quick access to various features of a tool you might be using. See Figure 2-12.

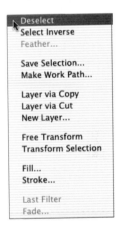

figure | **2-12**

Context menu for the Marquee tool. Right click (Windows) or Ctrl-click (Mac) to get to the context menus.

Marking the Stage

1. Place the cursor (don't click!) over the Rectangle tool in the toolbox. Note that a text equivalent of the tool name appears. This is called a tool tip. Next to the tool name there is also a shortcut key indicated. See Figure 2-13.

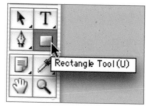

figure | 2-13 |

The tool tip for the Rectangle tool is revealed.

2. Now, click and hold on the Rectangle tool to open up further shape tool options. See Figure 2-14. Select the Ellipse tool.

3. Click on the Foreground color swatch in the toolbox to choose a color. See Figure 2-15.

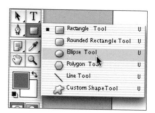

figure | 2-14 |

Click and hold on the Rectangle tool to reveal other shape options.

4. Select a color in the Color Picker and select OK. See Figure 2-16.

5. Click and drag on the Document window to create an elliptical shape. Draw four or five of

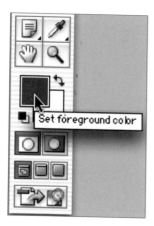

figure | 2-15 |

Set a foreground color.

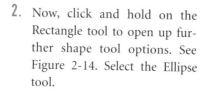

figure | 2-16 |

Select a color from the Color Picker.

different sizes. To create a perfect circle, hold down the Shift key as you click and drag to make the shape. See Figure 2-17.

NOTE: If you want to undo something, go to the History palette (Window > History, if not already opened). Each step you perform in Photoshop is recorded in the History palette (up to 20 states by default). To go back a step, click on the state above the step you just made.

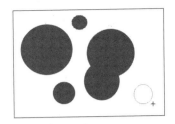

figure | 2-17 |

Create elliptical shapes.

6. Unless you're up to playing around some more with this file, we're done with marking up the stage. However, save this file for use in the next lesson. Choose File > Save As. For Format choose Photoshop. Name the file *myfile.psd* and save it to your *lessons* folder.

NOTE: You might be wondering what's the ".*psd*" at the end of your file name. This is the native file extension for all Photoshop files. If you see a file with this extension on the end you know it was created in Adobe Photoshop.

Lesson 2: Customize Your Experience

Photoshop is smart—it remembers what you like. Every time you open Photoshop and begin to do things like dock palettes to your palette well, set ruler units, or change how your cursor displays, Photoshop saves these preferences in a Preferences file located on your local hard drive. This is so great when you want to open up the program again on your computer and have everything exactly where you left it. Let me show you how this works.

Setting Preferences

1. Open the Photoshop program.

2. Choose File > Open and find the file *myfile.psd*.

   NOTE: If you don't have a *myfile.psd*, choose *chap2L2.psd* in the *chap2_lessons* folder.

3. Completely close any palette windows (except for the toolbox) by clicking on the Close icon in the upper bar of each palette. See Figure 2-18.

figure | 2-18

Close unneeded
palette windows.

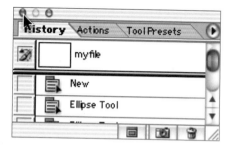

4. Choose Window > Layers to open the Layers palette.

5. Select the layer called *Shape 1*.

6. In the Layers palette, select the black arrow in the upper right corner of the window to open the palette's options. Choose Blending Options from the drop-down menu. See Figure 2-19.

figure | 2-19

Options for the
Layers palette.

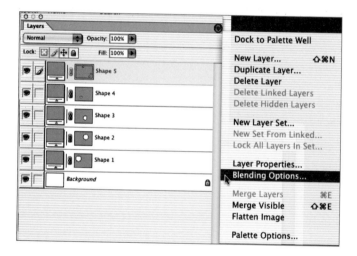

7. In the Layer Style dialog box, choose the Drop Shadow and Bevel and Emboss style options. Be sure Preview is selected in the dialog box, so that you can see the styles applied automatically to the document. Select OK. See Figure 2-20.

8. Select other layers (*Shape 2, Shape 3, Shape 4,* and so on) and apply other styles found in the Layer Style dialog box. For example, choose the Outer Glow and Satin effects.

NOTE: Yes, I know, the Layer Style dialog box can be a bit overwhelming—no worries. I guarantee you that this will eventually be one of your favorite places to visit in Photoshop.

9. Without really knowing it, you've already been setting some file preferences. Let's set some more using the Preferences dialog box. Choose Photoshop > Preferences > Display & Cursors (Mac) or Edit > Preferences > Display & Cursors (Windows). Any change you make in this box is recorded in a preferences file for the next time you open the program. There are a lot of preference options. We'll only tinker with a few. However, it's a good idea to look through all of them just in case you want to make a change down the road.

10. Under the Display & Cursors option, go to Other Cursors and select Precise. This changes the cursor of a selected tool from its standard icon to a more precise crosshair indicator. See Figure 2-21. This crosshair indicates a precision cursor; that is, the center of the cursor is the exact spot where you will select, draw, or edit. This is much more accurate than an icon cursor.

11. Select OK to close the Preferences window.

12. Save your file. Name it *myfile2.psd.*

13. Choose Photoshop > Quit Photoshop to completely shut down the program.

14. Now, open the program again and open your saved *myfile2.psd.*

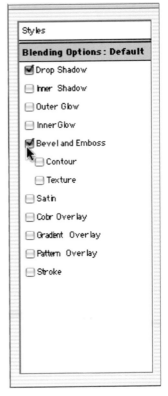

figure | 2-20

Select style options.

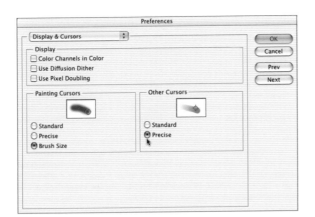

figure | 2-21

Change preferences in the Preferences dialog box.

15. Note that your preferences have not changed. Precise cursors are still indicated in the Preferences dialog box, and even the Layers palette is still open on your workspace.

Deleting Preferences

1. It's quite possible you might want to go back to Photoshop's default Preference settings. To do this, first close down the Photoshop program (Photoshop > Quit Photoshop for Mac users, File > Exit for Windows users).

2. Now, depending if you are on a Mac or a Windows computer, do one of the following:

   ● Press and hold Alt + Control + Shift (Windows) or Option + Command + Shift (Mac OS) immediately after launching Photoshop or ImageReady.

   NOTE: The keys must be pressed after Photoshop or ImageReady has started, but before the program actually opens. You will be prompted to delete the current settings file.

   Alternatively:

   ● In Windows, go to the *Documents and Settings\username\ Application Data\Adobe\Photoshop\8.0\ Adobe Photoshop CS Settings* folder. Delete the *Adobe Photoshop CS Prefs.psp* file.

   NOTE: Before deleting the preferences file, you might want to rename the preferences file and move it to the desktop as a safety copy.

   ● In Mac OS, go to the *Preferences* folder in the *System* folder (Mac OS 9.x) or *Library* folder (Mac OS X), open the *Adobe Photoshop CS Settings* folder and place the *Adobe Photoshop CS Prefs* file in the trash.

   NOTE: Before deleting the preferences file, you might want to rename the preferences file and move it to the desktop as a safety copy.

3. Once you've deleted the preferences file, reopen Photoshop to view the default setup. It will look something like that shown in Figure 2-22.

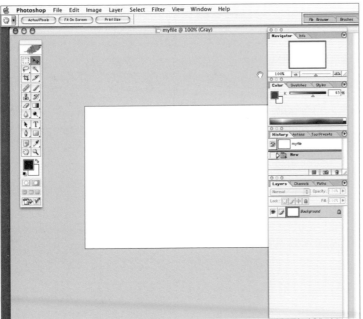

figure | 2-22

Photoshop with its
default setup.

SEEING IS BELIEVING

Have you ever been in the unfortunate situation where you paid
$60 to see your favorite rock star in concert only to find yourself in
the farthest row of the concert hall wishing you had a telescope in
your back pocket? Well, you'll be happy to know that you'll never
have that problem working in Photoshop. No matter how many
layers of objects you find yourself accumulating there is no lack of
a tool to help you see clearly where you are and what you are doing.
In this next lesson get up close and personal with Photoshop's navigational features, such as the Hand and Zoom tools, the Navigator
palette, and the screen and view modes.

Lesson 3: Navigational Features

Magnification Tools

1. In Photoshop open the file *chap2L3.psd* in the *chap2_lessons*
   folder.

   NOTE: If you receive a dialog box stating that "Some text layers might need to be updated…," choose Update.

2. Choose View > Fit on Screen to magnify the image to fit in the window area.

3. Note that the document title bar indicates the current magnification of the image. See Figure 2-23. This number varies depending on what view you've indicated for the document. For example, now choose View > Print Size, which shows you the image size if it were to be printed.

```
chap2L3.psd @ 40.7% (photo, RGB)
```

4. Next, choose View > Actual Pixels. This shows you the image size at 100% of the screen resolution (you will learn more about resolution in Chapter 3).

5. Select the Zoom tool in the toolbox (see Figure 2-24).

6. Click once with the Zoom tool over the image. It zooms even closer to you. Click again to zoom even closer.

7. Hold down the Option (Mac) or Alt (Windows) key to reverse the Zoom tool (note the minus sign in the Zoom tool cursor). Continue to hold the Option/Alt key down has you click once on the artwork to zoom back. Click again three (3) more times to zoom even further away.

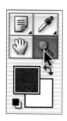

8. Let's zoom into a particular area of the photograph. With the Zoom tool selected, click and drag from upper left to lower right a rectangular shape over the copyright notice in the lower left corner of the document. With this area marqueed, let go, and note how the area selected zooms in close. Whoa! See Figure 2-25.

9. Select the Horizontal Type tool in the toolbox. Then select the text *2003*. Change the text to *2004*. See Figure 2-26.

10. Select the Hand tool in the toolbox (the tool right next to the Zoom tool). Click and drag with the Hand tool over the document, pushing it down until you see the *Tyrone* text at the top of the photo.

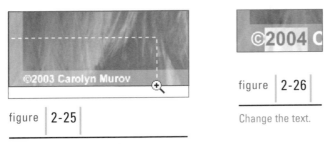

figure | 2-25

Select an area to zoom close.

figure | 2-26

Change the text.

11. In the Layers palette, select the layer called *Tyrone*. Change the blending mode for the text from Normal to Color Burn. See Figure 2-27. Note that the text blends with the background colors of the photo.

   NOTE: There are a lot of different types of blending modes. Feel free to explore the others (such as Difference and Luminosity). Blending modes are used a lot, so this won't be the last time you get to play with them.

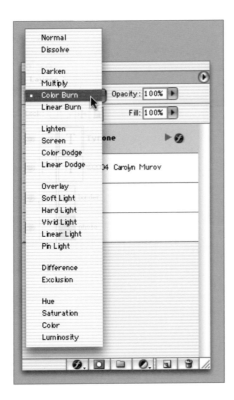

figure | 2-27

Located at the top of the Layers palette is the drop-down menu to change the blending modes of a layer.

12. Be sure the Hand tool is selected in the toolbox. Note the options available for the Hand tool in the options bar right below the main menu. In the options select Fit On Screen (alternatively, you can also choose from the main menu View > Fit on Screen). See Figure 2-28.

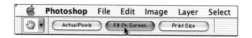

The Navigator Palette

1. Another way to get a good view of your work is to use the Navigator. Choose Window > Navigator to open the Navigator palette (if not already open). Note in the palette window a small view of the image with a red border around it. See Figure 2-29.

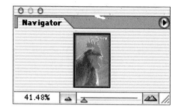

2. In the Navigator palette, slide the small arrow in the lower part of the window to the right to magnify the document or to the left to reduce it. Note that the red border adjusts in the viewing window to indicate what area is viewable in the document.

figure | 2-29

The Navigator palette.

NOTE: Alternatively to moving the slider to zoom in and out you can click on the mountain-looking icons on each side of the slider. Also, you can type in a zoom percentage in the lower left corner of the Navigator palette.

3. Magnify the image by sliding the arrow in the Navigator palette to the right. The red border area should grow smaller in the window.

4. Locate a specific area of the image by placing the cursor over the red border area in the Navigator palette (note that the cursor changes to the Hand tool). Now, click and drag the red border area.

Screen Modes

1. Choose View > Fit on Screen to see the complete image.

2. In the toolbox (lower part), select the Full Screen Mode with Menu Bar option. See Figure 2-30.

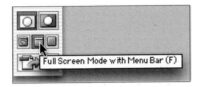

figure | 2-30

There are three screen mode options located in the lower part of the toolbox. From left to right they are: Standard Screen Mode, Full Screen Mode with Menu Bar, and Full Screen Mode (no menu bar).

3. Now, try the next option, Full Screen Mode.

4. Go back to Standard Screen Mode.

5. Close the file. You're done with this lesson.

SUMMARY

This chapter familiarized you with the Photoshop staging area—the workspace and navigational elements of the program. You also learned how to set your own preferences and if necessary delete them. Additionally, you got a first insight into how easy (dare I say "magical") it is to do such useful things as change your cursor icon, create a drop shadow behind a shape, and blend the colors of two layers.

in review

1. What does Shift-Tab do?

2. What does *.psd* at the end of a file name indicate?

3. What's the File Browser? How is it useful?

4. What's the difference between View > Fit on Screen and View > Print Size?

5. What is a precise cursor? Where can you change the cursor from Standard to Precise mode?

6. What are two ways to reset your preferences to the default settings?

7. What's the purpose of the Navigator palette?

↗ EXPLORING ON YOUR OWN

1. In the Photoshop program, go to Help > Photoshop Help and read the section "Looking at the Work Area."

2. Create a new file. Use the Rectangle and Ellipse tools to make shapes. Fill each shape with a different color. Use the Zoom and/or Navigator palette to practice zooming in and out of the Document window. Move the file around with the Hand tool. Reset your preferences.

notes

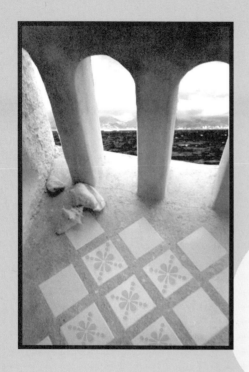

| image essentials |

3

charting your course

Getting acquainted with the Photoshop staging area was the essence of Chapter 2. It allowed you to get comfortable in the space, so that the real show can begin.

As you might already know, any well-trained artist has a background in the classics. If you're an actor you study Shakespearean sonnets; a painter, Renaissance art; a musician, Mozart's symphonies; a dancer, ballet. The study of the classics not only provides some perspective from the past but more importantly becomes a fundamental sounding board to grow creatively. Such a sounding board for a graphic artist would be an understanding of how computer graphics are generated, and that's what this chapter is all about. Your classical training begins with a study of vectors and bitmaps; particularly bitmaps, since that's what Photoshop knows best. It also begins with some other vital stuff, such as bit depth, resolution, and image formats. You'll also get some more practice working with Photoshop's main ingredient—pixels.

 goals

- Develop a firm grasp of the two types of digital images: vector and bitmap
- Discover the meaning of zeros and ones
- Master some tricks to make resolution your friend
- Learn about image formats and get an overview of common image format types
- Wrap your brain around how images are created and edited using pixels
- Explore hands-on more tricks of the program with bitmaps and pixels in mind

IMAGE CONSTRUCTION

No doubt you're eagerly awaiting to get your hands back on Photoshop. However, it just wouldn't be right to send you on the next phase of the journey ill equipped. It would be like sticking a light saber in your hand without guiding you in the art of the Force; you would survive a little while, probably create some really star-studded stuff, but eventually you'll want finesse on your side. Filters and effects only get you so far. The real advantage is to become one with the mind of the program—to know exactly what makes it tick. This applies not just to Photoshop but to any computer graphics program you might encounter. Your training begins with an initial understanding of how images are constructed in the digital world. They come in two forms: bitmap and vector.

The Brief on Bitmapped Images

Let's start by examining a basic black-and-white photograph (see Figure 3-1). To reproduce this image on paper is pretty straightforward: some black ink is deposited dot by dot on white paper. But, how is this photo reproduced on your computer? Imagine this image is formed from a mosaic of tiles. However, instead of each tile being made of ceramic or glass it's made of something called pixels, square-shaped elements. When lined up side by side, in a grid, these pixels form a complete image or pattern (see Figure 3-2). This grid of pixels is called a bitmap, and it's the manipulation of these types of images that is the heart of Photoshop.

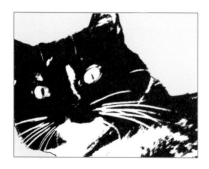

figure | 3-1 |

A photograph reduced to only black and white.

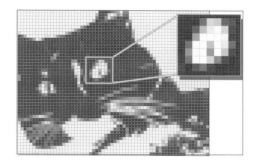

figure | 3-2 |

A photograph constructed from a grid of pixels.

Bit Depth

Two important concepts related to bitmaps are bit depth and image resolution. Let's start with bit depth. Going back to our black-and-white visual in Figure 3-1, how does the computer know to designate which part of the visual is black and which is white? Let me explain without getting too "techie." First, you must know that the brain of the computer knows only two numbers: zero and one. Yep, no deep math here—just zeros and ones. Amazingly, how the computer calculates different combinations (or strings) of zeros and ones produces every image, letter, and movement made on the computer. For instance, if you type the word *shazam* on your keyboard, the computer translates that word into its own language of zeros and ones—a string of data that looks something like 011100010101.

Okay, here's where it gets interesting. A single zero (0) or a single one (1) has a measurement called a "bit." Furthermore, a certain number of zeros and ones (bits) is represented in each pixel (tile) of a bitmapped image. (Are you still with me? Hang in there; it will soon be made clear.) This representation is an image's *bit depth*. In the instance of our black-and-white photo, a white pixel you see (or don't see) is translated as zero (off) in the computer brain and a black pixel is translated as one (on). Each pixel in this example is equal to one bit of color information, which can be either black or white.

Not surprisingly a black-and-white image is sometimes referred to as a *one-bit image*. We will discuss the relationship of image color to bit depth further in Chapter 5. For now, just remember that the larger an image's bit depth (accumulation of zeros and ones) the more variations of color an image contains. See Figure 3-3. In general, a larger bit depth also produces an image with a larger file size.

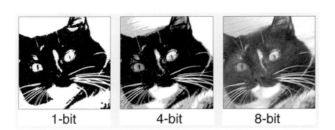

| 1-bit | 4-bit | 8-bit |

figure | 3-3 |

The larger an image's bit depth the more variations of color (for example, shades of gray) the image contains.

Resolution

Resolution plays an important role in Photoshop, and the concept of resolution is going to crop up again and again throughout the pages of this book. It's somewhat of an illusive term because it can be discussed in many different contexts, depending on how an image is being used. Ultimately, though, resolution works as a measurement for how much information a file contains. For our purposes right now, resolution is a way to describe the amount of pixels in an image, which results in what size an image might be when reproduced for print or the screen (i.e., the Web).

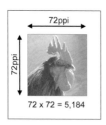

72ppi

72ppi

72 x 72 = 5,184

figure **3-4**

A 1-inch by 1-inch image in Photoshop is set, by default, at a resolution of 72 ppi.

In Photoshop, an image with a resolution of 72 pixels per inch (ppi) and measuring 72 pixels in width and 72 pixels in length equals a 1-inch by 1-inch image when set to a magnification of 100%. This makes an image with a total of 5,184 pixels. Huh? See Figure 3-4 if you need a visual.

Why 72, you might be wondering? Well, that's the default screen resolution (the resolution set for viewing images on a screen) in Photoshop. If you don't believe me, go to Photoshop > Preferences > Units & Rulers (Mac) or Edit > Preferences > Units & Rulers (Windows) and see for yourself (or see Figure 3-5). I wouldn't mess around too much with this screen resolution setting. Keep it at 72 pixels per inch. The number 72 also represents the average screen resolution of your monitor (though newer monitors now have a resolution of 96 pixels per inch, which you should not let confuse you right now). Also, 72 ppi is the resolution of web images. This makes sense because web images are viewed via a screen. (I know you are wondering "Will my picture look better if I increase the ppi?" The answer is no. You are just squeezing more zeros and ones [bits] into the same area. The only thing you did was make your file larger in size.)

figure **3-5**

The Preferences dialog box for setting screen resolution.

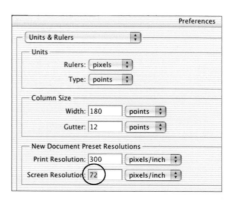

Now, by default Photoshop views images at 100% based on this 72 ppi screen resolution. However, if you wanted to create an image that came out 1 inch by 1 inch when printed, the resolution you would set depends on the resolution of the output device (i.e., your printer). Let's say you needed to create an image that needed to be 144 ppi. What would it look like in Photoshop if set to a screen resolution of 72 ppi? Well, let's find out:

1. Open the Photoshop program.

2. Choose File > New and enter the following information:

   ● *Name: res_72*

   ● *Preset:* Custom

   ● *Width:* 1 inch

   ● *Height:* 1 inch

   ● *Resolution:* 72 pixels/inch

   ● *Color Mode:* RGB Color

   ● *Background Contents:* White

3. Select OK.

4. Choose View > Actual Pixels to ensure that the document is at 100% magnification. You should see a blank document that looks approximately 1 inch by 1 inch in size. See Figure 3-6.

5. Keeping your *res_72* document open, choose again File > New and enter the following information:

   ● *Name: res_144*

   ● *Preset:* Custom

   ● *Width:* 1 inch

   ● *Height:* 1 inch

   ● *Resolution:* 144 pixels/inch

   ● *Color Mode:* RGB Color

   ● *Background Contents:* White

6. Select OK.

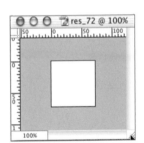

figure   3-6

A 1-inch x 1-inch document with a resolution of 72 ppi, 100% magnification, in Photoshop.

7. Choose View > Actual Pixels to ensure that the new document is at 100% magnification. You should see a blank document, but compared to the first document *(res_72)* it's visually four times the size. See Figure 3-7. Why is this, even though the document's dimensions were set to 1 inch by 1 inch, just like the first document? Well, that's because you are viewing it at a default screen resolution of 72 ppi (remember that setting in the Photoshop preferences?). For *res_144* to show all of its pixels set at 144 ppi (a total of 20,736 pixels) at a screen resolution of 72 it must visually expand the document size, precisely four times the size of *res_72*.

figure | 3-7

Comparing at 100% magnification the size of a 72-ppi document to a 144-ppi document.

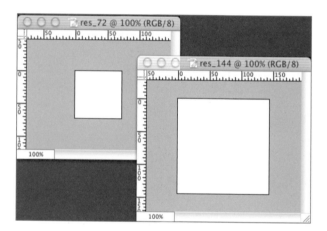

8. There's more. When the file *res_144* gets to its final output source—a printer, which in this case is requiring an image of 144 ppi—it will print at the intended 1-inch x 1-inch size. Choose View > Print Size to see this calculation.

NOTE: One more thing to be aware of is the size of each of the documents created. The *res_144* file is 4x bigger than *res_72*. See Figure 3-7 again and note the document size in the status bar at the bottom of each window: 61K versus 15K.

I totally understand if you are still unresolved about the concept of resolution. Perhaps you even feel the urge to slam this book shut. Before you do, however, bookmark this page—you'll probably want to refer to it again later. If it's any comfort, this whole resolution idea really begins to sink in when you find yourself in an actual predicament (or two or three) using the program. Until such a predicament arrives you'll get plenty of practice with resolution throughout the lessons in this book.

The Brief on Vector Graphics

As you've discovered when dealing with bitmap images, an image's resolution and pixel dimensions are interdependent. Adjusting the amount of pixels in an image affects its resolution, not to mention its visual quality, and vice versa. This is a fact of life, and there's no way around it, unless of course you're working in vectors. Vectors are another way digital images are constructed. As part of our classical training, it's very important that we discuss vectors, but only briefly. Photoshop does have some vector support (which comes in handy when you need some flexibility with free-form drawing in the program or when importing vector-based graphics created in other programs, such as Adobe Illustrator), but as you know it's not the heart of the program (bitmaps are!).

Vector graphics are made up of points and lines that describe an object's outline or shape. See Figure 3-8. Instead of being comprised of a grid of square pixels (see Figure 3-2), a vector image is drawn based on mathematical calculations of X and Y coordinates. Because of this, vectors are described as *resolution independent.* This means that they can be scaled big or small and printed to any output device without loss of detail or clarity. Hey, that sounds pretty good—why not use vectors for all digital images? I hate to break it to you, but there is no one-stop shop. Vector graphics are great for a certain type of image design and for free-form drawing, including bold and illustrative types of graphics, such as logos and text treatments, which can be easily scaled while retaining crisp lines and solid colors. On the flip side, bitmaps are a great way to represent continuous-tone images, such as photographs or digital paintings that have subtle gradations of color and shading.

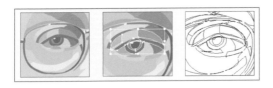

figure | 3-8 |

Anatomy of a vector graphic from full shade view to outline view.

Seeing All Sides

Now that you've got some idea of the differences between bitmap and vector graphics, I must confess that it's not all black and white. With the inundation of so many kinds of computer graphic software programs and variations thereof, you might find yourself sifting through a lot of digitized gray matter. Programs such as Adobe Photoshop and Macromedia Fireworks are designed to work specifically with bitmap-constructed images. Adobe Illustrator, Macromedia Freehand, and CorelDRAW are designed to work with vector-based graphics. However, most programs, to some extent, have the ability to import and translate both vector and bitmap graphics. At first this convergence of image types might seem a bit confusing, but once you understand how digital images are constructed your work as a graphic artist becomes much more productive.

Before moving on, it's also good to know there are different image formats for different types of images. A format is described by an extension at the end of the file name, as in *image.jpg* or *mywork.tiff*. An image's format indicates the makeup of the image; that is, whether it's made of bitmaps or vectors. It also determines an image's file size and visual quality. There are many kinds of image file formats, depending on where you are going to use the image (i.e., print or Web).

Most graphic programs support the use of the following:

Bitmap-only formats

- *BMP:* Limited bitmap file format not suitable for web or pre-press.

- *GIF:* Compressed format mainly used for Internet graphics with solid colors and crisp lines.

- *JPEG:* Compressed format used for Internet graphics, particularly photographs.

- *PNG:* Versatile bitmap-compressed format used mainly for Internet graphics.

- *TIFF:* Saves bitmap images in an uncompressed format (although in Photoshop there are options for some compression capability); most popular for artwork going to print.

Vector and bitmap-based formats

- *EPS:* Flexible file format that can contain both bitmap and vector information. Most vector images are saved in this format.

- *PICT:* Used on Macintosh computers, and can contain both vector and bitmap data.

- *SWF:* The Macromedia Flash file format. A common vector-based graphics file format for the creation of scalable, compact graphics for the Web and hand-held devices.

- *SVG (Scalable Vector Graphics):* Emerging XML-based vector format for the creation of scalable, compact graphics for the Web and hand-held devices.

PIXELS: THE MAIN INGREDIENT

Photoshop manipulates pixels like a sculptor molds clay. Pixels are the main ingredient from which all images are formed in the program. Just as a sculptor has numerous implements to mold his vision, the tools in the Toolbox of Photoshop are designed specifically to shape pixels. The Magic Wand tool selects them, the Crop tool deletes them, the Smudge tool smudges them, and the Clone Stamp tool duplicates them. You get the idea.

Lesson: Playing with Pixels

The purpose of this next lesson is to show you that no matter what mysterious tricks we get into in the upcoming chapters the underlying truth is always the same: Photoshop is just a playground for pixels. See Figure 3-9.

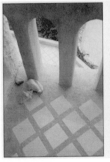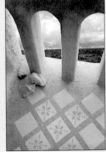

Lightening and Darkening Pixels

1. In Photoshop, choose File > Open. Open the file *chap3L1.psd* in the *chap3_lessons* folder.

figure | **3-9**

The lesson before and after playing with pixels.

2. Right away, save a copy of this file in your *lessons* folder: choose File > Save As and name your file *chap3L1_yourname.psd*.

3. From the main menu, choose Image > Adjustments > Auto Levels to have Photoshop automatically adjust the brightness and contrast (light- and dark-colored pixels) of the image. Ah, already much better.

Deleting and Transforming Pixels

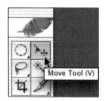

1. Keeping your *chap3L1_yourname.psd* file open, choose File > Open and open the file *tile.tif* located in the *chap3_lessons/assets* folder. In the next step you are going to move this tile pattern onto your *chap3L1_yourname.psd* file.

2. Select the Move tool in the toolbox. See Figure 3-10.

3. Now, click and drag the selected tile pattern over the top and center of the *chap3L1_yourname.psd* file, and then let go of the mouse button. A copy of the image will appear on the file (see Figure 3-11). Right on!

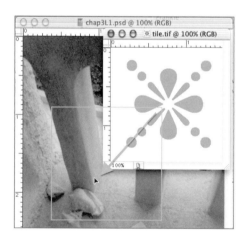

4. Close the *tile.tif* file. You are done with this file.

5. Now, get rid of the white pixels around the tile pattern. Select the Magic Wand tool in the toolbox. See Figure 3-12.

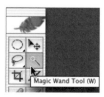

6. With the Magic Wand tool, click over a white section of the tile pattern. All white areas of the image are selected. Hit Delete on the keyboard or choose Edit > Clear. Ta-da! No more white pixels. The Magic Wand really is magic.

7. Choose Select > Deselect (apple/Command-D on the Mac or Ctrl-D on Windows).

8. Select Window > Layers to open the Layers palette if it is not already open.

9. Double click on the text *Layer 1* and rename the layer *tile pattern*. See Figure 3-13.

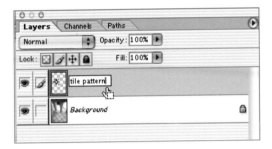

figure | 3-13

Rename the layer.

10. Be sure the tile pattern layer is selected. Choose Edit > Free Transform. In the options bar below the main menu, type in the following (see Figure 3-14):

- *Width (W):* 32.0%

- *Height (H):* 32.0%

- *Rotation:* 55.0 degrees

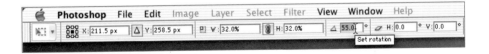

figure | 3-14

Scale and rotate pixels by typing in exact increments in the options box for the Free Transform command.

NOTE: Alternatively to typing in exact scaling and rotation numbers in the options box you can scale and rotate the transform box that surrounds the selected image. See figures 3-15 and 3-16.

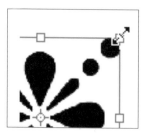

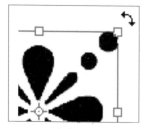

figure | 3-15

Scale interactively by clicking and dragging on a corner of the Free Transform box.

figure | 3-16

Rotate interactively by clicking and dragging right above a corner of the free transform box. Note the rotation icon.

11. Select the Move tool in the toolbox. A dialog box will come up asking if you want to apply the transformation. Click Apply. (Double clicking on the transformed image or hitting Return or Enter will work as well.)

12. Move the tile pattern over one of the floor tiles in the photograph. See Figure 3-17.

13. Choose File > Save and save your work thus far.

figure | 3-17

Move the tile pattern over a tile in the photograph.

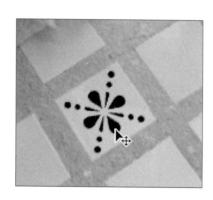

Altering, Blending, and Duplicating Pixels

1. Be sure the tile pattern layer is selected.

2. Choose Filter > Texture > Craquelure from the main menu.

3. Adjust the Crack Spacing to 10, Crack Depth to 2, and Crack Brightness to 10.

4. Select OK to apply the effect on the tile pattern.

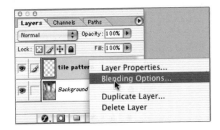

5. Right click (Windows) or Ctrl-click (Mac) over the tile pattern layer and choose Blending Options from the drop-down menu. See Figure 3-18.

6. In the Layer Style dialog box, check and highlight (by selecting the name) the Bevel and Emboss option. The Bevel and Emboss options will appear to the right of the dialog box.

figure | **3-18**

Select Blending Options.

7. Be sure the Preview option is selected, so that you can see the following Bevel and Emboss options applied to the pixels of the tile pattern (see also Figure 3-19).

figure | **3-19**

Select options for Bevel and Emboss.

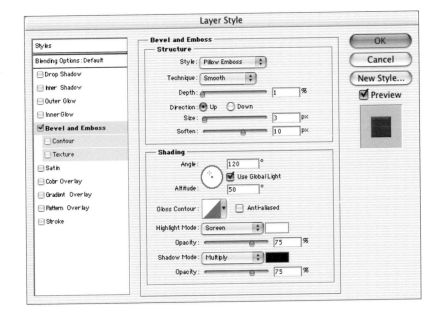

For Structure:

- *Style:* Pillow Emboss
- *Technique:* Smooth
- *Depth:* 1
- *Size:* 3
- *Soften:* 10

For Shading:

- *Angle:* 120
- *Altitude:* 50
- *Highlight Mode, Opacity:* 75
- *Shadow Mode, Opacity:* 75

8. Select OK to apply the effect.

   To further blend the tile pattern into the photograph, be sure the tile pattern layer is selected and in the Layers palette choose Multiply for the blending mode and 60% Opacity. See Figure 3-20.

figure | 3-20 |

Use a blending mode and opacity to further blend the tile pattern pixels with the photograph's pixels.

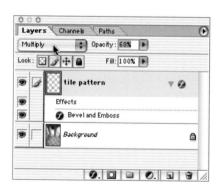

9. Select the Move tool in the toolbox.

10. Place the cursor over the tile pattern, hold down the Alt (Windows) or Option (Mac) key, and then click and drag to make a duplicate of the pattern with all of its effects. Move the duplicate over another tile in the photograph.

11. Create several more duplicates and place them over other tiles in the photograph. For reference, see the completed image in Figure 3-9.

    NOTE: Each time you create a duplicate tile pattern it creates a new layer for that tile object in the Layers palette. To move an individual tile pattern you need to select that tile pattern's layer in the Layers palette. To delete a tile pattern, select its layer and click on the Trash Can icon in the lower right corner of the Layers palette.

12. Save the file with the new changes.

Hiding and Revealing Pixels

1. Let's open another file to add to your scene. Choose File > Open and open the file *ocean.tif* in the *chap3_lessons/assets* folder.

2. Select the Move tool in the toolbox. Place the cursor over the ocean photo and drag a copy of the photo to your *chap3L1* file.

3. Close *ocean.tif*.

4. Position the ocean photo in the upper top area of the file.

5. Choose Select > Load Selection from the menu bar.

6. In the Load Selection dialog box, select *Channel: arches*. Click OK.

7. A selection (marked by marching ants) is indicated on the file. This selection was pre-made and saved for purposes of this lesson. You'll learn how to make your own saved selections in Chapter 8.

8. Choose Layer > Add Layer Mask > Reveal Selection in the main menu. Amazing! The selection reveals the ocean scene, masking out all other pixels. Now the photo has taken on a whole new perspective—much more inviting, I think.

9. Save your file. You're done with playing with pixels (at least temporarily).

SUMMARY

This chapter was heavy duty! It was a big bite into the nitty-gritty of bitmap and vector graphics, bit depth, resolution and image formats, not to mention an opportunity to practice playing with pixels. Just like studying the classics in any field, however, it was important to get this fundamental information out of the way, so that you can more easily, productively, and creatively progress to the next level of Photoshop know-how.

in review

1. Briefly describe the differences between bitmap and vector graphics.

2. What are bits? Why is a black-and-white image considered a one-bit image?

3. How does resolution affect a bitmap image's dimensions?

4. Bitmap images are most common for what type of images? Why?

5. Text and logo treatments are created best as what type of a graphic? Why?

6. What's an image file format?

7. What's the main ingredient in Photoshop? Name five ways you altered this ingredient in the lesson.

↗ EXPLORING ON YOUR OWN

1. In Photoshop, go to Help > Photoshop Help. Choose the topic "Getting Images into Photoshop and ImageReady" and read the sections "Working with bitmap images and vector graphics" and "Understanding image size and resolution."

2. Play with blending other tile patterns and background images in the *chap3L1.psd* file. Some sample patterns and background images you might want to use are located in the *chap3_lessons/samples* folder. You can also bring in your own tile patterns and background photos. For example, what would the image look like with an outer-space or underwater scene revealed through the arches?

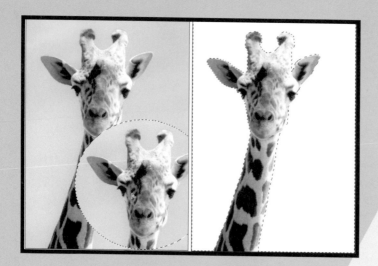

| selecting and transforming |

4

charting your course

After reading the last chapter, it's clear Photoshop knows pixels. And so will you, starting with this chapter. Using Photoshop's versatile and varied selection tools (such as the Marquee, Lasso, and Magic Wand tools), and transform commands (such as Scale, Rotate, and Skew), you get up close and personal selecting and transforming individual squares of color.

 goals

- **Get versatile with Photoshop's selection and transform tools**
- **Practice building a composite image**

ABOUT SELECTING AND TRANSFORMING

Selecting pixels and transforming them work hand in hand. You select an area of your Photoshop image and then move, scale, or rotate it in some way (or add a fill or effect to it, which comes up in later chapters). Learning to select and transform pixels are critical steps in your study of Photoshop.

How Do Selections Work?

When you select something on your Photoshop document—that is, when the marching ants appear (see Figure 4-1)—what exactly are you selecting and how do you control these selections? When examined closely, each pixel produced is its own shade of color, and because of this the computer can smartly select pixels based on these shades or tones (see Figure 4-2). For example, the Magic Wand tool knows what pixels to grab onto by where you apply it to an image and what you have determined is its *color tolerance*. Tolerance defines how similar in color a pixel must be to be selected, ranging from 0 to 255 (you'll learn more about the 0-to-255 thing in the next chapter). Similar to how tolerance works is feathering of selections. This type of selection determines how much transparency is created in each pixel.

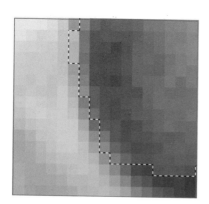

figure | 4-1 |

A selection is indicated by a dashed line, affectionately known as "marching ants."

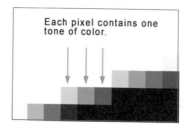

figure | 4-2 |

Each pixel is its own tone of color. Photoshop selects pixels based on their color range, or tolerance.

I must mention here that the selection accuracy is also controlled by the frequency and/or proximity of pixels in a given area. For example, the lasso tools control what pixels they snap onto not only by the contrast of colors from pixel to pixel (edge contrast) but by the number of pixels within the tool's positioned area. The accuracy settings for the selection tools are always found in the selected tool's options bar (see Figure 4-3).

figure | 4-3 |

Options available in the Magic Wand tool's options bar.

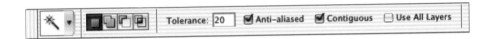

All that being said, the concern here is not so much what feature of what tool does what (that's next) but to know that the big picture is simply this: selections and their accuracy are determined by the color settings and location of pixels within a given area.

Overview of Selection Tools

Before you start playing with selection tools in the next lesson, here's an idea of what each type does and why one tool might be better suited for particular selections than another.

Select Menu

The quick and easy way to select all items on a layer is to choose the layer from the Layers palette and then from the main menu choose Select > All (Command-A for Mac or Ctrl-A for Windows). From the main menu, you can also choose to deselect all items on a layer, reselect them, or invert the selection.

Marquee Tools

A marquee, in its most common definition, is a permanent canopy or bulletin board that projects over the entrance of a building, like those seen over Broadway theaters. They highlight, usually in bright neon colors, the performance and performers of the evening. In Photoshop, the Marquee tools are used to highlight (select) an area as a shape, such as a rectangle, ellipse, or row or column of pixels (see Figure 4-4). The Marquee tools are the most convenient way to select areas of an image. However, because the selections are defined within a specific shape they are not designed

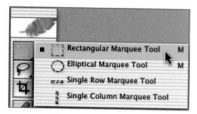

figure | 4-4 |

The Marquee tools available in the tool-box.

figure | 4-5 |

Select circular areas with the Elliptical Marquee tool.

to select odd areas of pixels. For instance, if I wanted to select the eye of the giraffe in Figure 4-5 with minimal effort, I would use the Elliptical Marquee tool. If I wanted to select an area of the giraffe's neck to create a pattern or tile effect from it I would use the Rectangular Marquee tool (see Figure 4-6). If I wanted to select one of the irregular spots on the giraffe I would use another tool, such as the Lasso tool (coming up soon).

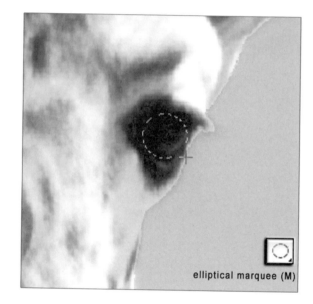

elliptical marquee (M)

There are three styles of selecting you can choose in the selected marquee's option bar:

- *Normal:* In normal style you select the specific Marquee tool you want and then click and drag the tool over the area of your document you want to select. To constrain the shape proportionally, hold down the Shift key as you drag with the tool. When you let go of the tool, the marching ants appear, indicating the selection.

- *Fixed Aspect Ratio:* In this style you can define a selection with a fixed height-to-width ratio. An example would be an image compatible for the NTSC TV format, which requires a 4-by-3 aspect ratio.

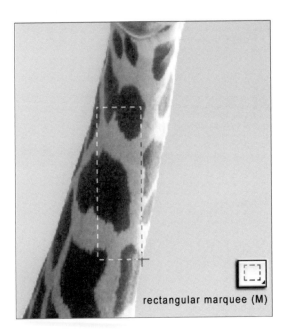

rectangular marquee (M)

figure 4-6

Select rectangular areas with the Rectangular Marquee tool.

● *Fixed Size:* If you already know exactly what size you want a selected area to be, you can enter this size in the Fixed Size style of the Marquee tool's options bar. Keep in mind that the number of pixels needed to create a 1-inch selection depends on the resolution of the image (this concept is covered in Chapter 3).

Magic Wand

If you recall, I revealed the secret of the Magic Wand tool to you at the beginning of this lesson. The Magic Wand tool selects pixels based on a color range or color tolerance, which is set in the tool's options bar (see Figure 4-7). Enter a low value to select the few colors very similar to the pixel you click, or enter a higher value to select a broader range of colors. The pixels can be selected contiguously (sharing a boundary or touching each other) or noncontiguously.

figure 4-7

Select the Magic Wand tool in the toolbox to access its tolerance settings in the options bar.

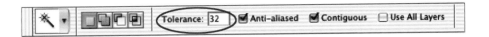

For the giraffe on the left in Figure 4-8, the Magic Wand tool's tolerance is set at 45 and is applied to the sky area around the giraffe. The range indicated is low enough that it selects the light pixels of the sky but not the darker pixels that define the giraffe. In the same figure, the giraffe on the right side has a tolerance set at 100— opening the range of color possibilities that can be selected. The Magic Wand tool is super for selecting odd areas of similar color in a photograph (see Figure 4-9). To use the Magic Wand tool you choose the tool in the toolbox, set the tolerance in the options box, and click down with the tool on the area you want to sample for the selection.

figure | 4-8

On the left, the color tolerance for the Magic Wand tool is set at 45 and is applied to the sky area of the image. On the right, the color tolerance is set at 100, expanding the selection area.

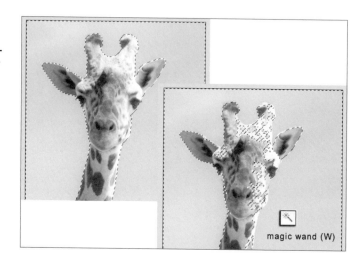

figure | 4-9

You can use the Magic Wand tool to select areas of similar color, such as the patch on the hide of the giraffe.

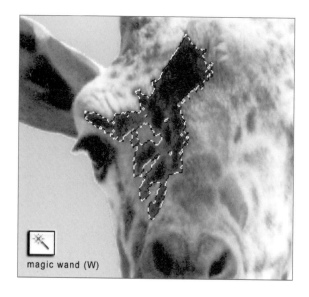

Lasso Tools

Unless you're a surgeon or can thread a needle with a steady hand, the Lasso tools can be tricky to master. It just takes practice, which is well worth the effort when you want to select odd areas of an image that might otherwise be impossible to do. There are three types of Lasso tools (see Figure 4-10).

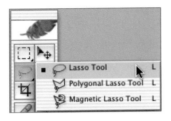

figure | **4-10**

The Lasso tools in the toolbox.

● *Lasso:* Lets you draw selections with freehand or straight-edged segments. See Figure 4-11. To create freehand segments, simply click and drag around an area. To create straight-edge segments, hold down the Alt/Option keys and click where segments should begin and end. You can switch between both free-form and straight-edge modes as you draw—cool! To close (define) the selection, let go of the mouse button and the Alt/Option keys.

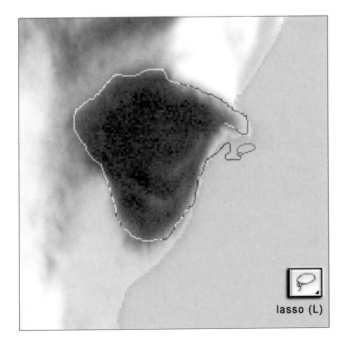

lasso (L)

figure | **4-11**

Use of the Lasso tool.

● *Polygonal Lasso:* Like the Lasso tool, lets you draw selections with freehand or straight-edge segments. To create straight-edge segments, click down on the area where segments should begin and end. To create freehand segments, hold down the Alt/Option keys and drag over the area. (Yes, it's the opposite commands for the Lasso tool). To close (define) the selection, double click with the Polygonal Lasso pointer tool. See Figure 4-12.

figure | 4-12

Use of the Polygonal Lasso tool.

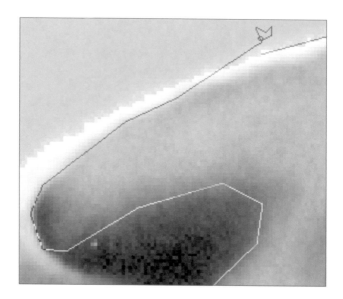

● *Magnetic Lasso:* Similar to the Magic Wand tool, the Magnetic Lasso tool is more or less attracted to pixels based on color and their proximity to each other. As you move along the edge of an object you want to select, the Magnetic Lasso tool attaches itself to pixels with fasteners. The more fasteners the more precise the selection border. If you draw free-form (click and then drag), the Magnetic Lasso tool will automatically place fasteners based on the *frequency* you set in the tool's options bar. You can also place fasteners at will each time you click down with the tool. The higher the frequency number the more fasteners are created, and therefore the more precise the selection border. You can also determine something called *edge contrast,* which defines the lasso's sensitivity to edges (contrasts of color) in the image. A lower percentage detects lower-contrast edges (a white pixel next to a light gray pixel, for example); a higher percentage detects edges that contrast sharply with their surroundings (a dark blue pixel next to a white pixel, for example).

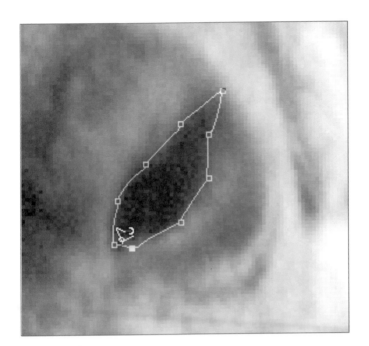

figure | 4-13 |

The Magnetic
Lasso tool
deposits fasteners
to define the
selection border.
In this example,
the frequency of
fasteners is set to
80, quickly and
more precisely
selecting the
intended area.

Like the Polygonal Lasso tool, to close (define) the selection double click with the tool. See Figure 4-13.

Adding and Subtracting Selection Areas

Inevitably your selections will not be perfect the first time around. You close and define the selection border and discover that you missed some areas. You have two options here. You can redraw the selection, which is good practice but not always very efficient. Or, you can add to or subtract from, or intersect, your selection area by choosing these options in the selection tool's options bar (see Figure 4-14). More quickly, you can add to a selection by selecting the tool you want to use (Lasso, Magic Wand, or Marquee) and holding down the Shift key as you draw over the areas you want to add. To subtract from a selection, you choose a selection tool and hold down the Alt/Option keys as you draw over the areas you

figure | 4-14 |

Add to and subtract
from, or intersect,
your selection by
choosing the option
in the options bar.

want to remove from the selection (see Figure 4-15). You can also right click (Windows) or Ctrl-click (Mac) over the selected areas and choose Add to Selection, Subtract From Selection, or Intersect Selection from the context menu.

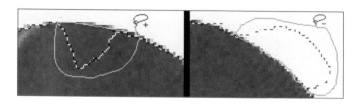

figure | 4-15 |

Hold down the Shift key to add to a selection. Hold down the Alt/Option key to subtract from a selection. Note the + or – signs next to the selection tool's pointer, depending on what you've chosen to do.

Selecting an Object on a Layer

When you begin to work with objects on multiple layers, often you will want to select items on a specific layer. In the lessons, there will be plenty of opportunities to practice this way of selecting, but just in case you need to know right now, follow these three simple steps:

1. Choose Window > Layers to open the Layers palette (if not already open).

2. In the Layers palette, select the layer containing the item(s) you want to select. Be sure it's an active layer, not the Background layer.

   NOTE: To convert the Background layer to an active, editable layer, double click on the Background layer thumbnail in the Layers palette and give it a new name.

3. Roll the pointer over the selected layer, and Ctrl-click (Windows) or Command-click (Mac) the layer's thumbnail.

4. Note that the opaque items on that layer are selected in the document.

Quick Mask

Photoshop's quick mask selection feature can rock your world. It's somewhat complicated to get the gist of at first, but within time could easily become your favorite selection tool (see Figure 4-16). I will share a lot more about quick masks and let you practice masking in Chapter 8. For now, try to wrap your brain around the idea of making selections using a paintbrush (sized to your liking) and letting color differentiate not only what is fully selected but what is partially (semitransparently) selected.

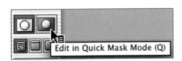

figure | 4-16 |

Get to Quick Mask mode from the tool-box.

One thing about selections is that once you have an area selected whatever you do next in the program (move, add a filter, paint, and so on) will be applied to that selected area only. On occasion you might select something inadvertently (or forgot it was selected) and then attempt to do something else, like paint on another layer. When this happens a warning circle comes up (see Figure 4-17). If this happens, don't freak out. Choose Select > Deselect from the main menu to remove all selected areas (even those you can't see) and then be sure you are on the layer you want to modify.

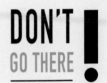

figure | 4-17 |

Warning: You can't do that! Deselect All and check to be sure you are on the layer you want to modify.

How Does Transforming Work?

Once you select something in Photoshop you might want to transform it in some way. This means moving, scaling, or rotating it. You can transform numerically—by entering an exact number(s) for the transformation in the options bar (see Figure 4-18). Or, you can use the Free Transform command, which lets you interactively (and in one continuous operation) transform (including rotate, scale, skew, distort, and set perspective) on a selected item using selection handles and specific keyboard commands (see Figure 4-19).

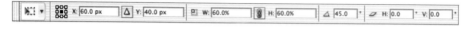

figure | 4-18 |

In a selection's options bar you can numerically enter a transformation.

figure | 4-19 |

The Free Transform command lets you transform an object interactivity and with keyboard commands by adjusting the bounding box handles.

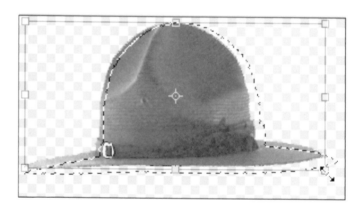

Overview of Transform Tools

Briefly, let's go over the transform tools in Photoshop:

- *Move:* Since moving (translating) things is so much a part of this program, the Move tool is probably the most used tool in the program (see Figure 4-20).

- *Scale and Rotate:* To change the size of a selected object or to rotate it, choose Edit > Transform > Scale or Rotate (see figures 4-21 and 4-22).

figure | 4-20 |

The Move tool in the toolbox.

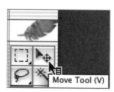

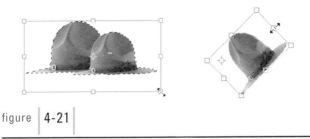

figure | 4-21 |

Scale proportionally by holding down the Shift key while dragging the scale handles on the corner of the selection. To scale disproportionally, just drag the scale handles on the corner or sides of the free transform bounding area. Note that the hat on the right is also being rotated.

figure | 4-22 |

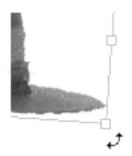

Position the pointer slightly outside a corner of the free transform bounding box to rotate the selection.

- *Skew:* To slant an item vertically or horizontally. Choose Edit > Transform > Skew.

- *Distort:* To stretch an item in all directions. Choose Edit > Transform > Distort.

- *Perspective:* To apply one point perspective to an item (see Figure 4-23). Choose Edit > Transform > Perspective.

  NOTE: When choosing Edit > Transform you also have the options to rotate a selection 180 or 90 degrees, or to flip it horizontally or vertically.

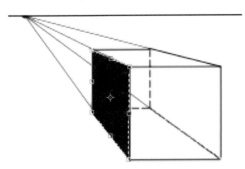

figure | 4-23 |

To create the illusion of a dimension, use a combination of the distort, skew, and perspective transformations.

More Options for Selections

There are other things you can do with selections than transform them. You can also copy, paste, delete, duplicate, paint, draw, adjust, or add an effect or filter to the selection. Most of these operations will become second nature to you as you work with the program, but let me go over them briefly.

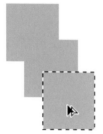

- *Copy, Paste and Duplicate:* Simple enough: make your selection, choose Edit > Copy, and go to where you want to paste it and choose Edit > Paste. If you paste it into the same document it will create a copy on a new layer, and perhaps directly over the original selection. Use your Move tool if you need to move one away from another. Similar to most programs, shortcut keys for copy are Command-C (Mac) and Ctrl-C (Windows) and for paste Command-V (Mac) or Ctrl-V (Windows). Another way to quickly duplicate a selection on the same document is to make your selection, choose the Move tool, and while rolling the pointer over the selection press Alt/Option on your keyboard. A duplicate icon appears (see Figure 4-24). Click and drag to make the duplicate.

figure | 4-24

To duplicate, make a selection, choose the Move tool, hold down Alt/Option on the keyboard, and click and drag to make the duplica-tion.

- *Delete:* Get rid of a selection by pressing Delete on your keyboard or by choosing Edit > Clear. Or, choose Edit > Cut if you want to remove the selection and paste it somewhere else (see Figure 4-25).

- *Add Effect or Filter:* Often you will want to adjust the color or add an effect or filter to just a part of an image. Easy enough: select the layer and area you want to work on and then choose a filter from the Filter menu.

figure | 4-25

On the left shows a duplicate of the giraffe's head. On the right shows the background select-ed and deleted.

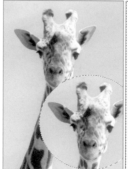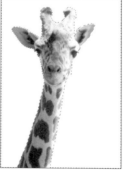

Alternatively you can invoke an image adjustment command (Image > Adjustments), such as for Brightness/Contrast, Hue/Saturation, or Replace Color. You can also edit color fills and gradients. See Figure 4-26.

● *Paint, Draw, and Erase:* You can also use the paintbrush, draw, and erase tools within a selection—a convenient way to stay within the lines.

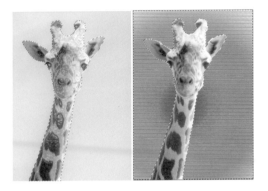

figure | 4-26

On the left the giraffe selection has been modified with the Plastic Wrap filter. On the right the background of the giraffe has been modified with a gradient and texture effect.

Lesson: Dressing Max

Finally here's your chance to select and transform pixels. While dressing Max (see Figure 4-27) for school (the Photoshop way), you learn how to use the Marquee, Magic Wand, and Lasso tools. You will also learn to move, scale, and rotate objects, and to transfer and organize selected pixels from one file to another.

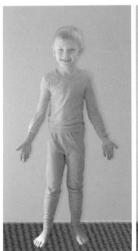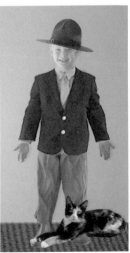

figure | 4-27

Max before and after.

Setting Up the File

1. In Photoshop, choose File > Open. Open the file *chap4L1.psd* in the *chap4_lessons* folder.

2. Save a copy of this file in your *lessons* folder. Choose File > Save As, and name your file *chap4L1_yourname.psd*.

   NOTE: If you get a "Maximize Compatibility" dialog box, keep the option checked and choose OK.

3. Choose View > Actual Pixels to see the document at 100% magnification. This is Max, a friend of mine.

4. Choose Image > Image Size. Note that the image is set at 72 pixels per inch (a good resolution if you want to use this image on the Web or for screen display).

5. Choose Window > Layers (if not already open) to view the three layers currently in the file. Each clothing item you bring into the file will have its own layer.

Selecting and Translating from One Document to Another

1. Choose File > Open and browse for *chap4_lessons/assets/ hat.tif*. Choose Open.

2. View the Layers palette. Note that the hat is located on a Background layer. The Background layer is the default layer of any new Photoshop file. All other layers go above the Background layer, and you cannot change the stacking order, blending mode, or opacity of a Background layer. It's not necessary, however, to have a Background layer. Actually I prefer to convert my Background layer into a regular layer, where I can create transparent content, move it anywhere in the Layers palette, and change its blending mode. To convert the Background layer of the hat image, double click on the Background layer and enter a new layer name (such as *hat*) in the New Layer dialog box (see Figure 4-28).

3. Now, select the Magic Wand tool in the toolbox (see Figure 4-29). In the options bar for the tool, set the tolerance to 10.

4. Click on the white background of the hat image to select it. Press Delete on the keyboard to remove the background pix-

els. The grid image you now see behind the hat indicates that area is transparent. The grid will not be saved when you convert the image into another format other than Photoshop (.*psd*) or when you print it (see Figure 4-30). You can change the grid size and colors in Preferences > Transparency & Gamut (Mac) or Edit > Preferences > Transparency & Gamut (Windows).

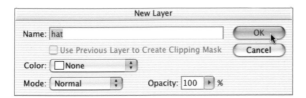

figure | **4-28**

Change the Background layer to a regular layer so that you have more options.

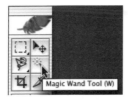

figure | **4-29**

Select the Magic Wand tool in the toolbox. Then, in the options bar, set the tolerance of the Magic Wand tool to determine how many pixels within a certain color range the wand will select.

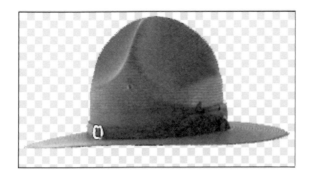

figure | **4-30**

The transparent areas of a layer are indicated by a grid pattern.

5. Now, choose Select > Inverse from the main menu to select the hat area (the part you want!) rather than the background.

6. Position the *chap4L1* document (Max) and the *hat* document side by side on the screen. Select the *hat* document.

7. Now, select the Move tool in the toolbox. Move the pointer over the hat image and note that the pointer now has a scissor icon next to it. The scissors indicates that you can copy the hat from one place to another by dragging it to its new location. Click and drag the hat to the *chap4L1* document (Max). Let go of the mouse to deposit the copy on the file—hey, that's sweet! See figure 4-31.

8. Close the *hat.tif* file. Don't save it; you're done with it.

figure | 4-31

With the Move tool, drag the selection from one file to another and it makes a copy of it.

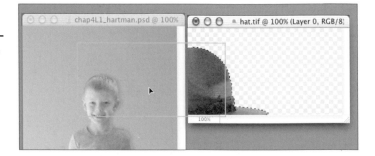

Transforming the Hat

1. First, note in the Layers palette that the hat has been placed on a new layer at the top of the stack. Double click on the layer title *(Layer 1)* and rename it *hat*. It is always good to keep your layers labeled intuitively. You never know when you're going to need to find them again later.

2. On the Max document it's obvious the hat is way too big to fit on his head. If you don't believe me, be sure the *hat* layer is selected in the Layers palette, select the Move tool, and then move the hat so that it's positioned over Max's noggin—huge!

3. With the *hat* layer selected, choose Edit > Free Transform. Click and drag inward on a corner of the transform bounding box to scale the hat to fit Max's head. To do this uniformly,

hold down the Shift key as you drag. If you make a mistake— no worries—Edit > Undo or reverse your steps in the History palette.

4. To position the hat, click near the center of the hat image (but not right on center, because that would move the object's registration point) and drag the hat to the desired location.

5. To rotate the hat, position the pointer slightly outside a corner of the free transform box. An icon with two curved arrows will appear. Click and drag to execute the rotation. See Figure 4-32.

figure | **4-32**

Three transformations occur to fit the hat on Max's head: scale, move, and rotate.

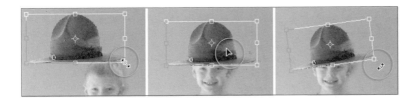

6. To complete the transformation do one of the following things: click on the check-mark button in the options bar, hit Return or Enter on your keyboard, or double click on the hat. If you don't want to commit to the transformation, choose the warning circle button in the options bar or hit Esc on the keyboard (see Figure 4-33).

7. Save your file.

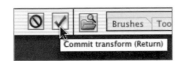

figure | **4-33**

Complete the transformation by clicking the check mark on the options bar.

Adding Another Clothing Item

1. Choose File > Open and open the *pants.tif* file in *chap4_ lessons/ assets*.

2. Be sure the pants document is selected (click on it to bring it forward).

3. In the Layers palette, double click on the Background layer to change it to a regular layer. Name it *pants*.

4. On the document, select the white background pixels with the Magic Wand tool.

5. Press Delete on the keyboard to remove the pixels.

6. Choose Select > Inverse to get just the pants.

7. With the Move tool, click on the pants and drag a copy of them to the *Max* document.

8. Close the *pants* file. No need to save changes.

9. On the *Max* file, rename *Layer 1* to *pants*.

10. Select the *pants* layer and choose Edit > Transform > Scale. In the options bar resize the pants numerically by typing in *65* (%) for both the width and the height (see Figure 4-34).

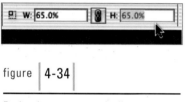

11. Position the pants to fit on Max.

figure | 4-34 |

Resize the pants numerically.

12. Note the stray white pixels around the edge of the pants. Let's clean them up a bit. Be sure the *pants* layer is selected. Choose Layer > Matting > Defringe. For the Defringe width, enter *4* (pixels) and select OK. Ahh, much nicer.

13. Save your file.

Adding to and Marqueeing a Selection

1. Choose File > Open and open the file *boots.tif* in *chap4_ lessons/assets*.

2. Be sure the *boots* document is selected (click on it to bring it forward).

3. In the Layers palette, double click on the Background layer to change it to a regular layer. Name it *boots*.

4. On the document, select the white background pixels with the Magic Wand tool.

5. Press Delete on the keyboard to remove the pixels. Look closely. There are still some white areas that need to be removed within the loops of the boots. These white areas are enclosed

by the red pixels of the boot and therefore were not detected by the Magic Wand tool.

6. Zoom in to the boot's loop on the far left-hand side of the document (see Figure 4-35).

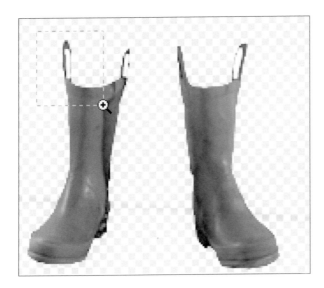

figure | 4-35

With the Zoom tool, marquee the area you want to see close up.

7. Select the Lasso tool and draw around the white pixels in the center of the boot's loops (see figures 4-36 and 4-37). Close the circle shape and let go of the mouse to see the marching ants selection. This takes a steady hand, so if you find yourself selecting everything but the white pixels choose Edit > Undo Lasso and simply try it again.

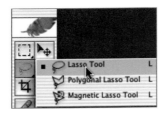

figure | 4-36

Select the Lasso tool.

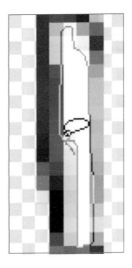

figure | 4-37

With the Lasso tool, draw around the white pixels within the boot loop.

8. Okay, let's add to this selection. It will take some coordination on your part, so be patient. Select the Hand tool and move the Document window to the left until you see the next boot loop.

9. Select the Lasso tool again and position the pointer over the white pixels in the center of the boot's loop. Hold down the Shift key and note that a plus (+) icon appears next to the lasso pointer. Keep the Shift key pressed and draw around the white pixels within the boot loop (see Figure 4-38). Close the shape, let go of the mouse, and see the marching ants selection (see Figure 4-39).

10. Keep adding to the selection. With the Hand tool, move the Document window to the left until you see the last boot loop on the right.

11. Select the Lasso tool again and position your pointer over the white pixels in the center of the boot's loop. Hold down the Shift key and draw around the white pixels within the boot loop. Close the shape.

12. The white areas within each boot loop are selected. Hit Delete on your keyboard to remove the unwanted pixels.

13. Choose View > Actual Pixels to view the boots at 100% magnification.

figure | **4-38**

Hold down the Shift key to add to a selection.

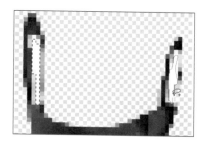

figure | **4-39**

Close the shape to define the selection.

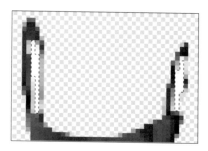

14. Now, let's move the boots to Max's feet. Position the *boot* document and *Max* document side by side on the screen. Select the Rectangular Marquee tool in the toolbox (see Figure 4-40).

15. Marquee around the boot on the left (see Figure 4-41). With the Move tool, click and drag a copy of the boot to the *Max* document. Position the boot over his right foot.

16. Select the other boot, and move a copy of it to Max's left foot.

17. Close *boots.tif*.

18. In the Layers palette, rename the right-foot boot *right_boot*, and the left-foot boot *left_boot*.

19. Select the *right_boot* layer and then choose Layer > Matting > Defringe. Type in *4* (pixels). Do the same thing for the *left_boot* layer.

20. Move the *pants* layer above the boot layers (see Figure 4-42). Position the boots if necessary to appear behind the pants.

21. Save the file.

figure | **4-40**

Select the Rectangular Marquee tool.

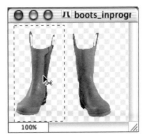

figure | **4-41**

Marquee around a boot and move to another document.

figure | **4-42**

The content of layers is stacked. You can move layers between stacks by clicking and dragging a layer between two other layers.

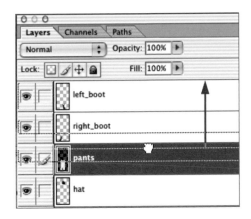

Selecting a Textured Background

1. Open *shirt_blazer.tif* in the *chap4_lessons/assets* folder.

2. With the Lasso tool, draw a cursory selection around the blazer. Be sure not to get any of the shirt in the selection. See Figure 4-43.

figure | 4-43

Cursorily select the
blazer with the
Lasso tool.

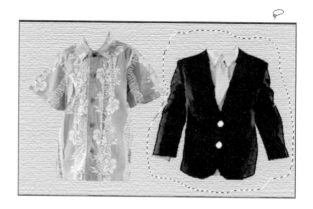

3. With the Move tool, click and drag a copy of the blazer selection to the *Max* file.

4. In the Layers palette, rename the new layer *blazer* and move it above the other layers.

5. Be sure the *blazer* layer is selected. Choose the Magic Wand tool.

6. In the options bar for the Magic Wand tool, enter *40* for the tolerance. Then click the green textured area to select it. Note that not all parts of the textured background have been selected.

7. Change the Magic Wand tool's tolerance to *65* and reselect the textured background. Do you get more or all of the background pixels? Play with the tolerance until you get the green pixels selected. You might also need to add or subtract from your selection if some of the green pixels are not contiguous, or try selecting an area with the Contiguous option deselected in the Magic Wand tool's options bar.

8. Press Delete on the keyboard to remove the selected background pixels.

9. Position and/or transform the blazer to fit Max. See Figure 4-44.

10. If you'd like more practice, on your own bring in the flowered shirt image to fit on Max. (You might want to turn the visibility off on the *blazer* layer while doing this.)

11. Save the file. Max is dressed and ready to head off to school.

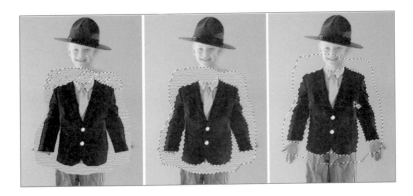

figure | 4-44 |

The stages of selecting a blazer for Max (steps 6 through 8).

SUMMARY

As you've learned, selecting and transforming objects is the most fundamental procedure you need to do in Photoshop. Identifying the best tools for the task makes these actions easier and more efficient to execute, letting you move on to more miraculous development in the program.

in review

1. Describe how the color tolerance setting works in Photoshop?

2. Name at least two ways to get better selection accuracy.

3. What selection tool is the least efficient in selecting irregular areas of an image?

4. What does the Contiguous option do when using the Magic Wand tool?

5. What shortcut key command lets you make straight-edge segment selections with the Free Lasso tool and freehand segments with the Polygonal Lasso tool?

6. Using any selection tool, what shortcut key command lets you add to a selection? Subtract from a selection?

7. One way to transform objects is numerically. What other way can you think of?

8. Describe what the Background layer is in Photoshop. How is it different from a regular layer?

↗ EXPLORING ON YOUR OWN

1. In the Photoshop program, go to Help > Photoshop Help. In the Help files read the sections "Selecting" and "Transforming and Retouching" (no need to get into the retouching parts of this section, which is covered thoroughly in Chapter 6). Also, refer to the section on keyboard shortcuts, "Keys for selecting and moving objects."

2. To complement Max, select and bring a copy of Mina the kitty *(chap4_lessons/assets/mina.tif)* into the *chap4L1* file that you created. For an example, see the "after" picture of Max (Figure 1 in the color insert) to see how I placed Mina, or the *chap4L1_final.psd* in the *chap4_lessons* folder. I removed the unwanted background pixels, scaled her, flipped her horizontally (Edit > Transform > Flip Horizontal), rotated her, defringed her (Layer > Matting > Defringed), and added a drop shadow (Layer > Layer Style > Drop Shadow).

notes

_____

_____

_____

_____

_____

_____

_____

_____

_____

_____

_____

_____

_____

_____

_____

_____

_____

_____

_____

_____

_____

_____

_____

_____

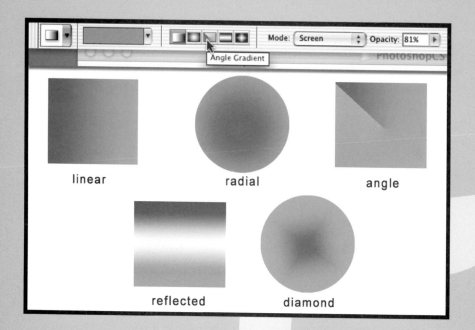

Mode: Screen   Opacity: 81%

Angle Gradient

PhotoshopCS

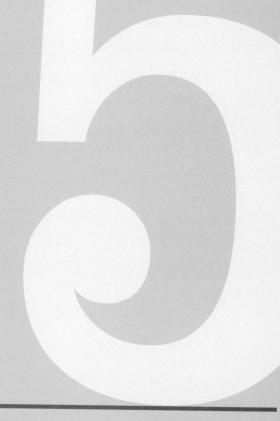

linear   radial   angle

reflected   diamond

| working with color |

charting your course

In the last chapter you selected and transformed pixels. Now you get to change the color of pixels. This chapter covers some fundamental concepts of color, such as how color is reproduced, color modes, and a hands-on study with color models that will pique your interest as a designer. Additionally, we get into some important aspects of color specifically related to Photoshop, such as tips for managing color in the program, dealing with channels, and using the color application tools.

 goals

- Understand the concept of a color gamut
- Get acquainted with color models
- Know what color mode to use
- Apply color to pixels
- Explore the color features and tools in Photoshop
- Make gradients
- Study, hands-on, the use of color models and tonal value

OPTICAL MIXING

Step away from your computer for a moment and find a painting somewhere. It could be the watercolor your child did last week in school or the acrylic piece you picked up at the local art auction. Look very closely at the painting. Examine how the brush strokes blend; how the mixing of pigment produces varied effects and transitions of color. When a color is blended with white it produces a lighter version of the color, and when blended with black a darker version of the color. This method of blending (mixing paint to produce colors) is different from how a computer produces color. In digital image-making each individual color produced is contained in its own pixel area (see Figure 5-1). The effect of colors blending, like what is actually occurring in a traditional painting, is only an illusion manifested by our own eyes, often referred to as "optical mixing."

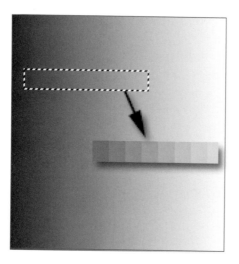

figure | 5-1 |

The image looks like a smooth gradient of color, but when we zoom in close to a selection we see that each pixel contains its own shade of color.

Optical mixing has been around awhile in traditional painting and drawing, often known as pointillism. Pointillism is a method of painting or illustration in which tiny dots (or shapes) of color are combined in such precision that when viewed from a certain distance the pattern forms a complete picture. Post-impressionist painter Georges Seurat (1859 to 1891) codified the technique of pointillism. Whereas other artists were blending paint colors on their canvases, he was creating the same effect by applying pigment in small dabs or points of pure color.

From *Understanding Art* (seventh edition) by Lois Fichner-Rathus, "Upon close inspection, the painting [Seurat's] appears to be a collection of dots of vibrant hues—complementary colors abutting one another, primary colors placed side by side. These hues intensify or blend to form yet another color in the eye of the viewer who beholds the canvas from a distance." A modern painter and photographer using this type of illusionary picture-making is Chuck Close, who combines detailed pattern shapes into famous portraits. The method of creating patterns by sewing colored patches together in quilting is also a form of optical mixing. In what other ways might you think images are formed optically? (See figure 5-2).

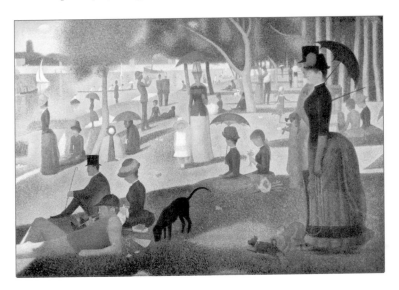

figure | 5-2 |

Example of a Georges Seurat painting, *A Sunday Afternoon on the Island of La Grande Jatte*. Using a technique called Pointillism, Seurat painted this picture with thousands of dots of color.

When we look closely at a digital image, each pixel is one shade of color, but when we step away from the image and view it from a distance it appears to be a completely blended image. Digital images produce form through optical mixing. One technique that encourages this illusion is *antialiasing*. Antialiasing smooths the jagged edges of a digital image by softening the color transition (with gradations of color or shades of gray) between edge pixels and background pixels. In other words, it makes an object that is made up of square pixels appear rounded, smoothed, or curved, not "pixelated." See Figure 5-3.

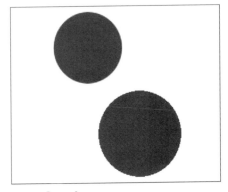

figure | 5-3 |

Image with and without antialiasing. The top circle has antialiasing applied and appears more rounded. The bottom circle doesn't have antialiasing and appears pixelated.

SPECTRAL ILLUSION

Okay, so we learned that our eyes have an uncanny way of optically mixing colors to form recognizable images. Now, discover that our eyes view different colors depending on where and under what conditions we are looking. Every device that has the capability to reproduce color (such as a computer screen, a printer, or a television set) has its own color range (or limits), which is defined as its *color space* or *gamut*. For example, although today's monitors can view millions of colors, what we see on a computer screen is not all the colors available in our universe. In fact, our human color device—our eyes—can view many more colors than any type of digitized screen or printer device.

Take a good look at Figure 5-4. The chart indicates the visual (human), computer screen (RGB), and printer color (CMYK) gamuts. (You'll learn more about RGB and CMYK in the next section.) Also, a color version is available to view in the color section of this book. What to notice are the marked areas indicating the gamuts. All of the gamuts overlap, each able to view some similar color shades. However, the print (CMYK) gamut, indicated by the smallest gamut area, has the least amount of viewable color possibilities.

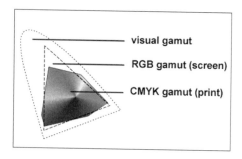

visual gamut

RGB gamut (screen)

CMYK gamut (print)

figure | 5-4 |

The visual, screen, and print gamuts.

So, you can imagine what might happen if you pick a color for your digital image in Photoshop (which by default uses the RGB screen gamut) only to find out when you print it that the color is completely different. Most likely the color you picked in Photoshop is not available in the printer's gamut. It gets even more particular. For example, a CRT monitor will show the same color blue differently than an LCD monitor, or a PC monitor versus a Macintosh monitor. No doubt this predicament is very frustrating, but once you understand why it happens there are many ways to achieve the result you want (this is what is referred to as "Color Management" or "Producing Consistent Color" in the Photoshop Help file). In fact, that's just another of Photoshop's many talents: the ability to simulate for us what colors will eventually look like once reproduced from different devices. We can't cover all the ways in this chapter, but I'll get you started with some explanation of color models and modes and provide you with some additional reading in the "Exploring on Your Own" section.

CHOOSING A COLOR MODEL

A *color model*, quite simply, is a system for describing color. You use color models when choosing, creating, and controlling colors in your digital images. All color models use numeric values to represent the visible spectrum of color. For instance, the truest red color on a screen is indicated as 255 Red, 0 Green, 0 Blue (or 255,0,0). There are many different color models, but in computer graphics and specifically in Photoshop we will look at the following: Grayscale, RGB, HSB, CMYK, and Lab.

Grayscale

The Grayscale color model is used to select tints of black ranging in brightness from 0 (white) to 100 % (black). In Photoshop, when you convert color images into grayscale the luminosity (tonal level) of each color in the artwork becomes a representation of a shade of gray (you get a taste of this in the lesson). To select colors in grayscale you choose Window > Color (if not already open) and from the Palette Options menu choose the Grayscale Slider (see Figure 5-5).

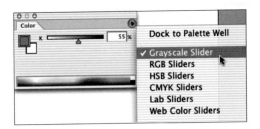

figure | 5-5

The Color palette with the Grayscale model selected.

RGB

The RGB model represents the primary colors of visible light: red, green, and blue (RGB). The mixing of red, green, and blue light in various proportions and intensities produces a wide range of colors in our visual spectrum. RGB color is also referred to as additive color. When R, G, and B lights are equally combined they create white, which is what you see when all light is reflected back to the eye. (The absence of colored light is black—what you get when you wander down a cave without a flashlight.) When R, G, or B overlap each other they create cyan, magenta, and yellow. See Figure 5-6 and the color insert (Figure 3). Devices that reproduce color with light are using the RGB color model. Examples are your television set, the miniscule screen on your PDA, and of course your computer monitor.

Each component (red, green, and blue) in the RGB color model is labeled a value ranging from 0 (black) to 255 (white). This means you can have a total of 256 shades of red, 256 shades of green, and 256 shades of blue, and any combination thereof (a lot of colors!). For example, the most intense red color is represented as 255 (R), 0 (G), 0 (B), and a shade of deep purple is represented as 40 (R), 0 (G), 100 (B). See Figure 5-7.

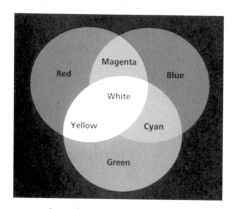

figure | 5-6 |

The RGB color model.

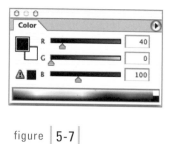

figure | 5-7 |

The Color palette with the RGB model selected.

Photoshop also includes the Web Color model, a modified RGB model that indicates a spectrum of colors most appropriate for use on the Web. The color components in the Web Color space are measured using hexadecimal, a number/letter system used to represent colors. For example, a color of red in hexadecimal is indicated as #FF0000.

HSB

Color can also be defined as levels of HSB—hue, saturation, and brightness. Hue identifies a main color property or name, such as 'blue" or "orange." It's measured by a percentage from 0 to 360 degrees, as if picking colors from a standard color wheel. (See Figure 5 of the color insert.) Saturation is the strength or purity of color. It is measured as an amount of gray in proportion to the hue, ranging from 0 (gray) to 100% (fully saturated). Brightness is the relative lightness or darkness of a hue, measured as a percentage from 0 (black) to 100% (white). See Figure 5-8.

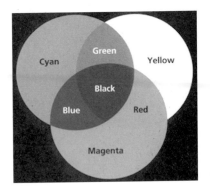

figure | 5-8

The HSB color model in the Color palette.

CMYK

You learned that the RGB color model reproduces color based on light. In contrast, the CMYK model reproduces color based on pigment or ink. The primary colors of CMYK are cyan (C), magenta (M), yellow (Y), and what you get when you mix them all together, which is black (K). We call cyan, magenta, and yellow subtractive colors because when you add these pigments to a white page or canvas they subtract or absorb some of the light, leaving what's left over to reflect back to your eye. When the colors overlap, interestingly they produce red, green, and blue (RGB). See Figure 5-9 and the color version in the color insert (Figure 4).

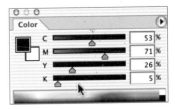

figure | 5-9

The CMYK color model.

Each color component of the CMYK model is represented by a percentage ranging from 0 to 100%. To produce a shade of mauve-colored paint, for example, you mix 53% cyan, 71% magenta, 26% yellow, and 5% black. See Figure 5-10. In the print industry this combining of the CMYK colors is called four-color processing. And the individual colors produced by the mixing of any of these four colors are appropriately identified as *process* colors. In addition to process colors, another color type used in printing is *spot* colors. These are special colors made up of premixed inks that require their own printing plate

figure | 5-10

The CMYK color model selected in the Color palette.

other than the one used for four-color processing. You'll run into the process and spot color types as you work with colors in Photoshop, but don't worry about them so much at this time. Preparing an image for a professional print job can easily become an advanced topic and beyond the scope of this book. A good start is to simply know that if your Photoshop graphic is eventually going to go to print you'll want to choose colors within the CMYK color model.

Lab

Specifically in Photoshop, color can also be defined as Lab, based on the human perception of color—the colors a person with normal vision sees. The primary color components of Lab separate out as luminance (lightness, or L) and two chromatic components: *a* for green and red and *b* for blue and yellow (see Figure 5-11). Interestingly, Lab color is not often used by the average Photoshop user. However, it plays a vital role behind the scenes. Lab describes color by how it looks to the human eye rather than through the lens (limited color range) of a particular device (a monitor, digital camera, or desktop printer). Because of this, Lab is considered a device-independent color model, which makes it a great color mode for Photoshop to use when it needs to convert colors based on a user's specified color management system. You could think of it as the color system used to transition colors between color systems. If I just lost you here, don't worry. It's good to know that Lab exists, but not necessary to completely comprehend in the initial stages of your Photoshop study.

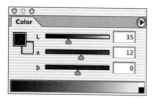

figure | **5-11**

The Lab color model.

GETTING IN THE MODE

While you can select colors from various color models, ultimately you'll want to set up your Photoshop image to a specific *color mode* or *working space* depending on the artwork's intended purpose. A color mode determines how your artwork will be output, either for display on screen (RGB) or for print (CMYK). When you create a new document in Photoshop you must specify the color mode. You can do this when you first create the document or switch modes while working on the document (see Figure 5-12). The main color modes are Bitmap, Grayscale, RGB Color, CMYK Color, and Lab Color.

Photoshop also includes specialized modes (such as Duotone, Multichannel, and Indexed Color) that I'll save for you to delve into on your own. You can change between the CMYK and RGB color modes at any time by choosing Image > Mode on the main menu. It's possible you'll want to change the color mode for a couple of reasons: (1) you'll want to use one of Photoshop's tools or filters, which can only be applied when the document is in RGB Color mode, and (2) you simply change your mind about where you want to output your artwork. Be aware that moving between modes can cause significant shifts in the colors you see on the screen, and can degrade the color accuracy of the image if moved between modes too many times.

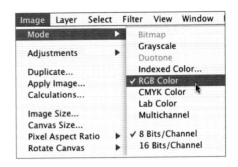

figure | **5-12**

Setting the color mode of the document.

Why all this color mode business, you might be wondering? Well, remember, when it comes to color reproduction what you see is not necessarily what you're going to get from print to screen and screen to print, but it doesn't hurt to try every means possible to get it close. Setting the proper color mode is one of those means by specifying the mode when you first make the document (File > New) or while working on the document (Image > Mode).

APPLYING COLOR

Applying color in Photoshop starts out easy enough. You first choose the color you want, and then you apply it to a selected area with a command or tool. The hard part comes in trying to decide what color you want. There are of course numerous "theoretical ways" in which to pick colors that work well together. One suggestion is to use a standard color wheel to identify complementary colors; colors that are opposite each other on the color wheel, such as blue and orange (see color insert Figure 5). The use of color models or wheels to mix and choose a color can help to identify color based on a numeric numbering system, but for the inquisitive-minded artist it might be just as well to play with colors until

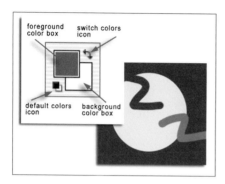

figure | 5-13 |

The foreground and background selection area of the toolbox, and erasing to reveal the background color.

you see something you like (just remember here that the color you see on the screen might not visually reproduce exactly as the same color to another medium, such as on a piece of paper).

In Photoshop you choose colors for either a foreground or background. The foreground color is used to paint, fill, and stroke selections, while the background color is used to make gradient fills and fill in the erased areas of an image (see Figure 5-13).

Color is applied using the Paint Bucket tool or a drawing or brush tool, or by choosing Edit > Fill or Stroke. See Figure 5-14. You can also take a sample of an existing color within an image with the Eyedropper tool (see Figure 5-15).

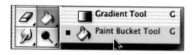

figure | 5-14 |

Select the Paint Bucket tool to fill in selections.

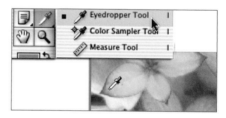

figure | 5-15 |

Select the Eyedropper tool and take a sample of color from an image.

You can choose colors in the Color palette, the Color Picker (accessed by double clicking the foreground or background color selection box in the toolbar), or the Swatches palette. You can also create graduated blends of color using the Gradient tool. Each of these color selection options is described in the sections that follow.

The Color Palette

The Color palette (see Figure 5-16) allows you to choose various color models in which to work and to switch between choosing and adjusting colors on either the foreground or background of a selected object.

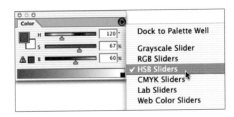

figure | 5-16

Go to Window > Color (if not already open) to open the Color palette.

The Color Picker and Custom Picker

The Color Picker (see Figure 5-17) is a somewhat sophisticated version of the Color palette, offering the option to view, select, and adjust colors from a number of color models in one window. It can be a little overwhelming at first, so let me break it down for you in the following figures.

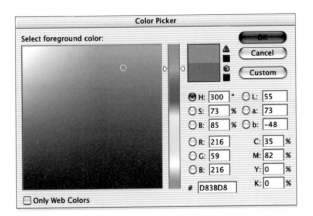

figure | 5-17

Full view of the Color Picker.

figure | 5-18

The left side of the Color Picker is for choosing colors

On the left side of the Color Picker (see Figure 5-18) you choose your colors. The spectrum bar on the right is where you pick the hue you would like, such as red, blue, green, or whatever. The large box to the left allows you to adjust the hue's saturation (moving horizontally) and brightness (moving vertically).

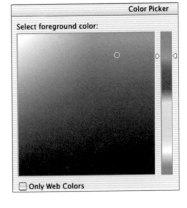

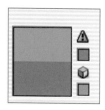

figure | 5-19

In the Color Picker there is
an area to preview a color
you have chosen next to the
color that is already applied
to the object.

The area shown in Figure 5-19 is where you preview the colors you are selecting in the Color Picker. Your current color selections are updated automatically in the top area of the box, while the lower part indicates the original selected color on the object. Next to the color indicator are gamut warnings. Gamut warnings pop up when you've chosen a color that's outside either the web-safe (the 3D box icon) or the CMYK gamut (alert triangle icon). When you click directly on the 3D box icon, the color shifts to the closest web-safe color. Similarly, when you click directly on the alert triangle the color shifts to the closest CMYK (print) color. This is a really handy feature!

On the right side of the Color Picker (see Figure 5-20) you can adjust colors numerically in all four of the color models: HSB, RGB, CMYK, and Lab. For those making web pages, included is the hexadecimal color code for selected colors.

By choosing the Custom button on the Color Picker a whole other world of color possibilities emerges. The Custom area (see Figure 5-21) lets you choose predefined color libraries, equivalent to those on printed swatch books, such as PANTONE or TRUMATCH.

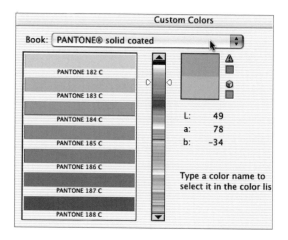

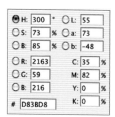

figure | 5-20

You can adjust colors numerically on the right side of the Color
Picker.

figure | 5-21

Custom area of the Color Picker.

The Swatches Palette

After spending long hours picking out your favorite colors, it's good to know you can save them in the Swatches palette (see Figure 5-22). You can apply your saved colors to selected objects by simply clicking on your saved swatches in the Palette window (see Figure 5-23). You can also make swatch libraries to reuse in other documents or use one of the many already provided for you. The Swatches palette will not only save and load your specific color selections but will load other custom color libraries.

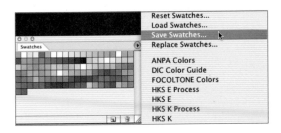

figure | 5-22 |

The Swatches palette.

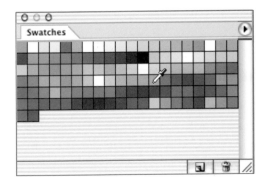

figure | 5-23 |

In the Swatches palette you can save and load specific swatch libraries.

The Gradient Tool and Gradient Palette

Gradients are graduated color blends, and are useful to create smooth transitions of color on an object or across multiple objects, giving them a more dimensional look. Gradients come in several varieties, including linear, radial, angle, reflected, and diamond, which you can choose from the Gradient options bar (see Figure 5-24). Gradients are created in the Gradient Editor (see Figure 5-25)

figure | 5-24

Gradient options bar
and examples of the
different gradient
blends.

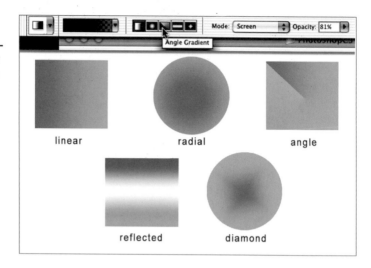

figure | 5-25

To modify or create
new gradients use
the Gradient Editor.

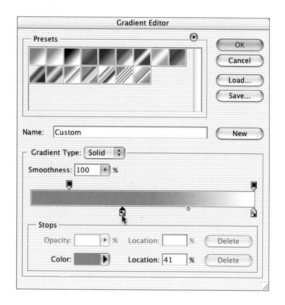

and then applied with the Gradient tool (see Figure 5-26) in the
toolbar. To get to the Gradient Editor, first select the Gradient tool
in the toolbar, and then click inside the gradient sample area in the
options bar to edit the gradient.

Solid gradients are the most common Gradient Type to choose in
the Gradient Editor, but you can also have fun with Noise gradients, a more random blending of color with variable roughness.
Expect to spend a lot of time in the Gradient Editor making and
saving new gradients. You'll get some practice in the next lesson.

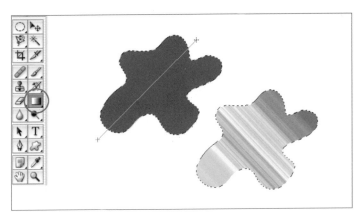

figure | 5-26

Gradient tool.

ADJUSTING COLOR

A big part of dealing with color in Photoshop is not just making color but adjusting color that is already in an image. There is a multitude of image adjustment options (Image > Adjustments) that can absorb your time and creativity, including options to change the tonal quality of a photograph (highlights, shadows, and midtones) and a photograph's hue and saturation levels. You'll get exclusively into adjusting color in Chapter 6. Before then, however, let me explain the importance of channels and bit depth.

About Channels and Bit Depth

I can't skip the concept of channels and the effect of bit depth when working with color in Photoshop. Inevitably you will run into both when working in the program. When you really start getting into the mysteries of color correction and manipulation, channels will provide the necessary clues to reach the result you want. Channels are grayscale images that store information about each of the primary colors of a color model. For example, the RGB model contains a red channel, green channel, blue channel, and composite channel (which is all three channels put together and what you normally see when viewing the image). You can view the channels available in any document by choosing Window > Channels, if not already open (see Figure 5-27).

Each channel can be edited separately, giving you full control over specific ranges of color in the image. If your photograph is too red, for instance, you can lesson the amount of red in the image with the Channel Mixer (Image > Adjustments > Channel Mixer). See figure 5-27

The Channels
palette.

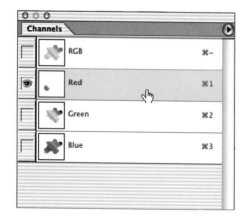

figure 5-28

Adjust the red pix-
els in the image
using the Channel
Mixer.

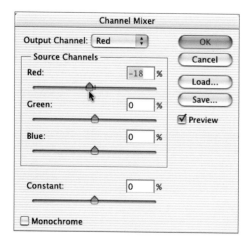

Figure 5-28. You can also create additional channels, such as a spot color to be used in the printing process or an alpha channel, which stores a specific selection or mask (see Chapter 8).

Also important to know is that the more channels in an image the larger the image file size, which is where bit depth comes back in. Remember in Chapter 3 I mentioned that the larger an image's bit depth (accumulation of zeros and ones) the more variations of color an image can contain? Moreover, the more variations the larger the image size. Well, all this bit depth info is stored in channels. A black-and-white image, sometimes called a one-bit image or bitmap, has one channel and a bit depth of 1, with the possibility of holding only two colors, black and white (see Figure 5-29). The same image saved in CMYK color, which has four channels and more room to store colors, has a file size of 351.6 K—heavy! See Figure 5-30.

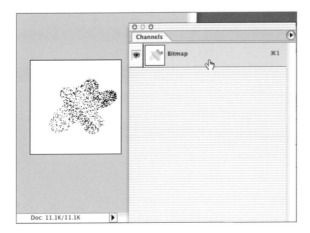

figure | 5-29 |

A one-bit image (or bitmap) has one channel, which supports a bit depth of two colors, black and white. Note the file size of the image in the lower left corner: 11.1K.

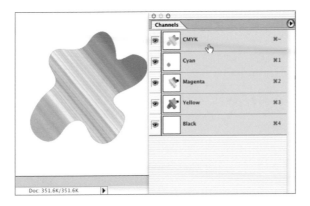

figure | 5-30 |

An image saved in the CMYK Color mode has four channels and more room to store colors. Note its file size: 351 K.

There actually is method to this madness, but I'm only going to take you so far as to understand that bit depth, channels, and color models are all interrelated.

● Bitmap images have one channel, and contain 1 bit of color (black and white).

● Grayscale images have one channel, but that channel contains 8 bits of color, which can produce 256 different shades of gray.

● RGB images have three channels of color, and contain 8 bits of color per channel, which can produce 256 shades of each of the colors red, green, and blue.

● CMYK images have four channels of color, and contain 8 bits of color per channel, which can produce 256 shades of each of the colors cyan, magenta, yellow, and black.

NOTE Living in the "more is better" world that we seem to be in, Photoshop also offers the capability of creating images containing 16 bits of color per channel—expanding the amount of color variations that can be stored in the image.

Lesson: Playing with Color Models

In this lesson, discover how to create complementary colors in Photoshop, blend them together with gradients, and adjust to grayscale. Refer to Figure 5-31.

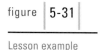

figure | 5-31 |

Lesson example shown in grayscale.

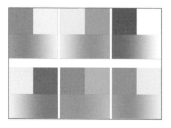

Setting Up the File

1. In Photoshop, choose File > Open. Open the file *chap5L1.psd* in the *chap5_lessons* folder.

2. Save a copy of this file in your *lessons* folder by choosing File > Save As and naming your file *chap5LI_yourname.psd*. This file contains a template and guides for you to build the color models lesson.

   NOTE: If you don't see the guidelines, choose View > Show > Guides.

3. Open the Layers palette if it is not already (Window > Layers). Select Layer 1 and name it *red*.

Creating True Opposites

1. Double click on the foreground color swatch in the toolbox to open the Color Picker.

2. In the RGB model settings area, enter *255* for red, *0* for green, and *0* for blue. 255 red is the truest red color you can create on the screen. Click OK. See Figure 5-32.

3. Select the Rectangle tool in the toolbox. See Figure 5-33.

4. In the options bar, choose the Fill pixels option. See Figure 5-34.

5. Also in the options bar, select the Geometry options pop-up to display the options for the Rectangle tool (the second down-pointing arrow from the left of the options bar). In the Rectangle Options box, choose Fixed Size, and then for W enter *.62* in and for H enter *.66* in. See Figure 3-35.

NOTE: Alternatively to setting a fixed size for the rectangle you can choose Unconstrained

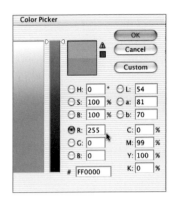

figure | **5-32**

Select a true red in the Color Picker.

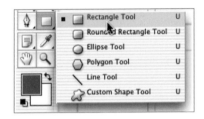

figure | **5-33**

Select the Rectangle tool.

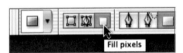

figure | **5-34**

Choose the Fill pixels option in the Rectangle tool's options bar.

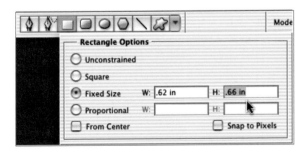

figure | **5-35**

Set a fixed size for the rectangle in its option bar.

and draw the rectangle free-form using the guides and template as positioning markers.

6. Click once on the down-pointing arrow of the Geometry options pop-up to close the window.

7. Place your cursor in the upper left corner of the first rectangle shape indicated on the file. Then, click to place the fixed-size rectangle (click and drag down if you are creating an unconstrained rectangle). See Figure 5-36.

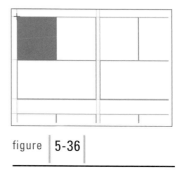

figure | 5-36 |

Place the rectangle on the document.

8. Select the Move tool, and place the pointer over the red rectangle you just created.

9. Hold down the Alt/Option key, and then click and drag to the right to make a duplicate rectangle. Place it right next to the first rectangle.

NOTE: As you drag the duplicate also hold down the Shift key to constrain its horizontal positioning.

10. Note that when you make a duplicate it creates a new layer in the Layers palette (red copy). Rename this layer *cyan*.

11. With the *cyan* layer selected, choose Image > Adjustments > Invert to create the complement (invert or dyad) of the red color, which is cyan.

NOTE: In the color insert of this book, visit the color wheel (Figure 5). Identify the red section in the wheel, and note the cyan section directly opposite it. Interestingly, the RGB and CMYK color models overlap in the color wheel to create a full spectrum of colors.

12. Create a new layer (Layer > New > Layer) and name it *green*.

13. Double click on the foreground color box in the toolbox to open the Color Picker.

14. In the RGB model settings area, enter *0* for red, *255* for green, and *0* for blue.

    NOTE: You can also set this color using the Color palette (Window > Color).

    Select the Rectangle tool in the toolbox.

15. Click on the upper left corner of the boxed area next to the cyan rectangle to deposit a green rectangle. See Figure 5-37.

16. Select the Move tool, hold down the Alt/Option key, and create a duplicate of the green box right next to itself.

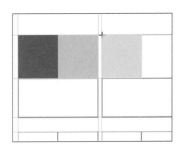

figure | **5-37**

Create another colored rectangle on a new layer.

17. Rename the duplicate layer *magenta*, the complement (invert or dyad) of green.

18. Choose Image > Adjustments > Invert to convert the color to magenta.

19. Double click on the foreground color swatch in the toolbox to open the Color Picker.

20. In the RGB model settings area, enter *0* for red, *0* for green, and *255* for blue.

21. Create a new Layer and name it *blue.*

22. Create a blue rectangle in the boxed area next to the magenta rectangle.

23. Duplicate the rectangle.

24. Rename its layer *yellow.*

25. Invert the color.

26. Save your file.

Creating a Gradient Between Two Complements

1. Select the Gradient tool in the toolbox. See Figure 5-38.

2. Click inside the gradient sample in the options bar to open the Gradient Editor. See Figure 5-39.

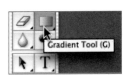

figure | **5-38**

Select the Gradient tool.

figure | 5-39 |

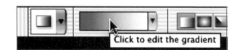

To open the Gradient
Editor, click inside the
gradient sample in the
options bar.

Click to edit the gradient

**DON'T
GO THERE**

Be sure to click inside the gradient sample area, not on the down-pointing arrow next to it. The options under the down-pointing arrow only give you the currently saved gradients, not the full Gradient Editor window.

3. Let's blend a custom gradient using the red and cyan complements. This will create all hues between the two, including chromatic gray in the center. Position the Gradient Editor so that you can also see the red and cyan rectangles on the document.

4. In the Gradient Editor, select the color stop on the left-hand bottom side of the gradient ramp (it will highlight in black). See Figure 5-40.

figure | 5-40 |

Select a color stop
to apply a color to
the gradient.

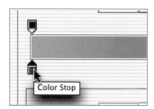

Color Stop

5. Position the pointer over the red rectangle in your document and note that the pointer changes into an Eyedropper tool. Click on the red to take a sample of the color, and the sample is automatically placed into the selected color stop of the gradient ramp. See Figure 5-41.

6. Now, select the color stop on the right-hand bottom side of the gradient ramp.

7. Take a sample of the cyan-colored rectangle in the document. The gradient between the two colors is created.

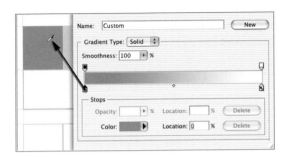

figure | 5-41

Take a sample of color to apply to the selected color stop.

NOTE: A wonderful thing you can do with gradients is change the opacity settings (levels of transparency) of any of the colors in the gradient. In this example we want the gradient color at full opacity, so be sure both opacity stops are set at 100% (see Figure 5-42). Also, for future reference you might want to add more colors to your gradient. To do this, simply click in the lower part of the gradient ramp to create more color stops (see Figure 5-43). To remove color stops, drag them down and away from the ramp and amazingly they disappear.

8. Select New to define (save) the gradient in the gradient sample area. Select OK to close the Gradient Editor.

figure | 5-42

Set the opacity stops at 100%.

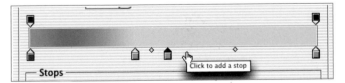

figure | 5-43

Add color stops to create more color blends.

9. Okay, you've made the gradient, now let's apply it to the document.

10. Create a new layer and name it *gradient1*.

11. Select the Rectangular Marquee tool in the toolbox (be sure it's the Marquee tool, not the Rectangle tool you were using before).

12. Select the rectangle area below the red and cyan boxed areas. Marching ants should appear indicating the selection.

13. Select the Gradient tool in the toolbox.

14. Click and drag the tool from left to right in the selected area, and then let go to apply the gradient. (See Figure 5-44).

15. Create a new layer and name it *gradient2*.

16. Following the steps above to create and apply another new gradient using green and magenta under the green and magenta boxed areas.

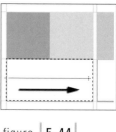

figure | 5-44

17. Ditto for the blue and yellow area.

18. Save your file.

Apply the gradient. Click and drag with the tool from left to right.

Exploring Complementary Hues

1. Let's do a little experiment. First, choose View > Show > Guides to turn off the guides in the document and to get a better look at what you are doing.

2. In the Layers palette, select the top layer and then link all other layers to it, except for the template layer set and Background layer.

3. In the Layers palette, click on the arrow in the upper right corner of the palette to open the drop-down options. Choose Merge Linked to combine the linked layers into one. See Figure 5-45. Rename the *layer top_color_set*.

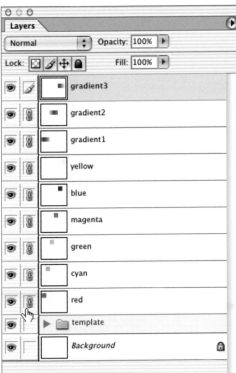

figure | 5-45

Merge linked layers.

4. It's not a bad idea here to save your file with a new name, preserving the original file with all layers intact (you never know
   when you might need access to those layers again). Choose File
   > Save As and save the file in your *lessons* folder as
   Chap5L1_yourname_merge.psd.

5. Make a duplicate of the color set and place it in a new layer
   below the top color set layer.

6. Rename the new layer *bottom_color_set*.

7. Be sure the *bottom_color_set* layer is selected, and then choose
   Image > Adjustments > Hue/Saturation. Check that Preview is
   selected in the Hue/Saturation display, and that you can see
   your document. Move the Hue slider all the way to the right
   and watch how the colors change through all the complementary hues and then back to the original color set. Move the Hue
   slider all the way to the left and you get the same result. Set the
   Hue slider to +25 to see the intermediate complementary colors within the spectrum. As a designer, these sets of colors are
   good starting points for creating colors that go well together.

8. While you are in the Hue/Saturation dialog, go ahead and play with the Saturation and Lightness settings. Saturation increases or decreases the intensity (vibrancy) of the colors. Lightness lightens and darkens the colors.

9. Save the file.

Go Grayscale

1. Every color in the spectrum has an equivalent gray tone. Identify the gray tones in the image by choosing Image > Mode > Grayscale. Choose the Don't Flatten option to preserve the layers in the document.

2. Note the variations of shades in the grayscale image. Once a file is converted to grayscale, it completely discards all color information. You can go back to RGB or CMYK mode at any time to add more color, but the parts originally converted to grayscale will remain that way. With this in mind, it's a good idea to keep a saved version of your file in full color before converting to grayscale.

3. Choose File > Save As and save a copy of this file as *chap5L1_yourname_gray.psd*. That's all for now.

SUMMARY

With such in-depth knowledge of how color performs in Photoshop (optical mixing, digital style) and how to apply it, hopefully your world is now coming up rainbows (or, if anything spinning color wheels and spectrum arrays). There is a definite correlation with where color is reproduced and how it appears to us visually. Lucky for us, Photoshop has the distinctive capability to translate different modes of color, preparing our artwork for all types of output.

in review

1. Describe how optical mixing works.

2. What's antialiasing in digital imaging?

3. Define color space or gamut? Name some devices that use gamuts.

4. What's the distinction between a color model and a color mode?

5. RGB is considered an additive color, CMYK subtractive. Why?

6. Why is the Lab color model considered device independent?

7. What are gamut warnings in Photoshop and where do you find them?

8. What kind of information is stored in channels?

9. What's a complementary color?

10. Where do you find and use color stops in Photoshop?

↗ EXPLORING ON YOUR OWN

1. I dare you to go to the Photoshop Help files and look up the topic of "Color Management" or "Producing Consistent Color." You'll find a lot of interesting information about how to best set up your work area and document, so that consistency of color is achieved when reproducing the image on different devices and platforms. Some of it you might find yourself ready to absorb. Other parts you might wait to read over when you start feeling more comfortable with using the program.

2. Practice saving and loading a swatch library. The commands to do this are located in the Swatches palette drop-down options menu.

3. Create a Georges Seurat Pointillism effect in Photoshop. Open any photograph and choose Filter > Pixelate > Pointillize.

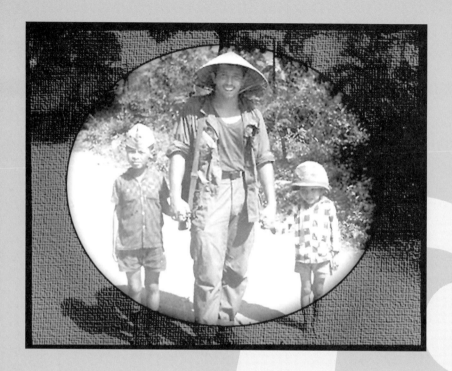

| image correction |

6

charting your course

It's no surprise that a good percentage of what Photoshop is used for is correcting photographs. After all, it was the curiosity of brothers John and Thomas Knoll with darkroom photography and computer programming that brought Photoshop into existence and into the hands of consumers in 1990. Like any great inventor, John kept asking questions: How can the personal computer save photographs into other formats, or adjust the contrast (lights and darks) in a photographic image? In all simplicity and complexity (depending on how you look at it), the answers are now at your fingertips in the form of Photoshop CS.

This chapter presents some fundamental techniques in the image correction process. A photograph's tonal and color quality, not to mention its subject matter, is unique, and in so many ways subject to the judgment of the artist. However, there are some general steps that can become a springboard for understanding the image correction process. Let's get into them.

 goals

- Experience six basic steps for image correction
- Know how to use levels to affect the brightness and contrast in an image
- Get familiar with the image retouching tools, such as Clone Stamp, Smudge, Dodge, and Sharpen
- Add an effect to a photograph

6 STEPS OF EN"LIGHT"ENMENT

So, you have a photograph and it needs some help. It's too dark, too light, the color is off, something is missing, and something has got to go. It's all so overwhelming that you wonder where to begin. When I teach students for the first time what the capabilities are in Photoshop for image correction, I start with six basic steps: import, resize, enhance, retouch, effect, and save. You might eventually choose to use all of these steps or some of them, depending on the photograph. Let me review these steps with you and then you can explore them yourself in the lesson.

Import

To get your photographic image into Photoshop it must be in a digital format. It could be taken from a digital camera or scanned in. Try to get the most high-resolution image you possibly can. It is better to have more pixels to work with than fewer. You could also obtain images from a stock image distributor, such as Corbis, Comstock, or PictureQuest. But those kinds of images are usually already beautifully corrected and wouldn't need much tonal adjustment. To import an image into Photoshop, choose File > Open and browse for the image on your hard drive.

Resize

It's unlikely your image will be exactly the dimensions and/or orientation you desire for its final output. You might need to change its dimensional size and resolution, add more or less area to the overall canvas, or simply crop out unnecessary parts. Whatever you do at this point, save a copy of the original image just in case you want to use it again in another context.

Image Dimensions, Resolution, and Mode

Right away you might want to check the image's resolution size to be sure it has enough pixels in it to do the task you want it to do. For example, if you want the image to be printed on a fine magazine cover, you will want the resolution of the image to be about 300 ppi (pixels per inch). If it's going to be printed in a newspaper, 150 ppi will suffice. For the Web or another digital environment, 72 ppi will work. We talked about the relationship of resolution to the size of an image in Chapter 3, if you need to review. To adjust the size and resolution of an image, go to Image > Image Size.

Another thing to check is what color mode the image is in (Grayscale, RGB, CMYK) and set it to the color mode you most likely would like to work in (review color modes in Chapter 5). Be aware that you can do certain things in some modes and not in others, which could determine when you work in one mode over another. For example, if you change to Grayscale mode, all color will be discarded from the image (and never to return on that part of the image again). If you choose RGB you can work with the many effects and filters in the program that are otherwise unavailable in other modes. And, when your image is toward completion, it's important to set the mode for its intended output. In general, use RGB for screen display, CMYK for print.

Canvas

It's possible you will want to add some more blank canvas area around the image, perhaps to include some text, a border, or other elements. To adjust the canvas size, choose Image > Canvas Size. See figures 6-1 and 6-2.

figure | 6-1 |

The Canvas Size dialog box. You can use several types of measurements (such as pixels, inches, and percentages) to determine the size.

figure | 6-2 |

The canvas of an image resized by 20 pixels all the way around.

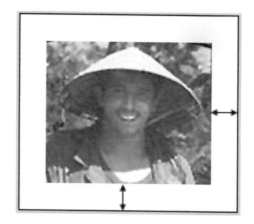

Cropping

When the composition of your photograph is just not right or it wasn't aligned properly during the scanning process, it's time for the Crop tool. Reminiscent of a bout of spring cleaning, the Crop tool can put everything in its place and remove unwanted or unusable areas. To crop, select the Crop tool and click and drag over the area of the image you want to keep. Once the area is defined you can then readjust or rotate the Crop tool more precisely before committing to the crop action. See Figure 6-3.

figure | 6-3 |

Specify and adjust a crop selection.

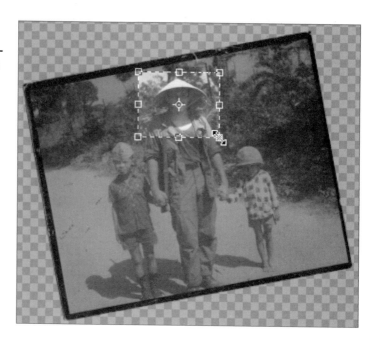

Enhance

Enhancing is where you begin to get into the heart of image correction, which includes adjustments to an image's tonal (brightness and contrast) levels and color balance. Under Image > Adjustments you will find many commands that relate to tonal and color balance editing (see Figure 6-4). Photoshop features auto-correction commands for quick fixes to photographs (Auto Levels, Auto Contrast, Auto Color). However, if you want the ability for more precise correction to specific pixels and their tonal quality, learn to use the Levels, Curves, and Channel Mixer options. See figures 6-5 and 6-6.

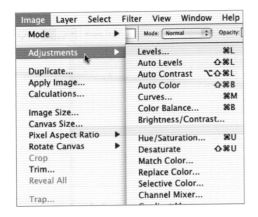

figure | **6-4**

Options available for image enhancements.

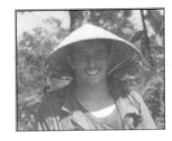

figure | **6-5**

An image before adjustments to its tonal range.

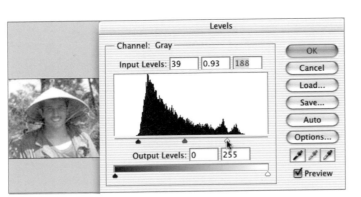

figure | **6-6**

An image after adjustments to its tonal range. For more precise control over the shadows, midtones, and highlights of an image, adjust the histogram (graph of the total distribution of colored pixels in an image).

Retouch

For some it's a full-time job retouching photographs—fixing the very large or very minute blemishes. There definitely is a talent to retouching so it looks transparent to the viewer, but Photoshop makes it easier (quite painless, really) with such tools as the Clone Stamp, Smudge, Blur, and Sharpen tools. See figures 6-7 and 6-8.

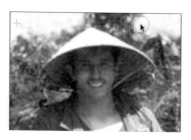

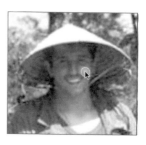

figure | 6-7 |

Use the Clone Stamp tool to take sampled areas of an image to use in place of unwanted areas.

figure | 6-8 |

The Dodge tool quickly lightens areas of an image.

Effect

Once the photograph is beautified the way you like it, consideration can be given to adding something more to it, such as an effect, a text element, a frame or border, or a filter or color enhancement. See Figure 6-9.

figure | 6-9 |

Using feathering, a soft effect is added around the image.

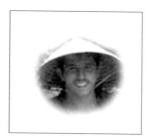

Save

Hopefully all along you save as you work on your image correcting, but final thought goes to output and creating copies of the work for its intended purpose. This might include saving the image in a compressed JPEG format for web publication or in TIFF format to head to the printer.

Lesson: Correcting the Mike Photo

In this lesson you'll experience the six basic steps of image correction, and then you'll be on your way to correcting and enhancing your own photographs. See Figure 6-10.

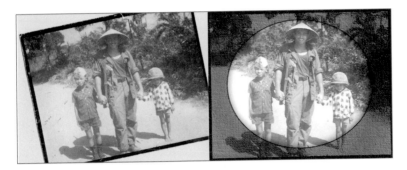

figure | 6-10 |

The lesson before and after. *Original photo compliments of Bruce and Linda Lord.*

Import

1. In Photoshop, choose File > Open. Open the file *chap6L1.psd* in the *chap6_lessons* folder.

2. Save a copy of this file in your *lessons* folder by choosing File > Save As and naming your file *chap6L1_yourname.psd*.

3. Choose View > Actual Pixels to see the document at 100% magnification. This is a photograph taken of my friend's brother, Mike, during the Vietnam War. Right away you can see the photo is quite faded and worn. With this photo, let's go through the six image-correction steps described previously. The first step, import, has already been completed.

Resize

1. Choose Image > Mode. The photograph is currently in RGB Color mode, but for simplicity in this lesson let's change it to Grayscale. Choose Image > Mode > Grayscale. A dialog box asks if you would like to discard all color information in the photo. Choose OK, and rest assured that you have a backup copy of the color version.

NOTE: For further study with color balance, the color version of the photo can be explored in the "Exploring on Your Own" section.

2. Now choose Image > Image Size. The photo's resolution is currently set to 300 ppi. At this resolution, if the photo goes to print it will be approximately 2.7 by 2.3 inches in size (see Figure 6-11). Uncheck the Resample Image option and enter 150 (ppi) for the resolution. The overall print size increases. 150 ppi is a good resolution for most print jobs (a higher resolution is needed for high-quality magazine covers and similar media, which you will learn more about in Chapter 10). Choose OK.

figure | 6-11 |

Always check the image size of your document, so that you know what you are working with.

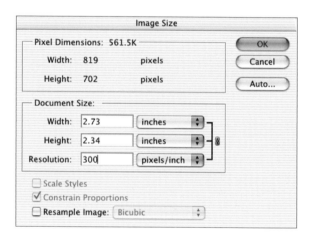

3. Choose View > Print Size to see the exact dimensions of the photograph if it were to be printed. Now, choose View > Actual Pixels to see the size of the image on screen (almost twice as big, because the screen views at about 72 pixels per inch, and if I just lost you here review the section on resolution in Chapter 3).

4. Okay, you've set the image size, but as you can see the image is crooked on the canvas, which can happen in the scanning process when the image is not properly aligned on the scanning bed. Select the Crop tool in the toolbox. Click and drag an area around the photograph. Scale and rotate the Crop tool around the edges of the photograph (see Figure 6-12), and then execute the crop (see Figure 6-13).

5. Save the file.

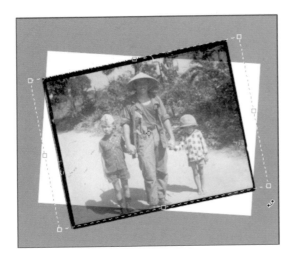

figure | 6-12 |

Using the transform handles, adjust the crop around the image.

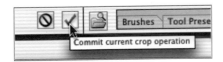

figure | 6-13 |

Choose the check mark on the options bar to execute the crop.

Enhance

1. Now the fun stuff. Choose Image > Adjustments > Auto Levels and note the automatic tonal correction made to the image. It's looking better already. Let's backtrack and try a different method—something with a bit more control. Choose Edit > Undo Auto Levels.

2. Open the Layers palette. Choose Layer > New Adjustment Layer > Levels. Keep the Levels 1 layer name and click OK. A histogram comes up. This is a graph that shows the distribution of shadows, midtones, and highlights in an image. The far left marker at the bottom of the graph indicates the end range for the darkest (shadow) pixels in the image. The far right marker indicates the end range for the lightest (highlight) pixels in the image. The marker in the middle adjusts all chromatic gray pixels between. See Figure 6-14.

figure | 6-14 |

Adjust the levels by moving the shadow, midtone, and highlight markers. Be sure to preview the document as you make changes.

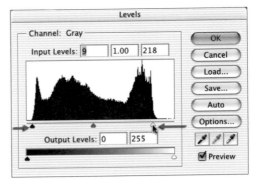

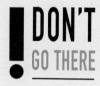

A more direct way to get to the Levels option in Photoshop is to choose Image > Adjustments > Levels. However, this option applies your level changes directly on the selected image layer. To avoid committing right away to your tonal adjustments, use an adjustment layer (Layer > New Adjustment Layer), which places a layer above the original image and works like a temporary overlay (see Figure 6-15). If you don't like the adjustment or just change your mind, simply delete the layer and the original image will remain intact.

figure | 6-15 |

A levels adjustment layer located above the image the layer is affecting. To edit the levels, double click on the histogram thumbnail in the adjustment layer.

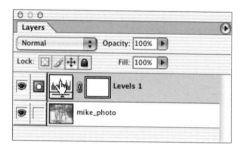

3. A quick way to find a good tonal balance in the image is to move the black (shadow) marker on the histogram inward until it aligns with the first vertical stretch of pixels in the histogram. Do the same with the white (highlight) marker. Note the changes occurring directly on the document. Adjust the midtones marker to the right or left to get a visual of how much control you have over the photo's brightness and contrast. See Figure 6-14.

NOTE: Adjusting the histogram is just the beginning of what you can do to manipulate the tonal range of pixels. There's more to play with in the Levels dialog, and we haven't even gotten to working with curves, but that's for later study (see "Exploring on Your Own" at the end of the chapter).

4. Once you get the levels to your liking, choose OK to close the dialog.

5. Okay, let's add some color back into the image—a sepia tone. To do this you must first change the image mode back to RGB via Image > Mode > RGB Color. Select the Don't Merge option.

6. Be sure the *mike_photo* layer is selected, and then choose Image > Adjustments > Photo Filter. Select the Sepia filter from the drop-down. Try a Density setting of about 75%. What do you think? Feel free to try the other filters if sepia is just not your color. See Figure 6-16.

NOTE: Alternatively you can colorize the image by choosing Image > Adjustments > Hue/Saturation, selecting the Colorize option, and setting the Hue, Saturation, and Lightness levels to your liking.

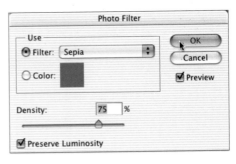

figure | 6-16 |

Colorize the photograph with a photo filter.

7. Let's work with the Sharpen feature. This next enhancement is optional, but it is sometimes necessary on images that have gone through a scanning process, which tends to overly blur some images. Sharpening is also a good idea when you want to bump up the readability of text in a photo. Be sure the *mike_photo* layer is selected. Choose Filter > Sharpen > Sharpen and note the subtle clarity in the image (if you didn't catch this the first time, choose Edit > Undo Sharpen and redo the step).

NOTE: Also available in the Sharpen filters is Unsharp Mask, which works like the sharpen feature but gives you more control over the effect. Give it a try, if you like; you can always undo the effect in the History palette.

8. Excellent time to save your work.

Retouch

1. Okay, on to some real magic. The Mike photo is pretty well worn. Note the stains and scratches on the photo, particularly those on the left-hand side (see Figure 6-17).

2. Let's change the pointer icon to a brush, so that it will work more accurately. Choose Photoshop > Preferences > Display & Cursors (Mac) or Edit > Preferences > Display & Cursors

figure | 6-17

The circled areas indicate scratches and stains in the photo.

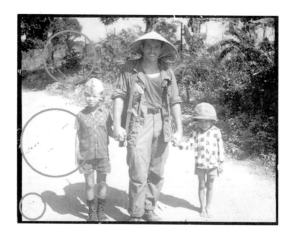

(Windows) and under Painting Cursors choose Brush Size (if it is not already selected).

3. Select the Clone Stamp tool in the toolbox (see Figure 6-18).

4. In the options bar click on the brush thumbnail to open the brush options. Click on the arrow to the right of the drop-down menu to open further options. Choose to view the brushes with Small Thumbnails (see Figure 6-19). The Clone Stamp tool takes a picture of an area of an image that can be brushed in elsewhere on the image. The brush size chosen determines the size of the picture area. Choose the Soft Round 27-pixel brush.

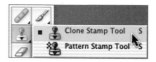

figure | 6-18

The Clone Stamp tool.

figure | 6-19

Select to view the brushes in small thumbnails.

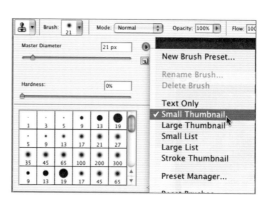

5. Place the Clone Stamp tool over an unstained, lighter area on the left-hand side of the image. See Figure 6-20. Hold down the Alt/Option key and click to take a picture (sample) of that pixel area.

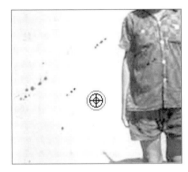

figure | **6-20**

Position the Clone Stamp tool over an area, hold down the Alt/Option key, and click to take a picture (sample) of the pixels.

6. Now, position the pointer over one of the stained areas of the image, and click once to apply the saved picture over the stained area. Click and drag (brush) lightly over the stained area to blend the area into the background pixels (see Figure 6-21). Note that when you click and drag over an area a crosshair comes up too. The crosshair indicates the area that is being copied by the brush in another area. Huh? Frankly, at first this relationship between the crosshair and the brush can be somewhat frustrating, but once you understand how the tool works it does make sense. The first picture taken with the Clone Stamp tool (when you hold down the Alt/Option key) is applied to a new area when you click elsewhere on the image. This indicates the relative starting point of what the crosshair will continue to pick up as you click and drag (brush) over the area. See Figure 6-22.

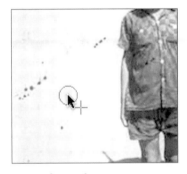

figure | **6-21**

Blending the area into the background pixels.

figure | **6-22**

First picture applied to a new area. Note the crosshair on the boy's nose. The pixels in this area are being applied by the brush above and to the left.

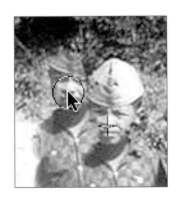

7. Continue to take samples of clean areas of the image and apply them to the stained or scratched areas. You might want to change your brush size, depending on the area size you are taking a sample of. You can do this quickly by Ctrl-clicking (Mac) or right clicking (Windows) over the area you are working with, which brings up the brush options box. See Figure 6-23.

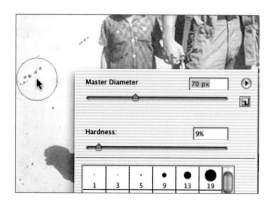

8. There are other retouch tools that might do the trick, other than the Clone Stamp tool. Select the Smudge tool in the toolbox (see Figure 6-24).

9. Zoom in close to the scratch on the boy's knee to the left of the photo.

10. Gently blend the darker pixels of the boy's knee into the light scratched area. See Figure 6-25.

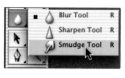

figure | 6-24

The Smudge tool is hiding under the Blur tool in the toolbox.

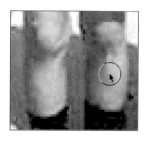

figure | 6-25

Hiding blemishes with the Smudge tool.

11. Zoom back out to 100% magnification. Note that Mike's face is quite dark under his hat. Zoom in close to his face.

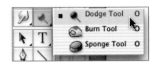

12. Select the Dodge tool in the toolbox (see Figure 6-26) and in the options bar set Exposure to 5%. In the options bar, also adjust your brush size, if necessary (I chose 5 for my brush size—quite small).

figure | **6-26**

The Dodge tool in the toolbox.

13. Gently brush the Dodge tool over Mike's cheeks to lighten them slightly.

14. Zoom back out to 100% magnification to see the subtle result. If you dodged too much, either undo actions in the History palette or use the Burn tool (under the Dodge tool in the toolbox) to redo the darker effect.

15. Using your newly found tools, retouch other areas of the photo, such as the scratches on its black border.

16. Save your document.

Effect

1. The effect step could involve any sort of added inspiration to a photo. For the Mike photo let's make a frame (see Figure 6-10, for example). Be sure the *mike_photo* layer is selected.

2. Select the Elliptical Marquee tool in the toolbox. Position the cursor on Mike's belt buckle and hold down Shift + Alt/Option, and then click and draw from the center a circle around the three figures.

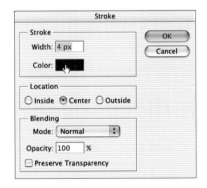

3. Choose Select > Inverse to inverse the selection area (marching ants should appear around the edges of the photo).

4. Choose Edit > Stroke, choose four pixels, and pick a dark gray color (see Figure 6-27).

5. Choose Filter > Texture > Texturizer. In the Texturizer dialog box choose the

figure | **6-27**

Add a stroke to the photo frame.

Canvas option (see Figure 6-28) and set the Scaling and Relief to your liking.

NOTE: You can preview the changes being made directly on your document without closing the Texturizer dialog box.

6. Choose Select > Deselect (Command-D for Mac, Ctrl-D for Windows).

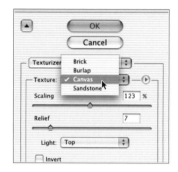

figure | 6-28

Add a texture to the selected frame area.

Save

1. You definitely want to save a Photoshop version of your corrected image (maybe even two or three versions along the way). Choose File > Save As and save a final .psd version in your lessons folder.

2. Now, let's save two other versions for different output. For print, choose File > Save As and under Format select TIFF. In the TIFF options box, select NONE for Image Compression and Discard Layers and Save a Copy for Layer Compression (see Figure 6-29).

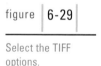

figure | 6-29

Select the TIFF options.

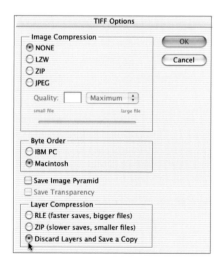

3. And, one for the Web. Choose File > Save As, Format: JPEG. Set the image compression quality to 8 (so there is some compression placed on the image, but not so much to ruin its quality).

NOTE: You can also choose File > Save For Web to save in JPEG format. However, this opens up another big dialog box of choices you might not want to deal with right now. We'll get into that in Chapter 11.

You are done with the image correction process.

SUMMARY

A whole new world—blemish-free—has opened up to you after this chapter. Using the powerful image-correction tools and processes available in Photoshop, now every photograph has the potential for perfection, if not totally true in content.

in review

1. What are the six basic steps for image correction?

2. Why is checking the resolution setting of an imported photograph or image important?

3. Why might someone work in RGB Color mode over other modes?

4. What are you adjusting when moving the sliders in the Levels histogram?

5. What keyboard command must you press to take a pixel sample with the Clone Stamp tool?

6. When working with the retouching tools, why would viewing your cursor as Brush Size be helpful? Where do you go to make this setting?

7. What's the advantage of using an adjustment layer to make color or tonal corrections on an image?

8. Why would you save backup copies of the original photograph before retouching it?

↗ EXPLORING ON YOUR OWN

1. In the Photoshop Help files (Help > Photoshop Help) expand your knowledge of levels and discover the wonders of curves. See the section on Making Color and Tonal Adjustments, parts "Using the Levels dialog box" and "Using the Curves dialog box."

2. Mike in color. Using the Channel Mixer, remove the red overcast in the chap6L1 file. For information on using the Channel Mixer, consult the Help files.

notes

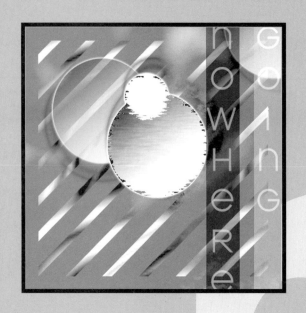

| drawing and painting |

7

charting your course

So far, we've spent a lot of time working with photographs in Photoshop—cropping, selecting, and transforming them, and altering tonal values and color. In this chapter, you get an introduction to the many drawing and painting tools of the program, which advances the possibilities of what you can do in Photoshop to another creative level. With little doubt, playing with the Paintbrush, Pencil, Pen, and Shape tools (not to mention path and type elements) will easily lose you in what could be a complex amalgamation of colors and shapes. It's like looking into and turning the tube of a kaleidoscope—where complex patterns and designs allure you into amazement.

If you were to take the kaleidoscope apart, however, you would find that how it produces this amazing eye candy is but an artifact of a simple design—a few reflective mirrors, some light, and a myriad of objects, confetti, beads, jewels, glass, and pressed flowers. The same goes for drawing and painting in Photoshop, except instead of spinning objects making these dazzling images it's another type of back-lit object. Yes, you guessed it, pixels.

 goals

- **Master pixel painting with the Pencil and Paintbrush tools**
- **Recognize how vectors serve as a temporary mold for more flexible and free-form drawing and offer cross-compatibility support between pixel-based and vector-based programs**
- **Make path, fill, and stroke geometric and free-form shapes**
- **Draw a nonrepresentational art piece**

PIXELS—A CONTEMPORARY ART MEDIUM

With pixels, you can simulate art styles through the use of the Pencil and Paintbrush tools (and filter effects, discussed later in this chapter). Want to paint with watercolors, an airbrush? Draw with charcoal or chalk? With your mouse or pressure-sensitive digitizing tablet you can. Additionally, from the brush libraries you can paint other elements, such as textured grass, scattered leaves and flowers, swirls, and patterns. And with custom brushes you can paint just about anything else you might think of. You can change brush sizes, opacity, blending modes, and flow attributes. (I fear if you're the doodling type, you'll never get beyond this chapter!).

Using the Pencil and Paintbrush Tools

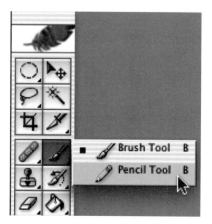

The Pencil and Paintbrush tools are found in the toolbox (see Figure 7-1). These let you paint with any foreground color you choose. In general, the Pencil tool creates hard-edged, freehand lines of color. The Paintbrush tool creates soft strokes of color. See figures 7-2 and 7-3 to compare and contrast the same styles used with both the Pencil and Paintbrush tools.

figure | 7-1 |

Pencil and Paintbrush (Brush) tools in the toolbox.

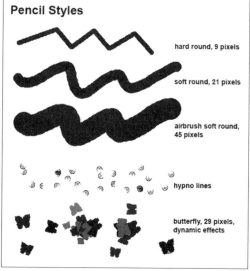

figure | 7-2 |

A small sampling of pencil styles and sizes.

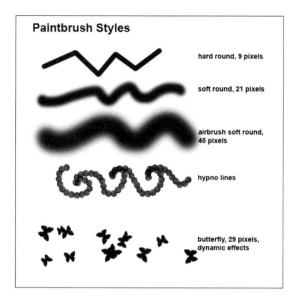

Paintbrush Styles

hard round, 9 pixels

soft round, 21 pixels

airbrush soft round, 45 pixels

hypno lines

butterfly, 29 pixels, dynamic effects

figure | 7-3 |

A small sampling of paintbrush styles and sizes.

When using these tools I recommend setting your cursor preferences to indicate the brush size you are using. To do this, go to Photoshop > Preferences > Display & Cursors (Mac) or Edit > Preferences > Display & Cursors (Windows), and under Painting Cursors choose Brush Size. There are several places to make adjustments and add variations to your pencil or paintbrush tool: in the options bar (see Figure 7-4), the Brushes palette (under Window > Brushes, Figure 7-5), and the context menu when you right click (Windows) or Ctrl-click (Mac) over an area with the tool (see Figure 7-6).

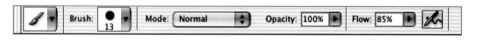

figure | 7-4 |

The Paintbrush (Brush) tool's options bar (Pencil tool options are similar).

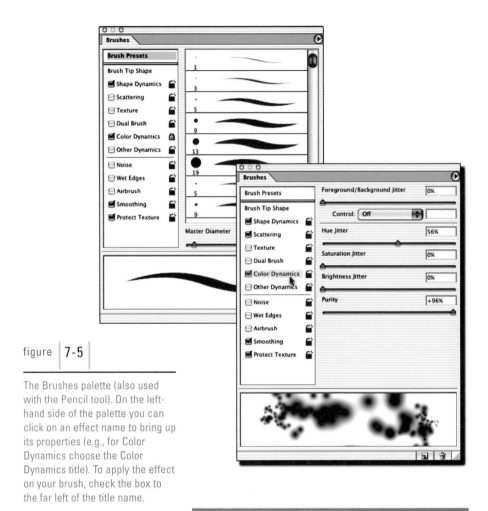

figure | 7-5

The Brushes palette (also used
with the Pencil tool). On the left-
hand side of the palette you can
click on an effect name to bring up
its properties (e.g., for Color
Dynamics choose the Color
Dynamics title). To apply the effect
on your brush, check the box to
the far left of the title name.

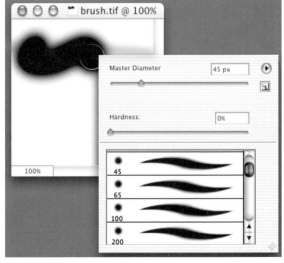

figure | 7-6

Context menu for the Paintbrush
tool. As you paint, you can quickly
change the tool's Diameter,
Hardness, or Style.

In the chapter lesson, you'll get to freely practice with the Pencil and Paintbrush tools, but I realize that's still a few pages away and the temptation to start messing around with these tools is usually urgent. So, let's do it—pronto!

1. In Photoshop, choose File > New and create a document any size you'd like.

2. Check the preferences to be sure that under Display & Cursors the Brush Size painting cursor is selected.

3. Set a foreground color in the toolbox. This is the color you will draw with.

4. Select the Pencil tool in the toolbox (see Figure 7-1). In the options bar click on the second inverted arrow to open the Brush (also Pencil) Preset picker. Choose a pencil in the scrolling list. See Figure 7-7.

   NOTE: Alternatively, you can go to Window > Brushes and open the Brushes palette, which contains these options and more.

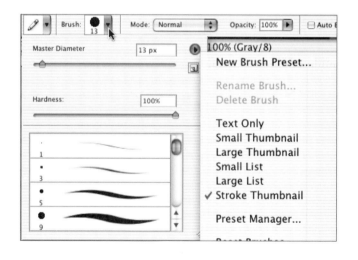

figure | **7-7**

Open the Brush (also Pencil) Preset picker. Note that in the Options drop-down menu for the Preset picker the view in this example is set to Stroke Thumbnail.

5. Note, for future reference, that in the options bar you can also adjust the Pencil tool's blending modes and opacity. Hold off on exploring these options until you feel comfortable with the basic settings.

6. Position the cursor over your blank document and click and drag to start drawing.

NOTE: To create straight lines, click down with the Pencil tool, hold the Shift key, and then click down in another place on the document. (Don't click and drag, just click-click-click...while holding down the Shift key. If you don't hold down the Shift key you just make dots. Try it and see!)

7. Draw to your heart's content, changing colors and pencil attributes.

8. To erase, use the Eraser tool (see Figure 7-8). Just like the Pencil tool's diameter (size), the Eraser tool's diameter can be set in the options bar. Whatever background color you have chosen in the toolbox is the color the Eraser tool reveals. So, if your document started out with a white background, make sure white is set in the background color swatch of the toolbox to completely remove whatever you are erasing.

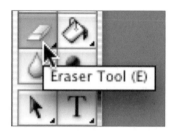

figure | 7-8

The Eraser tool. The color it reveals is determined by the background color.

NOTE: You can undo your strokes in the History palette.

9. Now, select the Paintbrush tool in the toolbox.

10. In the Brushes palette (Window > Brushes), select a Brush Preset. For more options (not that you need them right now) click the arrow in the upper right-hand corner of the palette and from the drop-down Options menu choose another brush library from the list at the bottom (i.e., from Dry Media Brushes or Special Effect Brushes). To add the brush library to the current list of brushes in the Brushes palette, select Append when the dialog box comes up. See Figure 7-9.

figure | 7-9

Choose Append to add brushes to your existing brush style list.

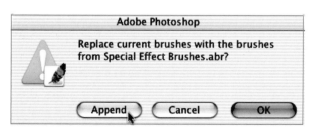

Adobe Photoshop

Replace current brushes with the brushes from Special Effect Brushes.abr?

(Append)   (Cancel)   (OK)

| figure 1 |

The ability to select and transform pixels is one of the first things to learn in Photoshop. This is practiced in Chapter 4 as you prepare Max to get ready for school.

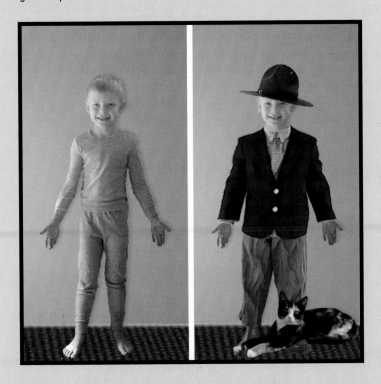

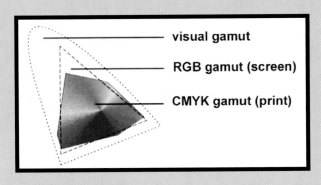

visual gamut

RGB gamut (screen)

CMYK gamut (print)

| figure 2 |

The visual (human eye), screen, and print color gamut areas.

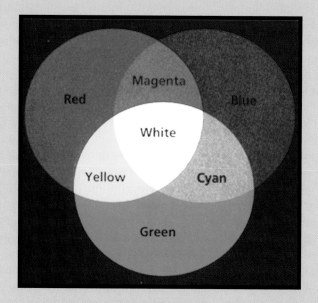

figure 3

The RGB color model. When RGB lights are added together, they create white. When R, G, or B lights overlap each other, they create cyan, magenta, and yellow.

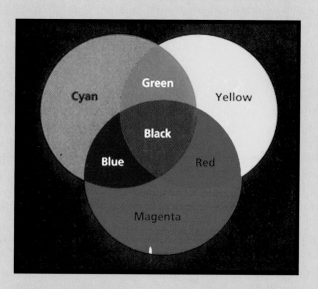

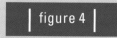

figure 4

The CMYK color model. When CMY ink colors are mixed together, they create black (K). When the colors overlap, they produce red, green, and blue.

figure 5

A standard color
wheel.

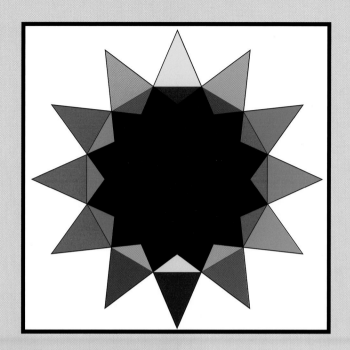

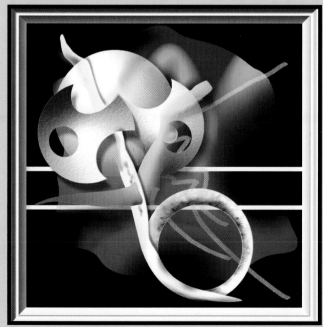

figure 6

An example of nonrepresentational art, which you create with the
drawing and painting tools learned in Chapter 7.

figure 7

An example of non-representational art—an art creation that may not make reference to anything in nature or reality.

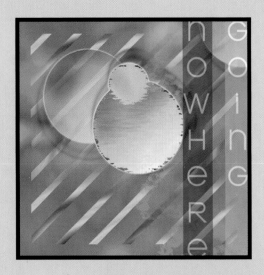

figure 8

With layer blending modes you can blend pixels from images on separate layers and produce many interesting effects. See Chapter 9.

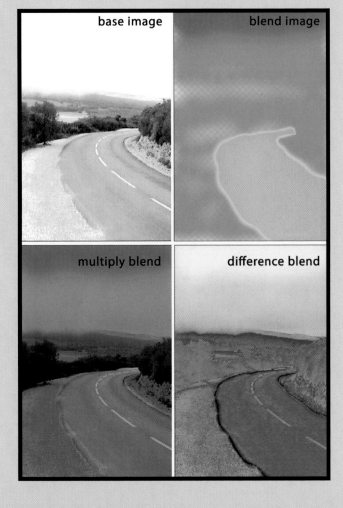

| figure 9 |

Student rendition of the CD Jacket project in Chapter 9. (Modesto Junior College, Photoshop class).

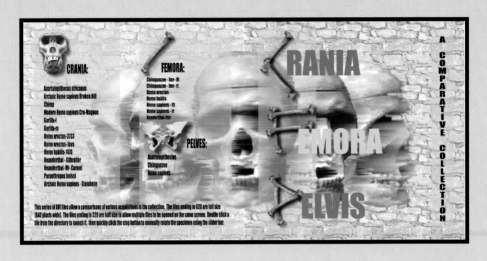

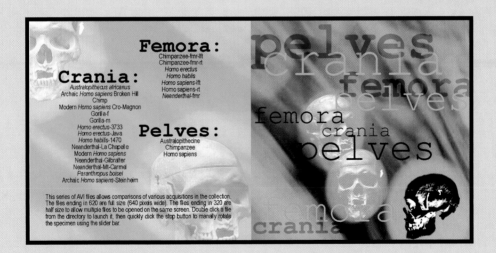

| figure 10 |

Student rendition of the CD Jacket project in Chapter 9. (Modesto Junior College, Photoshop class).

Retouched and print-
ready image from
Chapter 10.

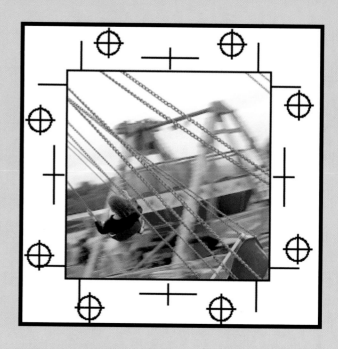

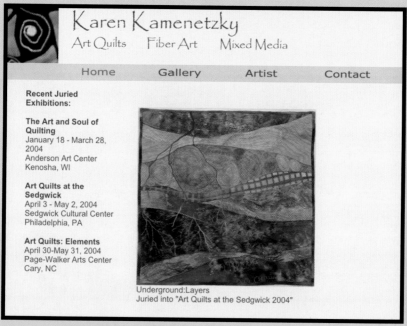

Web site home page whose images are optimized in Chapter 11
(www.karenkamenetzky.com).

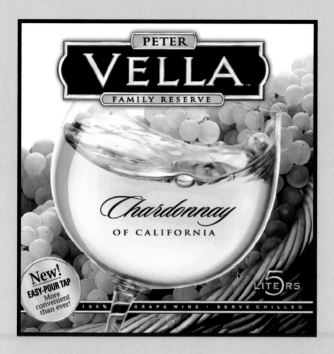

| figure 13 |

This wine box label was created by the artists at Gallo Winery, Modesto, California, using a combination of Photoshop and Illustrator. (Used with permission of E & J Gallo Winery.)

| figure 14 |

Montage, by graphic artist Christina Cross.

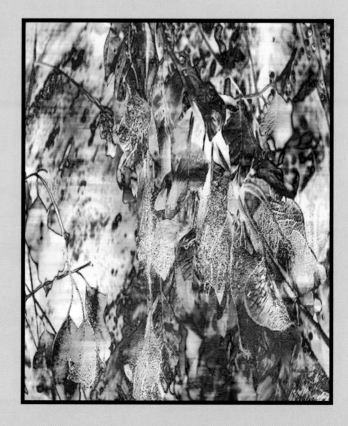

figure 15

Dance, by graphic
artist Christina
Cross.

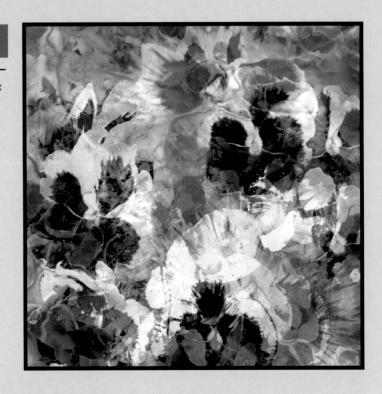

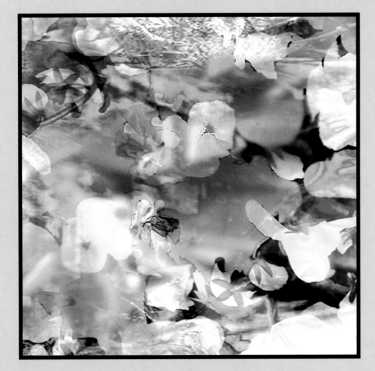

figure 16

Spring, by graphic
artist Christina
Cross.

| figure 17 |

Beach Boys, by graphic artist and animator Joe Summerhays.

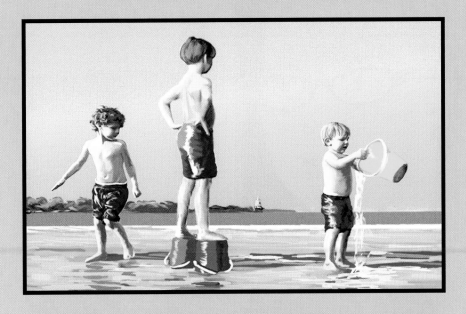

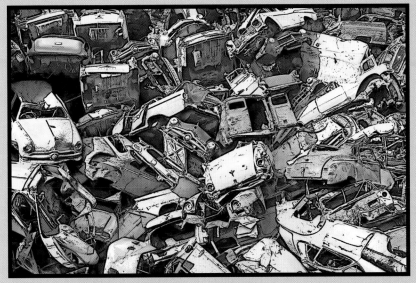

| figure 18 |

Autorama, by graphic artist Dave Garcez.

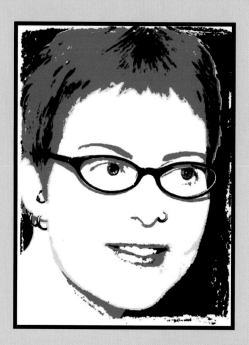

| figure 19 |

Stephanie, by graphic artist Dave Garcez.

| figure 20 |

Transformers, by graphic artist Fred Smith.

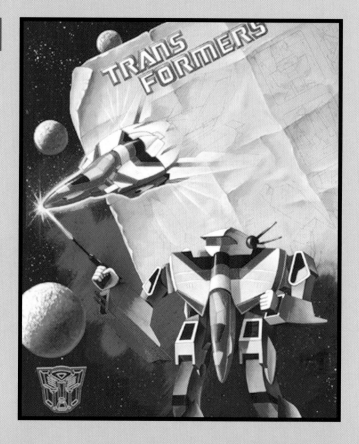

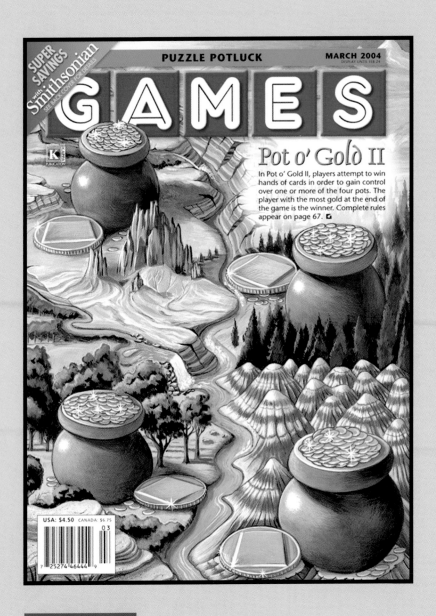

PUZZLE POTLUCK

MARCH 2004
DISPLAY UNTIL FEB 24

GAMES

K PUBLICATION

Pot o' Gold II

In Pot o' Gold II, players attempt to win hands of cards in order to gain control over one or more of the four pots. The player with the most gold at the end of the game is the winner. Complete rules appear on page 67.

USA: $4.50   CANADA: $6.75

03

7 25274 46444 9

| figure 21 |

Cover of *Games* magazine, by artist Fred Smith.

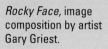

figure 22

Rocky Face, image composition by artist Gary Griest.

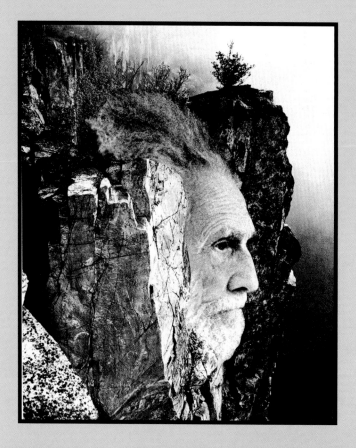

figure 23

Slow Star Willies, image composition by artist Gary Griest.

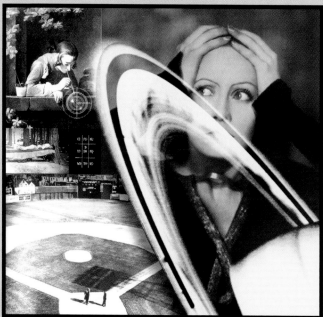

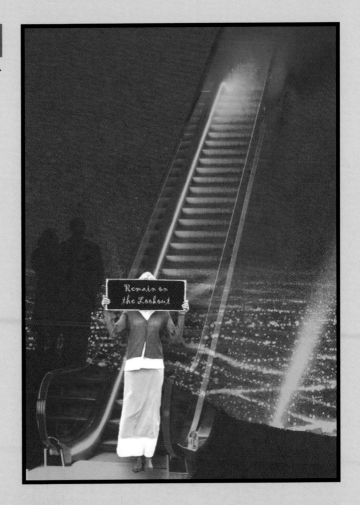

The Dead Are the
Closest Star, image
composition by artist
Gary Griest.

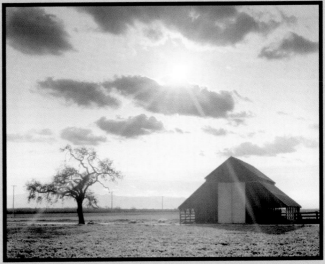

Barn and Lone Oak,
photograph with
Photoshop color cor-
rection and enhance-
ment. © Jeff Broome /
jeffbroome.com.

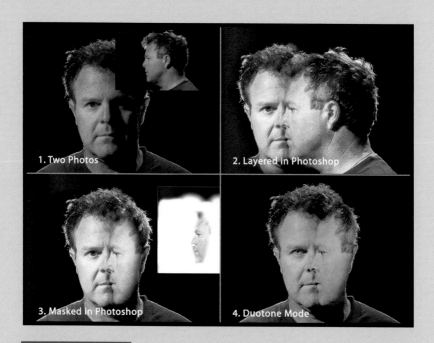

| figure 26 |

Stages of creation for *Self Portrait,* by Jeff Broome, photographer. © Jeff Broome / jeffbroome.com.

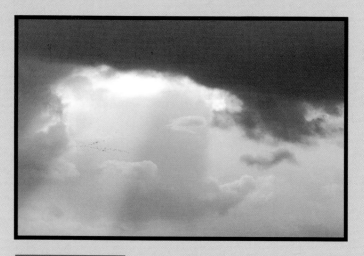

| figure 27 |

Birds in Flight, Winter Storm, color enhanced in Photoshop by photographer Jeff Broome. © Jeff Broome / jeffbroome.com.

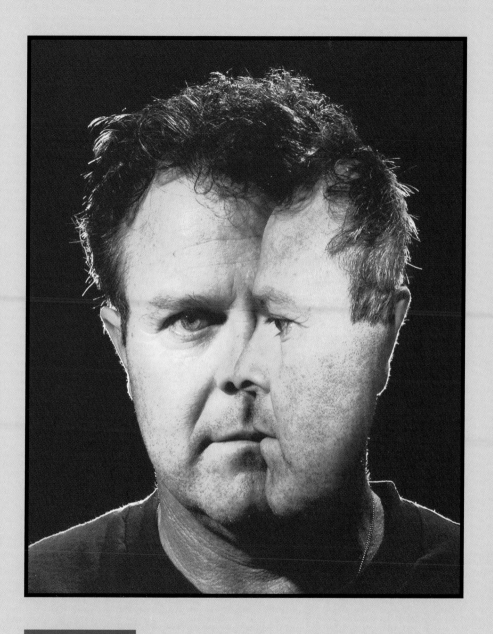

Self Portrait, completed image by Jeff Broome, photographer.
© Jeff Broome / jeffbroome.com.

| figure 29 |

Trees in Field of Mustard Seed Flowers, color enhanced in Photoshop by photographer Jeff Broome. © Jeff Broome / jeffbroome.com.

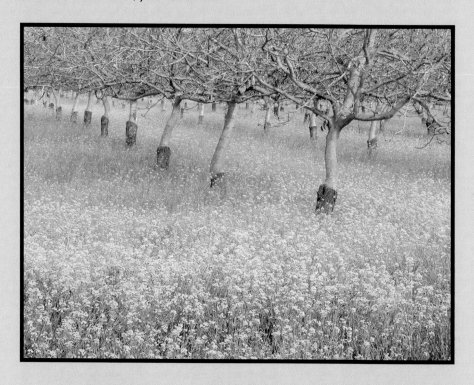

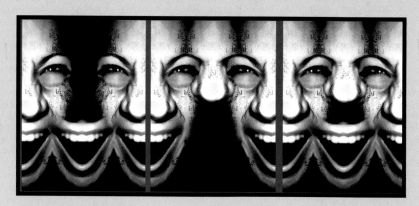

| figure 30 |

Laughing Hyenas, by Jeffrey Moring, artist. Images cloned and composited together in Photoshop. Compliments of Jeffrey Moring.

| figure 31 |

The Final Judgment, by artist Jeffrey Moring. Human models created in a 3D program, rendered and brought into Photoshop for retouching and lighting effects. Compliments of Jeffrey Moring.

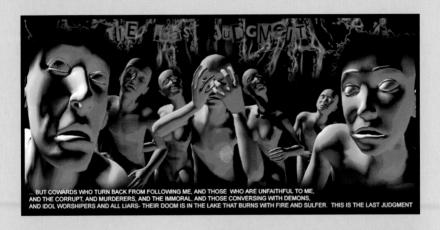

... BUT COWARDS WHO TURN BACK FROM FOLLOWING ME, AND THOSE WHO ARE UNFAITHFUL TO ME, AND THE CORRUPT, AND MURDERERS, AND THE IMMORAL, AND THOSE CONVERSING WITH DEMONS, AND IDOL WORSHIPERS AND ALL LIARS- THEIR DOOM IS IN THE LAKE THAT BURNS WITH FIRE AND SULFER. THIS IS THE LAST JUDGMENT

| figure 32 |

Unanswered Prayers, by artist Jeffrey Moring. Photo manipulation using Photoshop. Compliments of Jeffrey Moring.

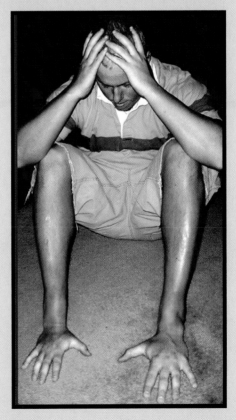

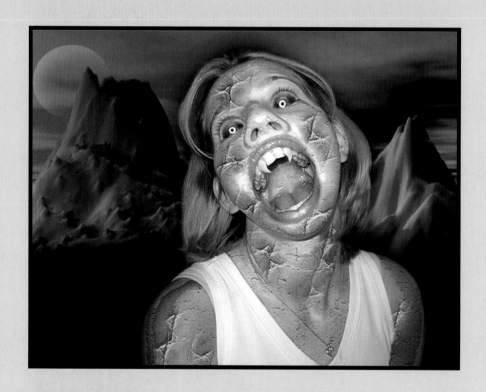

figure 33

Vamp'd, by artist Jeffrey Moring. Image composition and effects using Photoshop.
Compliments of Jeffrey Moring.

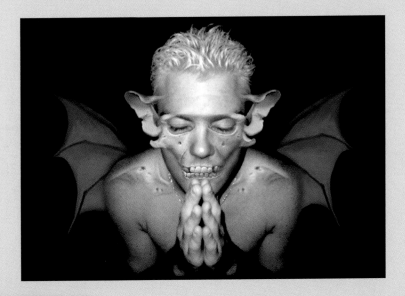

figure 34

Yesterday, Today, Forever, by artist Jeffrey Moring. See "Adventures in Design: From the Imagination" in this book for an explanation on how this image was created. Compliments of Jeffrey Moring.

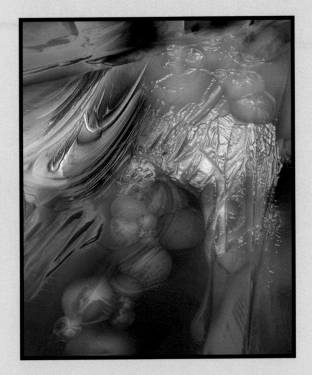

figure 35

Ice Ram, by digital artist and digital arts instructor Joel Hagen. Used with permission from Joel Hagen.

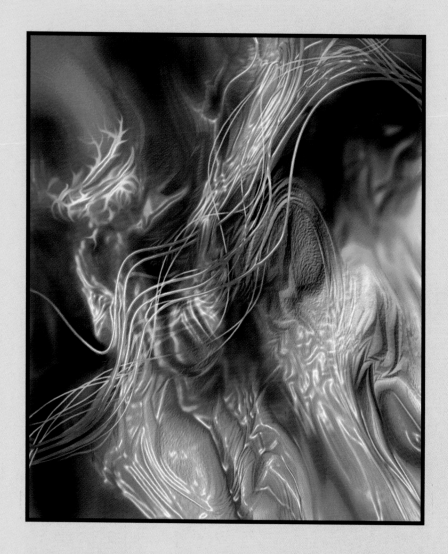

figure 36

Biowire, by digital artist and digital arts instructor Joel Hagen. Used with permission from Joel Hagen.

Wetware, by digital
artist and digital arts
instructor Joel Hagen.
Used with permission
from Joel Hagen.

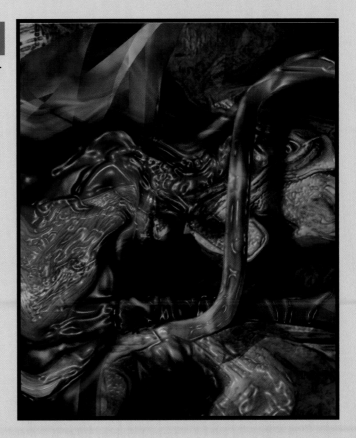

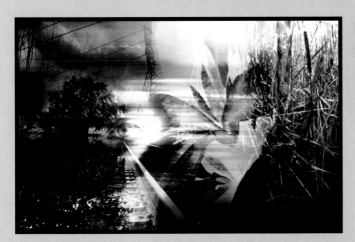

Image composition
by Mike Hagelsieb,
graphic artist.
Compliments of Mike
Hagelsieb.

Image composition by Mike Hagelsieb, graphic artist. Compliments of Mike Hagelsieb.

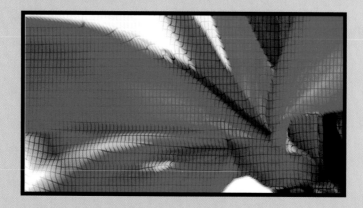

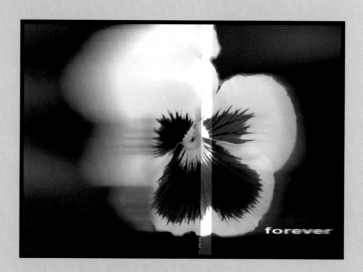

Forever, by Mike Hagelsieb, graphic artist. Compliments of Mike Hagelsieb.

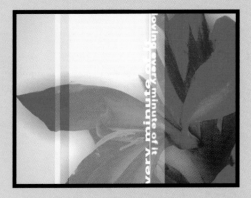

| figure 41 |

Time, by Mike Hagelsieb, graphic artist. Compliments of Mike Hagelsieb.

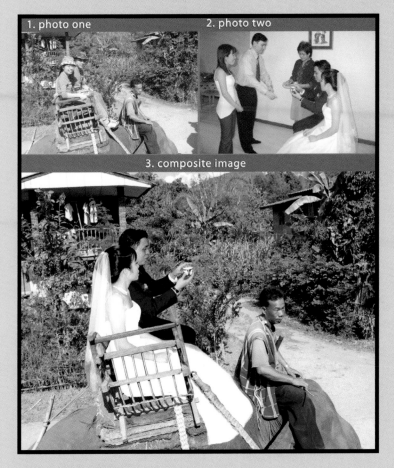

1. photo one

2. photo two

3. composite image

| figure 42 |

The making of an image composition by Wai Har Lee. Created by graphic artist Wai Har Lee.

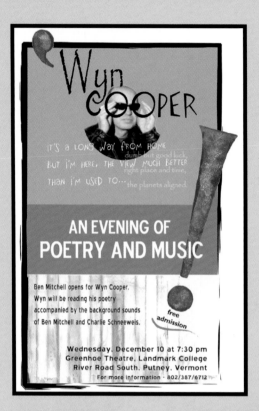

| figure 43 |

Poster design for Landmark College, by Annesa Hartman.

| figure 44 |

Golden Gate, photo manipulation by artist Zolton Baize. Compliments of Zolton Baize.

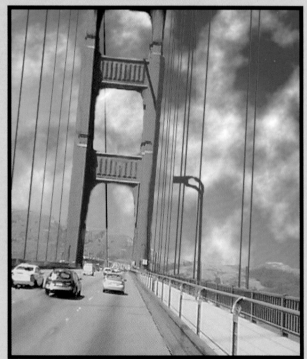

NOTE: If you are unable to find the arrow to click open the Options menu, you might need to detach the Brushes palette from the palette well. Click and drag down on the Brushes title tab to detach the docked palette. Also note that in the Brush palette's drop-down Options menu are settings for how you might like to view the brush styles in the Palette window. Such options are Text Only, Small Thumbnail, or Small List.

11. Freely paint with your chosen paintbrush. Alter the brush options in the options bar. Change the brush tip size and colors and adjust the Flow setting (see Figure 7-10).

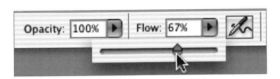

figure | **7-10**

Adjust the Flow settings of the paintbrush and see what effect this has when you paint.

12. Also, play with the adjustments in the Brushes palette, trying Scattering, for example. Click on the Scattering option on the left-hand side of the palette (it highlights in blue). Then adjust its settings in the options area to the right. To apply the scatter to the brush, click on the checkbox to the right of the Scattering option. See Figure 7-11.

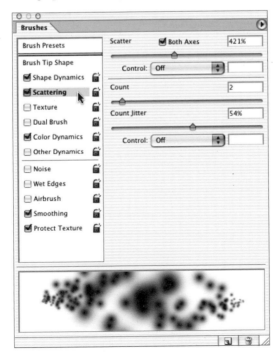

figure | **7-11**

Adjust settings for the Scattering effect in the Brushes palette.

Making a Custom Brush

Photoshop has provided a plethora of brush styles for your use, but inevitably, like anything in life, there will be need for something more and different. This is where making custom brushes comes in handy. A sample selection from any image or photograph can be used as a custom brush. First, marquee the area of the image you would like to use as a brush (be sure the correct layer in the Layers palette is selected as well), and then choose Edit > Define Brush Preset.

The custom brush shows up in the Brushes palette Brush Presets list. See figures 7-12 and 7-13. You can also draw or paint a pattern or shape, select it, and then choose Edit > Define Brush Preset. See Figure 7-14.

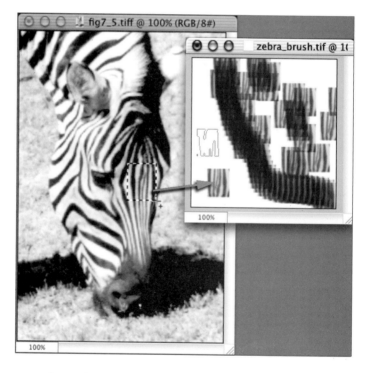

figure | 7-12

Need a brush of zebra stripes? Make a selection of part of a zebra picture and save it as a custom brush.

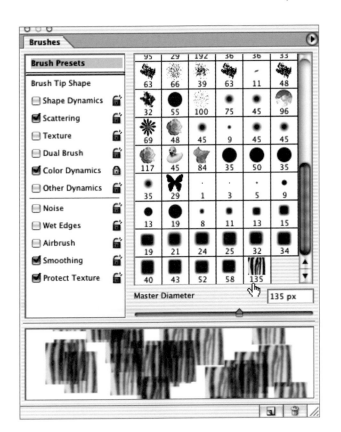

figure | 7-13 |

The zebra brush is saved in the Brushes palette under Brush Presets.

figure | 7-14 |

Draw your own shapes (hearts, for example) and make them into custom brushes.

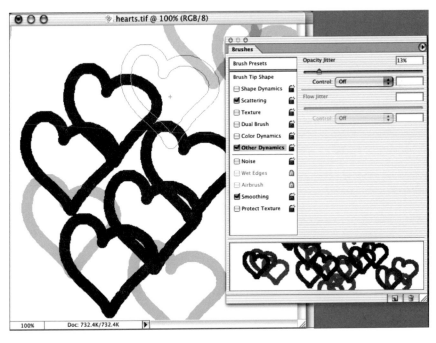

VECTORS: A GUEST APPEARANCE

I wish I could make it simple, tell you it's all black and white in regard to learning this program, but there are gray areas to tend to. Even though Photoshop is the pixel master, it can work with vectors on a minimal level—enough to use as a temporary solution for creating more flexibility in your drawing and for compatibility purposes when importing and exporting between programs. It's temporary in the sense that you can draw and make shapes using vector attributes, where no pixels are associated with the paths drawn, but that's only until the objects become rasterized (turned into pixels) with a fill or stroke color.

NOTE: Having a brain freeze on the difference between vectors and bitmaps (pixels)? See Chapter 3.

So you can understand the benefits of working with vectors rather than in pixels all the time, it's important to know when you have found yourself in this malleable gray area. In several places and processes within the program, vectors make a guest appearance, such as when using the Pen tool and creating paths, with vector masks, with type, and in saving in vector-supported file formats.

About Paths

Paths are vector lines you draw in Photoshop. Paths are used to define areas of an image and make new shapes or selections. You make paths using the Pen tool (see next section) or shape tools, or by converting a selection into a path. To see created paths, go to Window > Paths (see Figure 7-15).

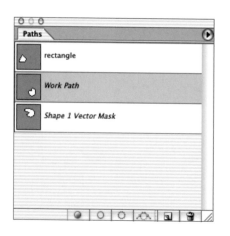

Let's make some paths in Photoshop to really wrap your brain around how these work.

1. In Photoshop, create a new document. Make it about 500 x 500 pixels in size.

2. Press Shift-Tab to hide unneeded palettes, if necessary.

figure | 7-15 |

The Paths palette.

3. In the toolbox, set your foreground and background colors to their defaults: black foreground, white background.

4. Choose Window > Paths to open the Paths palette. Note that no paths are indicated in the palette—yet.

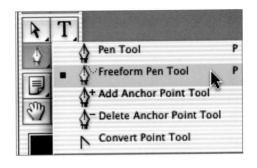

5. Select the Freeform Pen tool in the toolbox (see Figure 7-16).

figure | **7-16**

Select the Freeform Pen tool.

NOTE: The ways of the Pen tools are vast and somewhat complicated, which is discussed more in the next section. For now, just go with the flow.

6. In the options bar for the Freeform Pen tool, choose the Paths shape option, which is the second icon (the square with the Pen symbol in the middle). See Figure 7-17.

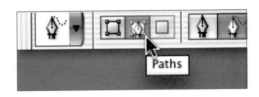

figure | **7-17**

Choose the Paths shape option.

7. Click and drag the Freeform Pen tool on your blank canvas, making a circular, closed shape. The shape is indicated as a work path in the Paths palette (see Figure 7-18). A work path is temporary. Unless you save it, when you draw another path it will be replaced.

figure | **7-18**

A path is indicated as a temporary work path in the Paths palette.

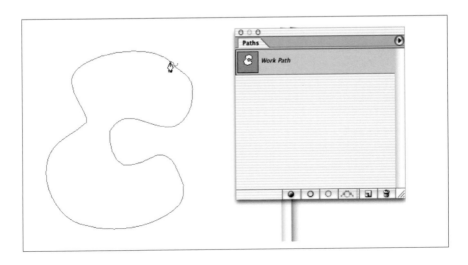

8. Before you save a path, let's replace the work path with another path. Try this: Select the Rectangular Marquee tool (first tool in the toolbox). Click and drag on your canvas to define the rectangle. Right now, it's considered a selection (indicated by marching ants). In the Paths palette, click on the arrow in the upper right-hand corner to open its options, and then choose Make Work Path (see Figure 7-19). Set the tolerance (smoothness) of the path to 2.0. Note in the Paths palette that the circular work path you made before has been replaced by a new, rectangular work path.

figure | 7-19 |

In the Paths palette, change a selection into a work path

Paths

| Work Path |

Dock to Palette Well

New Path...
Duplicate Path...
Delete Path

Make Work Path...

Make Selection...
Fill Path...
Stroke Path...

Clipping Path...

Palette Options...

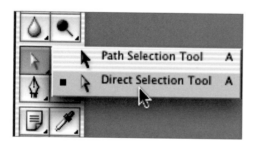

figure | 7-20 |

Select the Direct Selection tool in the toolbox to select individual anchor points on a path.

Path Selection Tool   A
Direct Selection Tool   A

9. With a work path you can modify the path freely (using vectors) before committing to the final, bitmapped version. Select the Direct Selection tool in the toolbox. This tool lets you select individual points on the path to modify it (see Figure 7-20). Click on a line of the rectangular work path to select it. Note the points on each corner (called anchor points). Click and drag one of the corner points to modify the rectangular shape into a triangular shape (see Figure 7-21). The work path is updated in the Paths palette.

10. From the Path palette's options (click on arrow in upper right) choose Save Path. Name it *mytriangle*.

11. Let's rasterize this shape; cast it in stone, so to speak. Choose Window > Layers. Double click on the Background layer to release it to a regular layer.

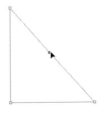

figure | 7-21

Move an anchor point to create a tri-angular shape out of a rectangular shape.

12. Now, go back to the Paths palette and select the *mytriangle* path. From the palette's options choose Fill Path (see Figure 7-22). A copy of the triangle path now becomes a permanent bitmap object in the current layer (you can no longer use the Direct Selection tool to select individual points on the object). In the Paths palette, however, the *mytriangle* work path is still available for further modification.

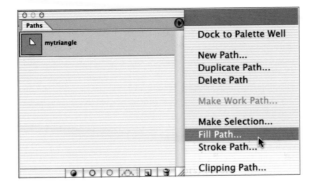

figure | 7-22

Make a work path a bitmapped object by filling the path.

More on the Pen Tool

Ahh, the Pen tool, an instrument that either wreaks havoc or invokes joy, depending on your experience with it. I'm not going to delve into the intricate workings of the Pen tool in this book. It's an available option for drawing in Photoshop, but truthfully it is best utilized in a vector-robust program such as Adobe Illustrator. In fact, its use is so important in that program that I spend almost a complete chapter on the Pen tool in my book *Exploring Illustrator CS*.

In brief, the Pen tool lets you draw straight and curved vector segments and paths, connected by anchor points. With each click of the Pen tool anchor points are deposited and can be selected and modified with the Direct Selection tool (what you experienced a bit in the last section on Paths). Through direction lines and direction points (together called direction handles), anchor points define the position and curve attributes of each line segment. See Figure 7-23. Because it is so precise, the Pen tool is excellent for tracing around complex shapes. In the following steps, practice drawing straight and curved lines with the Pen tool, first randomly to get a feel for it and then to more precisely trace images.

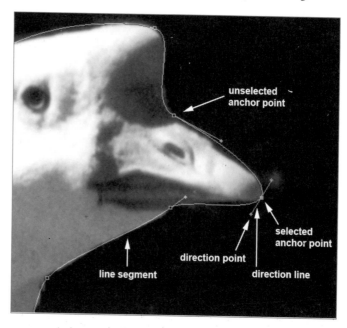

figure | 7-23

Anatomy of a path.

figure | 7-24

Select the Pen tool in the toolbox.

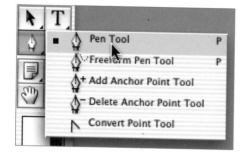

1. In Photoshop, choose File > New and make a new blank document (any size).

2. Select the Pen tool in the toolbox (see Figure 7-24).

3. As if you are doodling on a piece of paper, randomly click down anchor points on the document. To create straight line segments, click the Pen tool down and then pick it up and click somewhere else—keep click, click, clicking to make straight lines.

4. To end the path, Command-click (Mac) or Ctrl-click (Windows) anywhere away from all objects, or click on the first point of your path to close it.

5. To make curved lines, click and drag, keeping the mouse button pressed. Continue to click and drag to make curves. Fun, huh?

6. With no objective, continue click, click, clicking and click and drag, click and drag to make straight and curved paths. Use the Direct Selection tool to select and modify individual anchor points. Use the Path Selection tool (see Figure 7-25) to select a complete path, so that you can move it or delete it.

7. Now for more precision drawing. In Photoshop, open p*en_practice. psd* from the *chap7_lessons* fold-er.

8. Select Window > Layers and be sure *drawing_layer* is selected.

9. Select the Pen tool in the toolbox.

10. In the options bar for the Pen tool, choose the Paths shape option (see Figure 7-26).

11. Click down once on a corner of one of the diamonds in the first shape. This action makes an anchor point. Click the next cor-ner, then the next, and then close the shape by clicking on the first anchor point again (see Figure 7-27). If you make a mistake (which is highly likely when first attempting this tool), select the previous step in the History palette. If you're a perfectionist and want perfectly straight line segments between anchor points, hold down the Shift key as you click down each point.

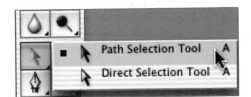

figure | **7-25**

Select the Path Selection tool.

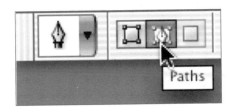

figure | **7-26**

Choose the Paths shape option in the options bar.

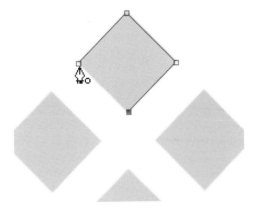

figure | **7-27**

Each time you click down with the Pen tool you create an anchor point.

12. Practice creating straight line segments on the other three diamond shapes. Choose Window > Paths to view the work paths you have created.

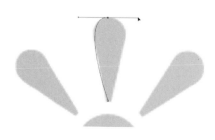

13. On the next tile shape (resembling a sunburst), click down once with the Pen tool on a tip of one of the teardrop shapes, and then click and drag on the rounded head of the teardrop to create a curve (with your finger still on the mouse you can continue to drag out to create a rounder curve and also move the direction handle up/down or in/out to make the line tangent with the tracing image). Click again on the anchor point at the bottom of the teardrop to close the shape. See Figure 7-28. Continue tracing the other teardrop shapes, and the circle in the middle. For fun: Can you draw the circle in the middle out of only two anchor points?

figure | **7-28** |

Create a curved line segment by clicking and dragging with the Pen tool.

14. Continue your Pen practice on the flower shape.

figure | **7-29** |

To quickly apply a stroke to a work path, select the shortcut at the bottom of the Paths palette.

15. Change your vector shapes into bitmapped shapes. First, choose a foreground color for the fill. Next, select the *Work Path* layer in the Paths palette. Click on the arrow in the upper right-hand corner of the Palette window, and then choose Fill Path.

16. See *pen_practice_final.psd* in the *chap7_lessons* folder for a completed version of this exercise. View the work paths in the Paths palette. The paths were stroked with a brush style with color dynamics turned on. To apply the stroke, choose Stroke Path from the Paths palette's options menu or by clicking on the shortcut at the bottom of the Palette window. See Figure 7-29.

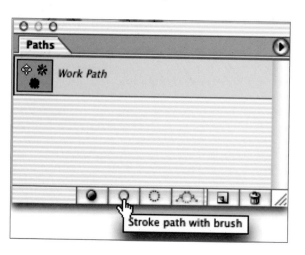

Vector Masks

Masks in Photoshop are a way to hide and reveal areas of an image. Masks are very useful in image editing and can create interesting effects, so much so that the next chapter is completely devoted to them. Since we are covering now the modes of working with vectors in the program, I want to mention that there is something called vector masks.

One nice thing about vectors is that they produce graphics with clean, sharp edges (not pixelated). To take advantage of this attribute, Photoshop offers you the ability to create vector masks. On a layer, vector masks produce a sharp-edged shape that is useful when you want to add a design element with clean, defined edges or for export into a vector-based program such as Adobe Illustrator. The vector mask itself is defined in the Layers and Paths palettes (see Figure 7-30). Use the pen or shape tools (see later section in this chapter) to draw a work path, and then define its vector mask by choosing Layer > Add Vector Mask > Reveal All or Hide All.

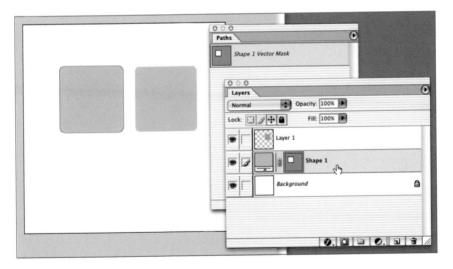

Type

When working in a word processing program, like Microsoft Word, have you ever noticed that when you print off a document of text that the text is very clean and crisp looking, and no matter what size you make it—12 pt or 60 pt—it always looks this way? On the other hand, when you print off a piece of clipart that was scaled really big on the document it looks kind of blurry and pixelated.

Why is this? Well, the type contains vector data that keeps the letter shapes sharp looking and that can be scaled big or small because, as you discovered in Chapter 3, vectors are not dependent on resolution. Therefore, when printed off on a printer that supports this vector data, the type looks really good and is easily readable. In contrast, the clipart is constrained by its resolution (made up of bitmapped pixels) and must remain a particular size to preserve its crispness when printed.

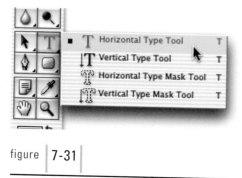

figure | 7-31 |

The Horizontal Type tool in the toolbox.

In regard to type in Photoshop, it works very similar to how it is reproduced in a word processing program. When first created, it locates itself on its own layer and contains vector data, so that you can easily modify it without worrying so much how good it's going to look when printed. To apply type to a Photoshop document, choose the Horizontal Type tool (see Figure 7-31), click down on the document, and begin typing.

Similar to editing type in a word processing program you can adjust a type's font, size, orientation, and color in the options bar. Alternatively, choose Window > Character for more formatting choices. See Figure 7-32.

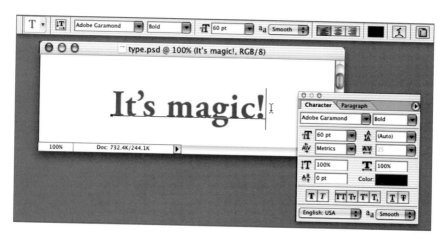

figure | 7-32 |

Format text in a Type tool's options bar and Character palette.

While I've made the analogy of how type works in Photoshop to how it works in a word processing program, I don't recommend using Photoshop as a word processing program. Even if you are going to create large bodies of text in an image or layout, I don't recommend doing it in Photoshop, but rather in a layout program such as Adobe InDesign, Illustrator, or Quark Express. These programs support type characteristics much better. I suggest in Photoshop using type only as a design element.

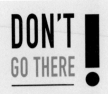

Vector Compatibility

As presented in Chapter 3, some image formats support vector data, some do not. When you work in Photoshop's native format (PSD), any vector masks, work paths, and type you create in the program is preserved in that temporary state until you decide to rasterize it (which you might need to do to add certain effects and filters to the element). When you go to save out your work, however, decisions must be made on whether or not you want to keep the vector data in the file, which depends on where it's going to go. If you save a file in the EPS or PDF formats, the vector data is preserved (see Figure 7-33) when opened in a vector-based program such as Adobe InDesign or Illustrator. You can select and edit individual objects and the anchor points of which they consist.

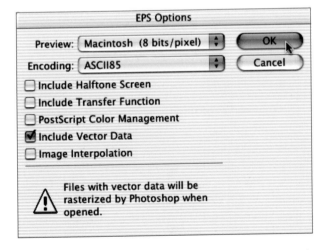

figure | 7-33

When saving out in EPS, the vector data can be preserved (indicated by check mark), but note the warning. It will not be preserved when reopened in Photoshop, only when opened in a fully vector-supported program such as Adobe Illustrator.

If saved in a TIFF or JPEG format and opened in a vector-based program, the vector data is rasterized (flattened into pixels). See figures 7-34 and 7-35. For your investigation, provided in the *chap7_lessons/samples* folder are several saved versions of an image

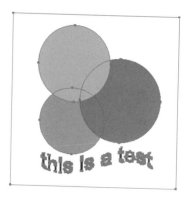

figure | 7-34 |

This EPS-formatted version of a file was saved in Photoshop and opened in Illustrator. When you click on the grouped item you can see the editable, individual anchor points that make up vector objects.

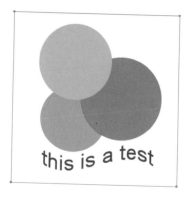

figure | 7-35 |

This JPEG-formatted version of a file was saved in Photoshop and opened in Illustrator. Because JPEG doesn't support vector data, when opened in Illustrator or Photoshop it is made up of bitmapped pixels only.

in different formats that, if you have Adobe Illustrator for instance, you can import into the program and then select the image or image parts to see what vector attributes of the image have remained. You can also import each version into Photoshop and see what occurs. Does the vector data remain intact or is everything rasterized?

MAKING SHAPES

In most any art class you learn how to draw geometric shapes first thing, and in previous chapters you have made shapes. However, now that you've finally learned about the characteristics of drawing with vectors and bitmaps you can better understand the shape-making tools and options. One way to make shapes quickly and easily in the program is to make a selection (draw with the Marquee or Lasso tools for instance) and then fill or stroke the shape by choosing Edit > Fill (or Stroke). There is also a set of shape tools you can use (see Figure 7-36). With the shape tools you have many options to choose from in the options bar (see Figure 7-37), such as the shape type (shape layers or vector masks, paths, or fill pixels), the characteristics of each of which were covered in the last sections on drawing with vectors versus pixels. And depending on what shape type you choose you also have the ability to add,

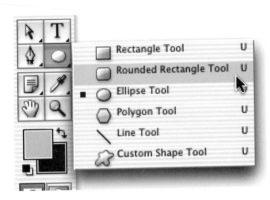

figure | 7-36|

The Shape tools available in the tool-box.

figure | 7-37|

The Shape tool's options bar.

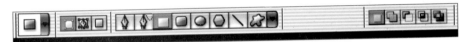

subtract, exclude, and intersect shapes as well as add styles (pre-made effects).

Practice the following steps for some familiarity with the shape tools.

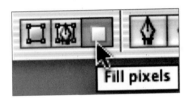

1. Create a new file in Photoshop, about 500 x 500 pixels in size. Make sure the background content is white.

2. Choose the Rounded Rectangle tool in the toolbox (see Figure 7-36).

3. In the options bar, select the Fill style option (see Figure 7-38).

   NOTE: In the option bar you can also modify the geometric options for the selected shape by clicking on the second inverted arrow. See Figure 7-39.

figure | 7-38|

Select the Fill option to make raster-ized shapes.

figure | 7-39|

You can alter the geometric options for a selected shape in the options bar.

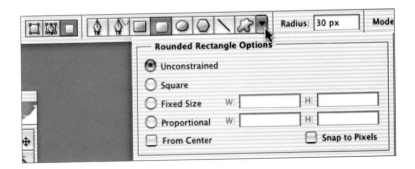

4. Set a foreground color in the toolbox.

5. Click and draw a rounded rectangle on the blank canvas.

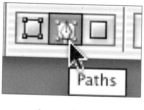

figure | **7-40**

Select the Paths style option.

6. Open the Layers palette and note that the rectangle is a rasterized image on the Background layer.

7. Now select the Paths style option in the options bar (see Figure 7-40).

8. Select the Polygon shape tool.

9. Draw a polygon on the document. It is a temporary work path that you can alter.

10. Open the Paths palette to see the work path.

11. Select the Shape layers style option in the options bar.

12. Choose a new foreground color.

13. Select the Custom shape tool and in the Shape Options drop-down menu choose a custom shape. See Figure 7-41.

   NOTE: You can also make your own custom shapes to put in the menu. See the Photoshop Help Files for details.

14. Draw the shape on the document. Note in the Layers palette a new layer containing the shape and its vector mask.

15. Select *Subtract from shape area* in the options bar, and then draw another custom shape overlapping the first custom

figure | **7-41**

Select a custom shape.

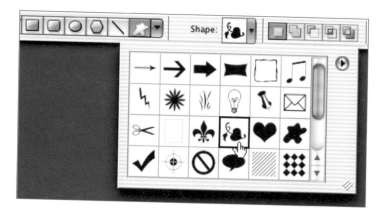

shape you made. See figures 7-42 and 7-43. Explore the other shape modification options (such as for adding, intersecting, or excluding a shape from another).

16. Select a Style option from the options bar. See Figure 7-44. The selected shape is updated with the style. Pretty sly, eh?

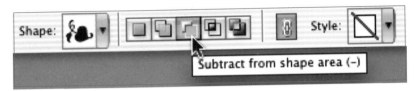

figure | **7-42**

Select the *Subtract from shape area* option in the options bar.

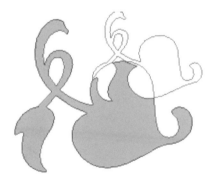

figure | **7-43**

The shape of one object subtracted from another.

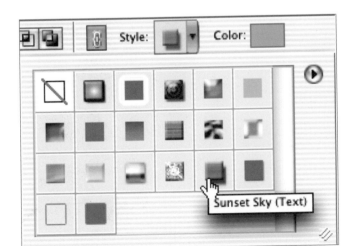

figure | **7-44**

Select a shape style.

Lesson: Nonrepresentational Art Creation

You'll be surprised to find that this lesson contains very little step-by-step instruction.

Since painting and drawing can be such an exploratory medium, I thought I would leave most of this lesson to your imagination. Using the various tools and techniques learned in this chapter, you create a *nonrepresentational* digital art piece—an art creation that may not make reference to anything in nature or reality (see Figure 7-45). As described in the book *Artforms* (revised seventh edition) by Duane Preble and Sarah Preble (revised by Patrick Frank), "Nonrepresentational art (sometimes called nonobjective or non-figurative art) presents visual forms with no specific references to anything outside themselves. Just as we can respond to the pure sound of music, we can respond to the pure visual forms of non-representational art."

figure | 7-45

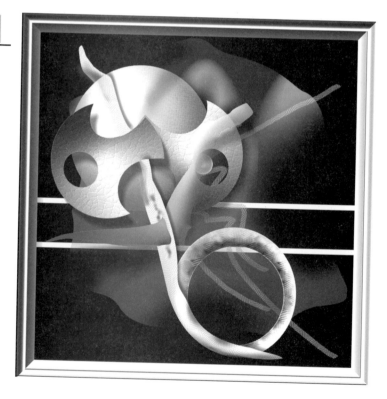

An example of nonrepresentational art using Photoshop. See also chapter opening image.

Setting Up the File

1. In Photoshop, set the background color in the toolbox to any color you'd like.

2. Next, create a new file about 500 x 500 pixels in size. Set Color Mode to RGB Color, the resolution to 150 dpi, and for Background Contents choose Background Color (which is the color you specified in the first step).

3. Open the Layers palette.

4. Make a new layer and name it *painting*.

5. Select the Paintbrush or Pencil tool. Set the brush style to your liking and start to paint on your canvas (it doesn't matter what you paint … and, if you don't like it, there is always the History palette). Open the Brushes palette (Window > Brushes) to explore more options.

6. Create another layer and name it *shapes*.

7. Create any number of Fill shapes using the Shape tool.

8. Make other shape styles, using vector shape layers and paths.

9. Save your file, if you haven't already (save often!)

10. Add some text as a graphical design element to the canvas.

11. Use Layer styles on any of the layers you have created, such as Drop Shadow, Bevel and Emboss, and Pattern Overlay. To do this, select the layer you want to affect in the Layers palette and choose Layer > Layer Style from the main menu.

12. If you recall how from previous lessons, place blending effects and filters on any of the layers you have created (there are more specifics on the "what" and "how" of blending effects and filters in Chapter 9).

13. Create another layer and name it *frame*. Draw or construct (using the Shape tool options such as Subtract or Intersect) a frame around your masterpiece.

14. Save your file in the JPEG format, quality amount about 8, and e-mail your art creation to a friend.

SUMMARY

After this chapter, there's no such thing as a blank Photoshop canvas. Usually it only takes a quick introduction to the drawing and painting tools and processes in this program to initiate a creative spark.

in review

1. What is the main difference between the Pencil and Paintbrush tools?

2. Name at least three features in the Brushes palette.

3. The Eraser tool erases with the foreground or background color?

4. Why would having some vector support in Photoshop be useful for drawing and painting?

5. Name three areas (features/tools) in Photoshop that incorporate the use of vector technology?

6. What's the difference between a "click" action with the mouse and a "click and drag" action when using the Pen tool?

7. What are paths in Photoshop? How do you make them? What tools do you use to select a complete path or parts of a path?

8. What file formats preserve vector data?

9. In what three styles (ways) can you create shapes in Photoshop?

10. Describe nonrepresentational (nonobjective) art.

↗ EXPLORING ON YOUR OWN

1. Create your own custom brush out of your signature (see Figure 7-46):

    ● Make a new document in Photoshop. For Background Contents choose Transparent.

    ● Select the Pencil tool in the toolbox.

    ● Choose a brush style with a small diameter (1 to 5 pixels in size).

    ● Choose a foreground color.

    ● Write your signature on the document.

    ● Choose Edit > Define Brush Preset, and name your custom brush.

- Set your brush settings in the Brushes palette (look for your custom brush in the Brush Tip Shape area).

- Paint with your signature.

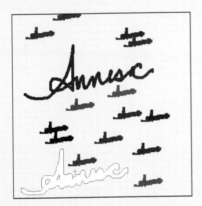

figure | **7-46**

Use the Scattering option in the Brushes palette with your new custom signature brush.

2. In the Photoshop Help files (Help > Photoshop Help) do a search for "brush dynamics" and find out what this feature does.

3. In the Help files, find out what the Convert Point tool does.

4. Using the Pen tool, trace around the images (*goose.tif* or *peacock.jpg*) provided in the *chap7_lessons/ samples* folder.

5. Practice creating some type on a path.

- Using the Pen tool, draw a simple path on your document.

- Select the Type tool and set the font and font size in the options bar.

- Click with the Type tool (the little I-beam) on the path and start typing some text.

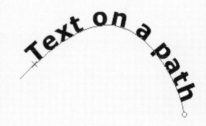

- Adjust the type by selecting it and modifying its formatting options in the options bar.

- Adjust the path the type is on by using the Direct Selection tool. See Figure 7-47.

figure | **7-47**

Text on a path—yeah!

6. Discover the wonder of kaleidoscopes. Visit these sites:

- Amazing Software Kaleidoscopes: *http://bindweed.com/kaleidoscopes. htm*

- Kaleidoscopes Heaven: *http://kaleidoscopeheaven.org/*

- Kaleidoscope Collector (how they work): *www.kaleidoscopesusa. com/how.htm*

- Make your own Kaleidoscope: *http://familycrafts.about.com/cs/ toystomake/a/blconnkaleid.htm*

notes

ADVENTURES IN DESIGN

DODGE AND BURN

In darkroom photography, "dodge and burn" is a technique whereby using light a photographer can selectively darken (burn) areas in a photograph, and just the opposite: selectively lighten (dodge) shadowed areas to bring out details. In glorified form, this technique is provided for you in Photoshop as the Dodge and Burn tools. Using any selected brush tip, these tools offer the artist localized and precise tonal control of the pixels in an image (see Figure A-1).

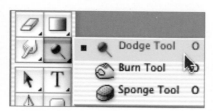

Figure A-1. The Dodge and Burn tools (along with the Sponge tool) offer localized tonal control on a photograph.

In the toolbox, the Dodge and Burn tools are grouped with another tonal control tool, the Sponge tool. These tools are great for localized manipulation of the highlights, midtones, and shadows in a photograph. However, for more global control use the Levels or Curves command. It's a wonderful-ly advantageous thing to be able to use the Dodge and Burn tools to subtly adjust the brightness and contrast in a photograph, as well as a simple way to paint more spatially enhanced objects. With these tools you can paint dimensional illusions quickly, as you will see in the next section.

Professional Project Example

If you have ever taken a traditional drawing or painting class (which I wholeheartedly recommend!), you've probably been assigned the onerous task of rendering an egg (in all its proportionally rounded splendor) using hard and soft lead pencils, charcoal, or a paintbrush. It sounds easy enough (after all, its only an egg), but after some initial sketches you might realize (at least I did) that it involves a very subtle play of dark and light pencil strokes and finger smudging to make the egg look somewhat realistic, rather than flat or oddly deformed. Using the Dodge and Burn tools in Photoshop, the digital art professional has found a more, shall I say, quick and dirty solution to putting the life into a flat image or photograph.

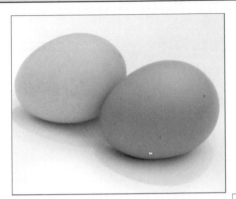

Figure A-2. A digital photograph of some eggs without photo retouching.

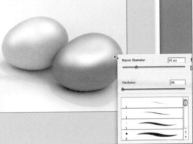

Figure A-3. With a soft-tipped brush, lighten areas of a photograph with the Dodge tool.

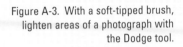

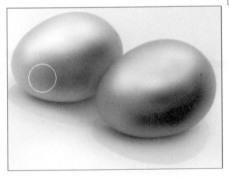

Figure A-4. With a soft-tipped brush, darken areas of a photograph with the Burn tool.

Figure A-2 is a photograph of some eggs. There are obvious lights and darks in the photo, but what happens if we enhance these tones for an even, more dimensional look? With the Dodge tool and a soft-tipped brush (or airbrush), areas of the eggs can be furthered lightened (see Figure A-3). Moreover, with the Burn tool and a soft-tipped brush (or airbrush), areas of the egg can be further darkened (see Figure A-4). The result is two "golden-looking" eggs (see Figure A-5). This same technique can be applied without a photo reference. Start with a gray-toned elliptical shape and build the shadows and highlights with varied brush strokes and tip sizes (see Figure A-6).

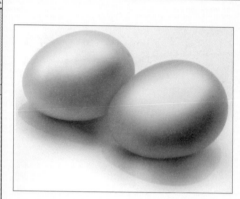

Figure A-5. A photograph of two eggs made more "golden-looking" using the Dodge and Burn tools.

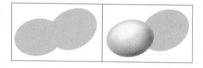

Figure A-6. Go from flat to spatial. Draw a dimensional-looking egg shape using the Dodge and Burn tools.

Your Turn

Using a sample file named *egg.psd*, located in the *aid_examples* folder, you will paint your own realistic eggs with a metallic sheen. If you'd like, you can further enhance the image with layer styles and/or artistic brush-stroke or sketch filters.

Self-Project Guidelines

1. Open the *egg.psd* document found in the *aid_examples* folder.

2. View the Layers palette, and be sure *overlay_adjustment_layer* is selected (see Figure A-7). This is the layer you will paint on with the Dodge and Burn tools. It is a special layer filled with a 50% gray background and set with an Overlay blending mode, located above and protecting the original photo you will enhance.

3. Select the Burn or Dodge tool in the toolbox, and set your brush tip size. For starters, I suggest a soft brush with a diameter of about 45 pixels, and for Range in the options bar of the tool select Midtones. See Figure A-8. You can also play with the Exposure setting to adjust the amount (or intensity) of lightness or darkness applied with each brush stroke.

4. After enhancing the egg photo on the *egg1* layer, save your file in your

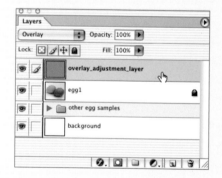

Figure A-7. Select the *overlay_adjustment_layer*.

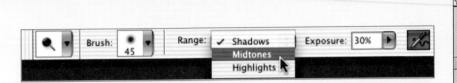

Figure A-8. Set options for the Dodge or Burn tools, such as Brush Size, Range, and Exposure.

lessons folder. Then hide the *overlay_adjustment_layer* and *egg1* layers in the Layers palette. This reveals another egg example: flat, elliptical shapes.

5. Expand the *other_egg_samples* layer set and select the *hand_drawn_egg1* layer.

6. Use the Burn and Dodge tools with soft-tipped brushes to bring the egg to dimensional life.

7. Add a drop shadow for further spatial impact via Layer > Layer Style > Drop Shadow.

8. Enhance the other egg example in the *hand-drawn_egg2* layer.

9. Save your golden eggs.

Things to Consider

For future explorations with drawing and painting such as this Adventures in Design consider the following:

- Whenever possible, use an adjustment layer to work on over your original image to protect it. When working with the tonal control tools, create a new layer with a 50% gray fill and set to the Overlay blending mode (as in the *egg.psd* file). Make global tonal adjustments, such as Levels and Color Balance, on an adjustment layer. Choose Layer > New Adjustment Layer.

- There are hundreds of artist's tips and techniques for using Photoshop. Step-by-step instructions are plentiful on the World Wide Web. Do a global search for "Photoshop tips and techniques," or a more refined search for the name of a Photoshop tool or function, such as "dodge and burn."

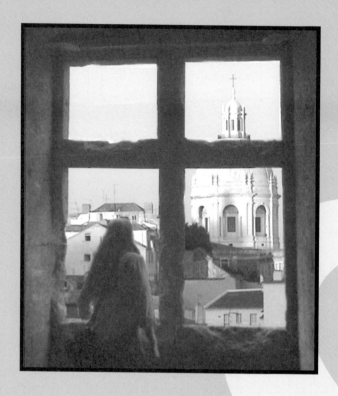

| masking |

8

charting your course

When I discovered the power of masking in digital illustration and design, I wondered how I managed so long without it. Masking is a technique for hiding or revealing areas of an image. Similar to how masking tape protects a window seal as you paint around it, a digital mask protects areas of an image as you apply effects to unmasked areas.

Masks are used a lot in animation and digital video editing. A scene transition where one frame wipes away another is a moving mask. A computer-generated character co-acting with a human actor is superimposed into a scene using masks. For the use in digital imagery, there are several types of masks in Photoshop, each of which contains specific attributes for different purposes. In this chapter, we cover how a mask works and the several types of masks you can create in the program, including layer and vector masks, type masks, clipping masks, and quick masks.

 goals

- Know what a mask is and how it works and is used in Photoshop
- Explore the types of masks available in Photoshop
- Paint full and partial selections using quick masks
- Hide and reveal content with layer and clipping masks

UNMASKING MASKS

First off, how does a mask work? I'll give you an overview, and then we'll take a closer look. Examine the four steps in Figure 8-1. Step 1 shows an original photograph taken at the rustic Pamela castle in Portugal. Step 2 shows part of the photo with a layer mask applied. The head area was selected with the Elliptical Marquee tool and then Layer > Add Layer Mask > Hide Selection was chosen. Step 3 indicates the layer (a picture of Max from Chapter 4) that will be affected by the mask created in step 2. The Max layer is then put below the mask layer and you get the result in step 4. The cardboard character no longer has my face (yes, that's me), is replaced with Max's face, and all of this magic was done without damaging the original photo.

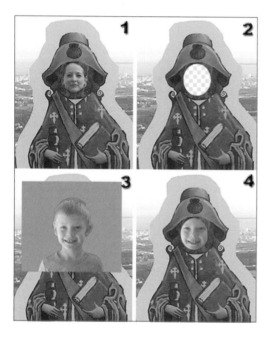

figure | 8-1 |

This four-part example shows how a mask can replace an area of a photograph with another photograph behind it. The cool part is that the mask really "protects" the original image—so it can appear that you've cut out (deleted) selected parts of an image without actually destroying the image. It's just another one of those illusions.

Now for an even closer look at a mask's characteristics, which might clarify things for you (or confuse you further). The confusion part is okay for now. Masks get easier to grasp when you actually play with them (like anything, of course!). So, once you've had the practice experience (by the end of this chapter, perhaps), you might want to come back and review this section.

Refer again to step 2 in Figure 8-1. When step 2 was executed on the photo example, the mask became part of the photo's layer in the Layers palette. See Figure 8-2, and note the mask thumbnail in the layer *cardboard_character*.

Hey, why not check it out for yourself? Open *example_mask.psd* in the *chap8_lessons/samples* folder. Then open the Layers palette and take a look. The black dot in the layer mask thumbnail shows the part of the mask to be transparent (in other words, the selection is hidden). An important distinction to make here is that the mask is not "deleting" the selection but "hiding" it. You can disable or delete a mask at any time and still have the original photo or artwork intact. To do this in this example, click on the mask thumbnail in the Layers palette, and then choose Layer > Disable Layer Mask (a big X appears over the thumbnail). To turn it back on, choose Layer > Enable Layer Mask. Here are a few more versatile things you can do with masks:

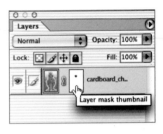

figure | 8-2

The layer mask thumbnail located on the same layer in which the mask is applied.

- You can unlock and move a mask to hide other areas of an image or photograph. In the example layer mask, unlock the mask thumbnail in the Layers palette from the photo it was masking, select it, and move it to a different location. See figures 8-3 and 8-4.

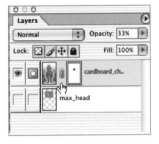

figure | 8-3

You can unlock the mask layer from the original object it was masking.

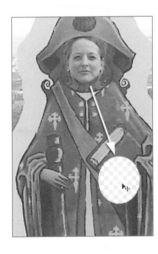

figure | 8-4

You can move an unlocked mask elsewhere on the image.

- As mentioned previously, you can also disable or delete a mask without any damage to the original work. See Figure 8-5.

- Masks can be made out of any selected shape. See Figure 8-6.

- You can load and save a selection from a mask. Selections you might want to use later can be stored (and reloaded at your convenience) as alpha channels. Alpha channels are located in the Channels palette and there's a lot to them (see Note). When you examine an alpha channel in Photoshop (see Figure 8-7),

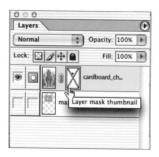

figure | 8-5 |

You can disable or delete a mask without damage to the original image.

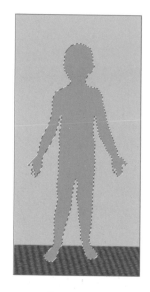

figure | 8-6 |

Masks can be made out of any selected shape, like that of Max's body.

figure | 8-7 |

An alpha channel, saved in the Channels palette, can be used to mask out areas of an image.

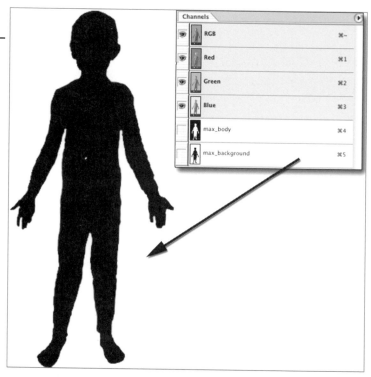

the black indicates the area you can see through the mask (like a window, it's transparent), and the white is the area that is opaque. In Figure 8-8 you can see how the black and white areas of an alpha channel can hide or reveal (mask) areas of an image. You can also have semitransparent masks at all different levels of transparency, which is indicated by varying shades of gray (see Figure 8-9). You'll learn how to create these soft transparency effects using a quick mask in the next section.

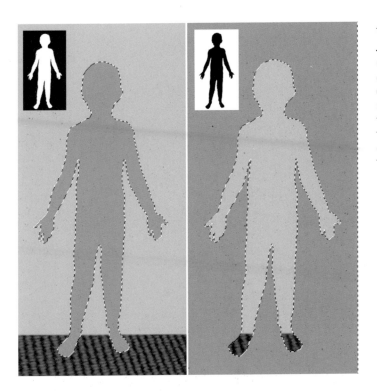

figure | 8-8 |

On the left the background is revealed (black) and Max remains isolated from the mask. On the right, the background is revealed through Max (black) and the rest of the background remains protected.

Some file formats, such as TIFF, will support an alpha channel in an image. This is useful when you want to use an alpha channel (to mask stuff, for instance) in another program (other than Photoshop) that supports the use of alpha channels, such as Adobe InDesign or Illustrator. See Figure 8-10.

NOTE: A little more about alpha channels: You can get into some sophisticated image editing and manipulation with alpha channels—something to look into in your more advanced studies of Photoshop. For now, keep in mind that channels, and alpha channels in

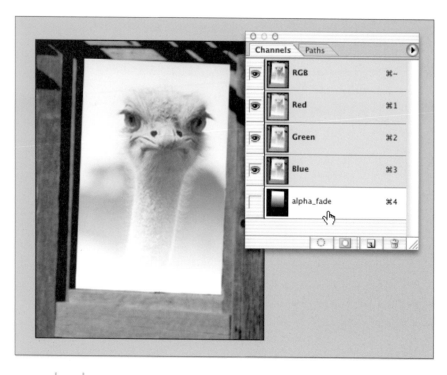

figure | 8-9 |

A gradient of grays can become a mask—each level of gray creating more or less transparency. Here, the ostrich is softly being revealed through the gradient mask.

figure | 8-10 |

The option to preserve an alpha channel appears when you save a file to the TIFF format.

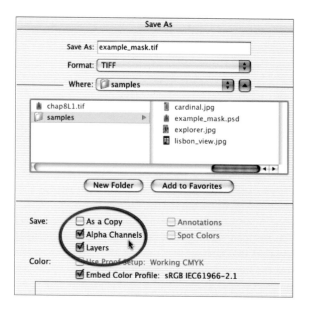

particular, have these properties (taken directly from the Photo-shop Help files):

- Each image can contain up to 56 channels, including all color and alpha channels.

- You can specify a name, color, mask option, and opacity for each channel. (The opacity affects the preview of the channel, not the image.)

- All new channels have the same dimensions and number of pixels as the original image.

- You can edit the mask in an alpha channel using painting tools, editing tools, and filters (see Figure 8-11).

- You can convert alpha channels to spot color channels.

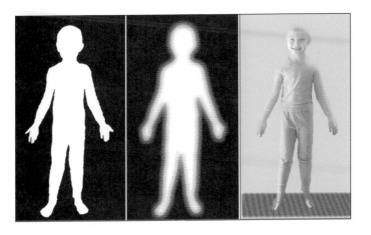

figure | 8-11 |

From left to right: alpha channel with-out filter effect, alpha channel with filter effect, and result of alpha chan-nel as a mask on the Max photograph (the edges of his body are transparent and appear "alien-like").

TYPES OF MASKS

While all masks work pretty much the same in Photoshop, there are different types of masks you can use, including layer and vector masks, clipping masks, type masks, and quick masks.

Layer and Vector Masks

Layer masks let you create a mask that is linked to an object on the same layer, and which therefore directly affects the object. A layer mask was used in our first example, shown in Figure 8-1. Vector masks are a variation on layer masks. They are created similarly. However, because vector masks consist of vectors the edges of a selection being used for the mask are much more crisp and clean-looking. To quickly make and edit a layer or vector mask:

1. Select an area on an image or photograph. Note that if you select the Background layer, you must double click on the layer to turn it into a standard layer for the next step to work.

2. Choose Layer > Add Layer Mask or Layer > Add Vector Mask, and determine whether you want the mask to reveal the selection or hide the selection.

3. To edit a mask, Command-click (Mac) or Ctrl-click (Windows) on the mask thumbnail in the Layers palette to select it.

4. Turn on Edit in Quick Mask Mode in the toolbox and add or subtract from the selection with the painting tools (details to follow in section on quick masks).

Clipping Masks

Clipping masks are a quick way to attach a sequence of layers to be masked by another layer. Here's how to do it:

1. Decide what item you want to use as a mask (text, shape, any filled object) and place it on its own layer.

2. Place items you want to be revealed through the mask in their own layers above the layer to be used as a mask.

3. Hold down the Alt/Option key and place the cursor between the layer edge of the item to be used as a mask and the layer you want to be revealed above it. A funky icon of two circles, one atop the other, appears. Click down on this edge line and the top layer will indent above the lower layer. The clipping mask has been executed. See Figure 8-12. Alternatively you can choose Layer > Create Clipping Mask.

figure | 8-12 |

Create a clipping mask.

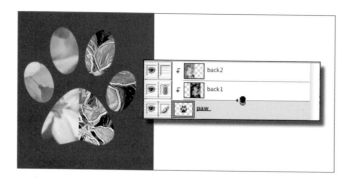

Horizontal and Vertical Type Mask Tools

With the Horizontal Type Mask or Vertical Type Mask tool you can make masks out of type. It's really quite easy:

1. In the toolbox, choose either the Horizontal Type Mask or Vertical Type Mask tool (see Figure 8-13).

2. Set the type's formatting options (font, size) in the options bar.

3. Click on the document and type a word or phrase. You'll be sent into Edit in Quick Mask Mode (indicated by the red transparent overlay) while you type.

4. Create a new layer in the Layers palette. Note that the type becomes a selection (but only temporarily) on the document for you to fill, add effects to, and use as an object for layer or clipping masks. See Figure 8-14.

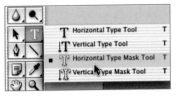

figure | **8-13**

The Horizontal Type Mask and Vertical Type Mask tools in the toolbox.

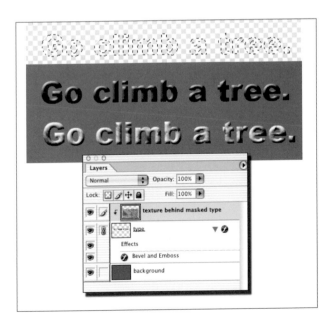

figure | **8-14**

The selected text in this example is filled, has a layer effect added to it, and is assigned a clipping mask that reveals a photographic texture through the letter forms.

Quick Masks

As mentioned in Chapter 4, there is a direct relationship between selections and color in Photoshop. The dynamics of this relationship open the possibility for very versatile and sophisticated mask making with the use of Photoshop's quick mask feature. A quick mask is not really a mask but a temporary mode in which to define and edit selections with the painting tools (or even a Photoshop filter effect). Paint with white to select more areas of an image. Paint with black to deselect areas. Paint with an opacity setting or shade of gray to create a semitransparent mask that's useful for soft-edged, feathered effects. (You can also uniformly soften selection edges with the Feathering option, accessed via Select > Feather.)

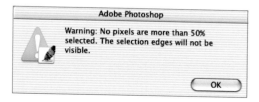

figure | 8-15 |

The "selection edge not visible" warning.

figure | 8-16 |

The original photo of Max, taken near a window with my digital camera. Admittedly, not the most professional setup.

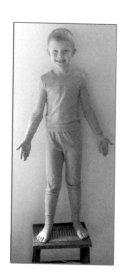

NOTE: When painting with black or white, the selection is either indicated or not by marching ants, but when painting with an opacity setting or a tonal color a selection may or may not be visible. A dialog box, as shown in Figure 8-15, might appear. However, although you cannot always see the marching ants of a semitransparent selection, the selection will be indicated by a level of gray when viewed as an alpha channel (saved mask).

When designing the Max lesson in Chapter 4 I used a quick mask to extract the background from the photograph, so that I could replace it with a different one. The background of the original photo was made up of many shadows and highlights, so regrettably I couldn't just click on it with the Magic Wand tool and be done with it. Moreover, I was hell-bent on protecting Max's body from the extraction. Check out Figure 8-16.

To get into Quick Mask mode I cursorily selected as much of the background as I could with the Lasso (or Magic Wand) tool and then chose Edit in Quick Mask Mode in the toolbox (see Figure 8-17).

Photoshop covers the nonselected areas of the image in a translucent color, which by default is red, like rubylith, but can be changed by double clicking on the Edit in Quick Mask Mode icon in the toolbox (see Figure 8-18). I then selected the Paintbrush tool in the toolbox. The swatches in the toolbox automatically become black and white, ready to mark out by color my selected or nonselected areas when painting. I painted with white to add to my selection (remove the translucent color) or black to delete areas of my selection (add the translucent color). Flipping between Edit in Standard Mode and Edit in Quick Mask Mode in the toolbox let me see how I was doing—showing what areas were selected or not selected (see Figure 8-19).

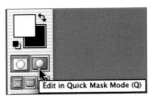

figure | 8-17

The Edit in Quick Mask Mode option in the toolbox.

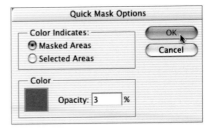

figure | 8-18

Double click on the Edit in Quick Mask Mode icon in the toolbox to get to its options.

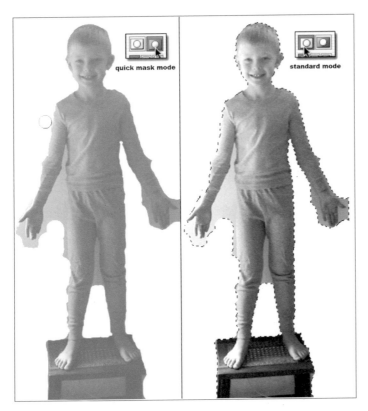

figure | 8-19

Move between Standard and Quick Mask modes to see how the selection process is going.

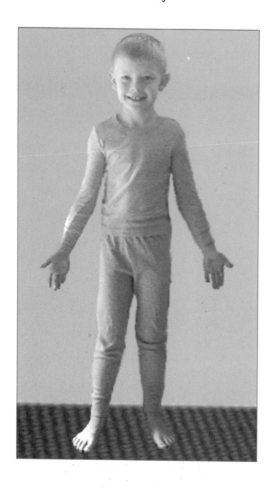

figure | 8-20 |

The final Max image used in the Chapter 4 lesson. Compare with Figure 8-16.

In Standard mode I saved a permanent version of my final selection to an alpha channel (just in case, after all that work, I wanted to use it or edit it again later) by choosing Select > Save Selection. Last, I created the layer mask out of the selection, made a new background on a separate layer, and placed it below the mask layer. The result is shown in Figure 8-20.

Lesson: Lisbon View

In this lesson you will create a new background in a photograph using Quick Mask mode and a layer mask (see Figure 8-21).

figure | 8-21 |

The lesson before and after a mask effect.

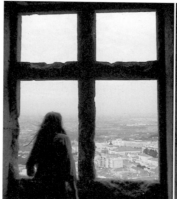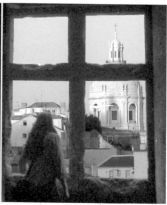

Setting Up the File

1. Open the *chap8L1.psd* file in the *chapter8_lessons* folder.

2. Choose View > Actual Pixels.

3. Press Shift-Tab to hide unneeded palettes.

Making and Refining a Selection

1. With the Rectangular Marquee tool draw a rectangle covering the top, left-hand open area of the window (the selection doesn't need to be perfect right yet). Hold down the Shift key and keep adding to the selection, defining each window area. For the window with the figure in it, select only the top area with the rectangular shape. See figure 8-22.

2. Select Edit in Quick Mask Mode in the toolbox. See Figure 8-23.

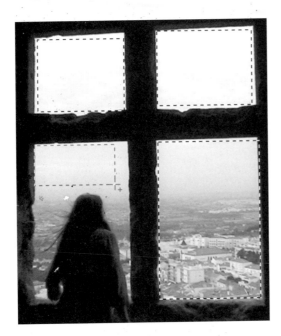

figure | 8-22

Select the open window areas with the Rectangular Marquee tool.

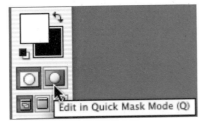

figure | 8-23

Select Edit in Quick Mask mode in the toolbox.

3. Zoom in close to the window area with the silhouette figure.

4. Select the Paintbrush tool and choose a hard brush about 9 pixels in diameter (see Figure 8-24).

5. Be sure white is the foreground color swatch in the toolbox.

figure | 8-24

Select an appropriately sized paintbrush.

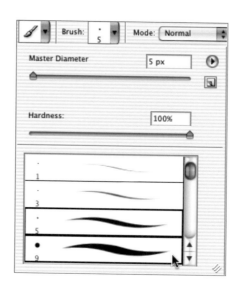

6. Begin to add to the selection by painting away the translucent areas of the open window. To more accurately select the corner crevices of the window you might need to change brush tip sizes. Leave a halo of the translucent color around the head and flying hair strands of the figure. Refer to Figure 8-25.

NOTE: If you get overly zealous with your painting you can undo brush strokes in the History palette, or paint with black to deselect areas.

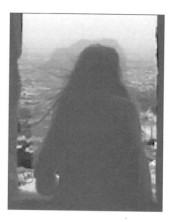

figure | 8-25

Keep part of the translucent color around the figure's head.

7. Switch to Standard mode to see what you've selected thus far.

8. Let's refine this selection a little more. Go back to Edit in Quick Mask mode. Set your brush to a soft round brush about 9 pixels in size (see Figure 8-26). As well, adjust its opacity setting in the options bar to about 92%. Paint carefully around the edge of the figure's head and over the flying strands of hair. You won't see it in the selection, but by using a softer brush and adjusting the opacity setting (or, alternatively painting with a shade of gray) you can create a softer, more realistic mask effect around the hair (you'll see this in a later step).

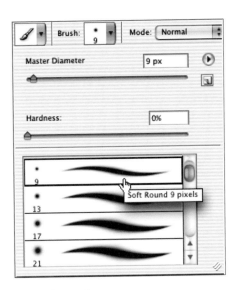

figure | 8-26

Set the brush with a softer tip to produce subtle, semitransparent mask areas.

9. Keep refining the selection with the paintbrush tools to your liking. All open parts of the window should be selected.

10. Go to Standard mode and choose Select > Save Selection from the main menu bar. Enter a name for the new channel (see Figure 8-27).

11. Choose Window > Channels to view the alpha channel mask you just saved.

12. Save the lesson in your *lessons* folder.

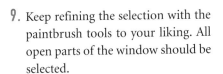

figure | 8-27

The saved alpha channel mask is located in the Channels palette.

Create a Layer Mask

1. In the Layers palette, select the *lisbon_view* layer. Your selection should still be selected. If not, choose Select > Load Selection and in the options box under Channel choose the alpha channel you just saved.

2. Choose Layer > Add Layer Mask > Hide Selection.

3. Choose File > Open and from the *chap8_lessons/samples* folder open *background1.jpg*.

4. Move a copy of the background image to the lesson file (to do this: with the move tool drag the image over the lesson file and let go of the mouse to drop the copy) .

5. Push Layer 1 (with the new background image) below the *lisbon_view* layer. Position the background image to your liking behind the *lisbon_view* layer mask.

6. With the background revealed through the mask you might notice that your mask needs a little more touch-up. Select the layer mask thumbnail in the Layers palette. Select a brush (set the opacity to 100%) and paint with black to reveal more of the background (the black, transparent area of the mask) or with white to hide more of the background (the white, opaque area of the mask).

7. Save the file in your *lessons* folder. Feel free to try other background images (a couple more are provided in the *samples* folder).

SUMMARY

The mystery of masks is uncovered in this chapter. Solutions for how to use layer, vector, type, clipping, and quick masks were examined, and practical application for their use revealed.

in review

1. What's the advantage of using masks to hide and reveal content?

2. Name at least four types of masks in Photoshop.

3. When you save a selection, where does it go?

4. What's the trick (or two) for making soft-edged effects or semitransparent masks in Photoshop?

5. What's the difference between a layer mask and a clipping mask?

6. What's the shortcut key to define a clipping mask in the Layers palette?

7. What first two steps must you do before you can see a quick mask?

8. In Quick Mask mode, how do black, white, and gray tonal colors affect the selection process?

✦ EXPLORING ON YOUR OWN

1. Explore your own mask effects on the sample cardboard character photographs located in the *chap8_lessons/samples* folder (*cardinal.jpg, pope.jpg,* and *explorer.jpg*).

2. Access the Help > How to Work with Layers and Selections > *Soften the edge of a selection* how-to in the menu options. Also read the related topics in the How To.

3. Using the Horizontal Type Mask or Vertical Type Mask tool, create textured mask effects with the words *earth, wind,* and *fire.*

4. Do a search for "image masking" on the Internet and find at least two examples that demonstrate the technique of masking.

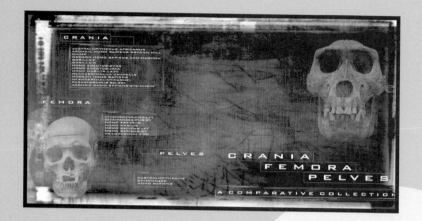

CRANIA
AUSTRALOPITHECUS AFRICANUS
ARCHAIC HOMO SAPIENS-BROKEN HILL
CHILD
MODERN HOMO SAPIENS CRO-MAGNON
GORILLA-M
GORILLA-M
HOMO ERECTUS-3733
HOMO ERECTUS-JAVA
HOMO HABILIS-1470
NEANDERTHAL-LA CHAPELLE
MODERN HOMO SAPIENS
NEANDERTHAL-MT-CARMEL
PARANTHROPUS BOISEI
ARCHAIC HOMO SAPIENS-STEINHEIM

FEMORA
CHIMPANZEE-FM-LFT
CHIMPANZEE-FM-RT
HOMO ERECTUS
HOMO HABILIS
HOMO SAPIENS-LFT
HOMO SAPIENS-RT
NEANDERTHAL-FMR

PELVES
AUSTRALOPITHECINE
CHIMPANZEE
HOMO SAPIENS

CRANIA
FEMORA
PELVES

A COMPARATIVE COLLECTION

| compositing and the design process |

9

charting your course

The previous chapters have focused almost exclusively on specific concepts, tools, and ways of doing particular things in Photoshop. In other words, how to get around its interface, manage color, select and transform pixels, retouch photos, draw and paint shapes, use type, and mask areas of an image. Next is to cover the process and methods by which to composite, link, blend, merge, and organize graphical elements into more complex images or graphic layouts. This includes a significant overview of image compositing and the design work process, using layers and alignment tools, merging images with blending modes or filter effects, acquiring content, and producing a CD cover where you can freely utilize all that you've studied thus far in the program.

 goals

- Learn workflow and organizational techniques for developing image compositions and layouts
- Cover some specifics using the Layers palette
- Review the options for content acquisition and copyright compliance
- Composite images together with blending modes, the Liquify effect, and filter effects
- Define the sequential steps of a basic design process
- Construct a CD cover for a mock client

ABOUT COMPOSITING AND COMPOSITION

I think it's important to make a distinction between image compositing and composition in regard to using Photoshop. In the book *Digital Retouching and Compositing: Photographers' Guide*, author David D. Busch describes image compositing as "…combining two or more images or portions thereof, to create a new image that didn't exist in that form previously." Artist, Jeffrey Moring's other-worldly images found in the color insert of this book are good examples of images derived by compositing. Also, see the "Adventures in Design: From the Imagination" in this book.

Composition, on the other hand, "…refers to the aesthetic arrangement of elements within a work of art," as described by author Lois Fichner-Rathus in *Understanding Art*, Seventh Edition. It's the artful use of design principles (including line, shape, value, texture, and color) in a visual image or design layout, such as a web site splash page, brochure, or poster. See "Adventures in Design: Wine Box Composition" in this book and the finished color version of the label in the color insert. I don't cover design principles specifically in this book, but I do in relation to using Adobe Illustrator in my book *Exploring Illustrator CS*. By nature of what Photoshop is commonly used for, more emphasis in this book has been placed on image compositing. However, I have provided in the next section a brief overview of the work process by which a design layout or composition might be constructed.

A DESIGN PROCESS

As much as we might like to snap our fingers in an instantaneous epiphany, and have an idea materialize from our head to reality (that would truly be magic), it just doesn't work that way. Thought to conception, conception to actuality, is a process—there's no way around it. So you might as well make the process your modus operandi. Of course, the process can take shape in numerous fashions. It's just learning the one that fits right for you as a graphic designer and for the needs of your clients. (I'm assuming here that a goal might be to do work for hire, to actually make money playing with Photoshop.)

In this section, I introduce a general process in which to organize and produce an image composition or layout and also share with you some of the tools available in Photoshop for organization and workflow. The parts to this process are: start with an idea, make a mock-up, gather content, assemble content, and fine tune.

Start with an Idea

As is the makings of anything, a design always starts with a vision or idea. In your mind sometimes the idea is perfectly realized, and it's simply a matter of getting it into a tangible form. Other times, the idea is further fleshed out as you go through the design process. Either way, you have to start with an idea, something that drives you to make it "real."

Make a Mock-up

Have you ever made a collage out of magazine clippings, perhaps as a kid? Usually before you permanently glue anything down you take your pile of clippings and artfully arrange them on your poster board. You move and rotate things around, group clippings based on topic or color, and inevitably place the most interesting clipping right in the center for visual impact. What's happening at this stage of development is your mock-up; thought is being put into the actual design of your collage and the initial placement of elements. At this point, nothing is set in stone, but ideas for how something will look best are thoughtfully considered.

The idea slowly forms into something tangible. Often it starts out as a cursory sketch, and is then reproduced into a more detailed drawing. Many artists will sketch the idea on paper first, scan it, and then use the sketch as a template for constructing the digital version. Others, who feel really comfortable drawing on the computer, construct the whole vision digitally, utilizing the flexibility of undo and redo (see figures 9-1 and 9-2). Once a mock-up is set up to your liking, or to your client's, you can then move to the next logical steps: gathering the actual content that will be used in the decided design and assembling it into the final product.

Gather Content

Once you have your mock-up, you now have a better idea of what kind of content you need for the final design. Gathering content for your layout can be the most time consuming and challenging

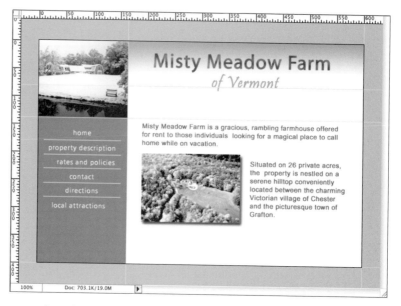

figure | 9-1 |

Design mock-up 1 of a web site home page.

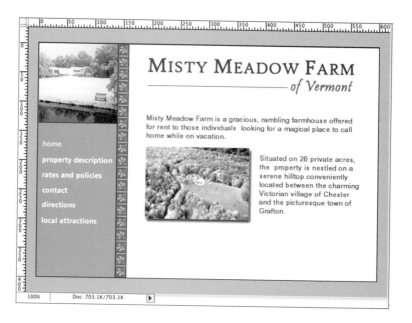

figure | 9-2 |

Design mock-up 2 of a web site home page.

part of the whole process, so be sure to leave plenty of time for it in your project timeline. Possibly you are in the situation where you must create all the content—images and copy—yourself, or procure the content from other sources, such as your client or possibly from an outside resource (such as another artist or writer, image, or font repository). At this point, consideration must be given to issues of copyright and content format.

Copyright Issues

If you create all your own content or use copyright-free material there's no need to worry about the permission process. On the other hand, many resources out there you might like to use, such as another company's logo or a photo of a famous person, could take a little investigative work to get the correct permissions for the materials' usage in your work. As an example, every digital image in this book is protected by copyright law whether explicitly indicated or not. As soon as it is created, copyright is automatically implied—no copyright notice or procedures are required to protect the image from unauthorized reproduction.

It certainly doesn't hurt, however, to register your work through the United States Copyright Office (that is, if you made your creation in the United States) at *www.copyright.gov*. You should a least put a copyright notice (© date, your name) on your work to deter individuals from using your work without contacting you for permission first. The artwork or photographs used in this book that were not created by myself (the author) I had to request permission for (and/or pay for) and acknowledge that permission was actually granted (e.g., "Printed by permission of…" or "Courtesy of…").

Since the proliferation of digital content into our society, copyright protections have been under renewed scrutiny. It has become easier than ever to procure and edit content without thought to the original artist who created the work. In regard to the protection of digitized content and the use of it for educational purposes, laws have recently been put into place, such as the Digital Millennium Copyright Act (see "Exploring on Your Own" for more information on this).

Important to know is a provision to U.S. copyright law called "fair use." Fair Use delineates the use of creative works for educational or nonprofit purposes, such as the photographs provided for the lesson project in this chapter.

When determining whether or not to use someone else's work as part of your own, ask yourself "Will copying of this image (or text, font, music, video, or data) make me money or take money out of someone else's pocket?" If the answer is "yes," proceed with caution—get permission and credit the author of the work.

Format

Another aspect of content gathering is getting the content into the right format for your use. For example, if Photoshop is to be used as the medium for assembling all your content (see next step), you want to be sure that the content can be successfully imported into the program. Are the images and photos you want to use in the correct file format for Photoshop or any other program you might be using to read? Is the written copy translatable in the digital environment? I'm not going to go into great detail about each of the importable file formats supported by Photoshop. However, the available formats appear in the File browser, the Open dialog box, or the Import submenu. Here's an abbreviated list: Photoshop, Photoshop EPS, CompuServe GIF, JPEG, PCX, Photoshop PDF, PICT file, PNG, Targa, TIFF, and Wireless Bitmap (WBMP).

Assemble Content

Once content is gathered, you assemble it in your layout program, which could be Photoshop, but also a more layout-friendly program such as Adobe Illustrator, InDesign, or Quark Express.

NOTE: If you are fortunate enough to have the whole Adobe Creative Suite at your fingertips, you have the option to assemble and edit your content between programs. For example, if you're working on an image in Photoshop that needs some work done in Illustrator or InDesign, you can choose File > Jump To and open the file in one of those programs.

There are two parts to integrating content into your final layout design: properly importing content from outside the program and accurately positioning content into the intended composition using placement and organization tools.

Import

Once you have the content in an importable format (see last section on gathering content), you bring it into Photoshop in two ways. You can use the Open and Open Recent commands, or the File browser (File > Browse). Also, you can copy and paste between many applications. You have been opening files all along in the book lessons, but here are the quick steps:

1. Choose File > Open.

2. Select the name of the file you want to open. If the file does not appear, select the option for showing all formats or documents from the Files of type (Windows) or Show (Mac) pop-up menu.

3. Click Open. A dialog box might appear, letting you set format-specific options. If a color profile warning message appears, specify whether to convert the pixels based on the file's color profile.

   NOTE: Image preview and file compatibility options can be found under Photoshop > Preferences > File Handling (Mac) or Edit > Preferences > File Handling (Windows).

Generally when importing native file formats—such as Illustrator (AI), Freehand (FH) or Flash (FLA)—from one program to another it's a hit-or-miss proposition. Sometimes the version of the program you are importing the file into will support it, sometimes not. Keeping files in more generic file formats (EPS for vector-based files, or TIFF for bitmap-based files) might prove a better solution, even if on occasion you loose some information in translation.

Another importing issue is if you attempt to open a newer version of a Photoshop file into an older version (i.e., CS to version 7) you usually get a dialog box that says something like that shown in Figure 9-3. The conversion will probably work, but you might loose some information. When you go to import artwork and you can't access the file you want to import even after you've chosen *Show all documents* from the *Files of type* (Windows) or Show

Adobe Photoshop

Unknown data has been encountered reading layer "Photo Filter 1" and will be discarded. Continue?

Read composite data   Cancel   OK

figure | 9-3|

Attempt to import a Photoshop CS file into Photoshop 7. It will work, but some information may be lost.

(Mac) pop-up menu, you know that the file has been saved in a format Photoshop cannot read.

Organizing

Once you've imported your content into Photoshop, or created it directly in the program, you should organize it some way. I emphasis the word *should* here because it's optional whether or not you want to organize your content. However, I highly recommend it. You can't just leave all of your content in one unnamed layer and expect to find what you need quickly and without frustration later on. Features to keep your work organized while integrating content in a document include Layers, the alignment commands, rulers, the grid, guides, and the Snap feature.

Layers

As you've probably surmised from working through past lessons, the Layers palette is your organizational Mecca. And, you're probably wondering why I've waited until Chapter 9 to impart this important bit of information. I figure the best way to learn how to use the Layers palette is to just practice using it, which by default you've had a chance too do in just about every document you've worked on in Photoshop, whether you wanted to or not. Additionally, you can do specific compositing techniques and effects when items are on individual layers, including layer styles (such as Drop Shadow, and Bevel and Emboss), blending modes, and filters. You have already explored these in other chapters, but they are officially covered in this chapter. The anatomy of the Layers palette (Window > Layers) is visually marked out for quick reference in Figure 9-4.

NOTE: By default every document in Photoshop starts on the Background layer. To change a Background layer into a regular layer (much more versatile), double click on the Background layer thumbnail in the Layers palette and give the layer a name. See Figure 9-5.

Layers are transparent except for any filled content that is placed on the layer, making it easy to move layer content elements above and below each other for dimensional reasons and for overlapping combinations of images and effects. See Figure 9-6.

Layers Palette

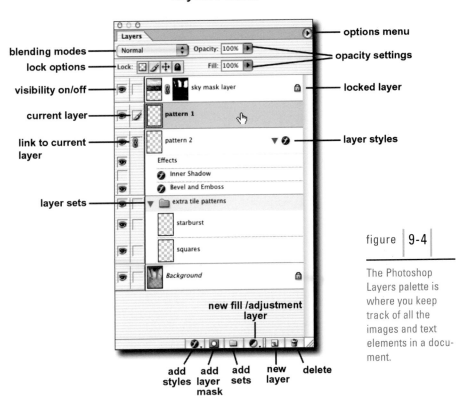

blending modes

lock options

visibility on/off

current layer

link to current layer

layer sets

options menu

opacity settings

locked layer

layer styles

new fill /adjustment layer

add styles　add layer mask　add sets　new layer　delete

figure | 9-4 |

The Photoshop Layers palette is where you keep track of all the images and text elements in a document.

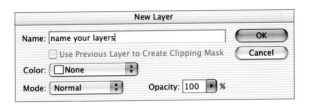

figure | 9-5 |

Give your layers intuitive names so that you can find what you need in the Layers palette.

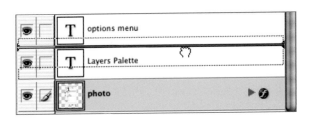

figure | 9-6 |

Layers can be selected and dragged up and down the layer stack, sending objects in front or in back of each other.

Items can be selected on any layer, by selecting the layer and then Command-clicking (Mac) or Ctrl-clicking (Windows) on the layer's thumbnail. See Figure 9-7.

figure | 9-7

Select all areas on a layer.

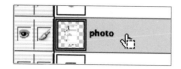

Layers can also be linked temporarily to transform or align objects as a group. You can also merge linked items into one layer, or group layers in subfolders, called Layer Sets. See Figure 9-8.

For plenty more details on layers visit Help > Photoshop Help > Contents > Using Layers.

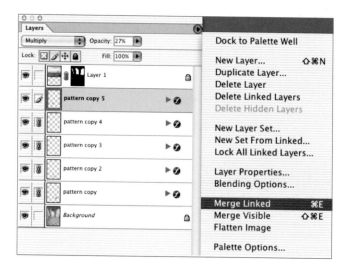

figure | 9-8

You can merge linked layers into one layer if necessary.

The Alignment Commands

The alignment commands located in the Move tool's options bar align objects on linked layers horizontally (right, left, or center) or vertically (top, bottom, or center). They also horizontally or vertically distribute linked layers evenly, using the object's edges for spatial reference. You can also get the alignment and distribution options by choosing Layer > Align Linked or Layer > Distribute Linked from the main menu bar. Being very precision-oriented, I use these commands a lot. See figures 9-9 and 9-10.

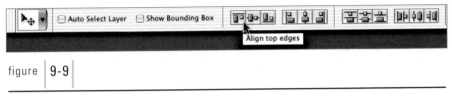

figure | 9-9

The alignment commands are located the Move tool's options bar.

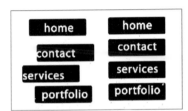

figure | 9-10

Before-and-after example of using the alignment commands. The buttons and text on the right are horizontally centered, with a vertically centered distribution of space between each object.

Rulers

Rulers, of course, are designed to accurately measure and place objects in the Photoshop work space. Rulers are toggled on and off by choosing View > Rulers. Both a horizontal and a vertical ruler are made available along the edges of the document. You can change a ruler's measurement by Ctrl-clicking (Mac) or right clicking (Windows) over a ruler and selecting a new measurement from the drop-down menu (see Figure 9-11). Alternatively, you can go to Photoshop > Preferences > Units & Rulers (Mac) or Edit > Preferences > Units & Rulers (Windows). In the upper left-hand corner of the document, where the vertical and horizontal rulers meet, you can also set what's called the ruler origin. Setting the ruler origin is useful when, for example, you are working on an object that's 2 x 3 on an 8-1/2 by 11 inch document. You can set the ruler origin at 0, 0 in the upper left-hand corner of the 2 x 3 area, rather than the 8-1/2 by 11 area, for more precise positioning. To set the ruler origin you move the cursor into the upper left-hand corner of the document where the rulers intersect and then click and drag the crosshair to the new origin edge. To restore default settings, double click on the upper left-hand corner where the rulers intersect.

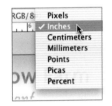

figure | 9-11

Ctrl-click (Mac) or right click (Windows) over the a ruler to change the measurement.

The Grid

The Grid function in Photoshop is located under View > Show > Grid. A grid of lines or dots appears behind your artwork. The grid can be used to symmetrically position objects. Grids do not print. You can adjust grid settings (such as color, style, and subdivisions) by choosing Photoshop > Preferences > Guides, Grid, & Slices (Mac) or Edit > Preferences > Guides, Grid & Slices (Windows).

Guides

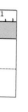

Guides are incredibly useful for aligning your work. You can quickly create guides by choosing View > Rulers and dragging guidelines from the horizontal and vertical rulers on the sides of the document (see Figure 9-12). Alternatively, choose View > New Guide. You can lock/unlock and clear guides in the View menu, and show guides under View > Show > Guides. Guides do not print. Adjust guide colors and style by choosing Photoshop > Preferences > Guides, Grid & Slices (Mac) or Edit > Preferences > Guides, Grid & Slices (Windows).

figure | 9-12 |

Drag guides from the horizontal and vertical rulers.

Snap

Snap allows for exact positioning of selection edges, shapes, and paths. Often, however, the Snap feature (on by default) is more a hindrance than a help, preventing you from properly placing items. Luckily, snapping can be enabled or disabled under View > Snap. With Snap on you can also choose to snap to particular elements, such as the grid (when visible), guides (when visible), and document bounds. Choose View > Snap To Guides, Grids, or Document Bounds.

NOTE: You can also snap to image slices that were made in Image Ready.

Fine Tune

The fine-tuning stage is where you fix the fine details of your image or layout, including adjusting colors, incrementally aligning items, and playing with subtle formatting of text (such as line and character spacing). In short, you make the document look as perfect as possible. At this time, you also prepare your final work for its intended output, such as choosing the proper color mode and settings for either screen or print.

BLENDING MODES, STYLES, AND EFFECTS

If you've spent any significant time playing in Photoshop, it's probable that you've already found and delved into the blending modes, layer styles, filter effects, and Liquify function. These are easy-to-use features with high visual impact (addictive, really) and that work miraculously with image compositing.

Blending Modes

Blending modes work with layers and layer sets. A blending mode is specified for a selected layer that affects (blends with) the layer below it or within a layer set.

Blending modes are true compositing of images on different layers, determining how pixels blend with underlying pixels in an image. See Figure 9-13.

NOTE: Blending modes are also available for the Paintbrush options, found in the Paintbrush tool's options bar.

Experience pixel blends by opening *chap9_lessons/samples/blend.psd.*

1. Open the Layers palette.

2. Two layers are already created for you. Select the layer *painted image.* From the drop-down menu in the Layers palette, choose the Multiply blending mode—a blend that simulates a look of transparent markers (see Figure 9-14). Explore the other modes. (Alternatively, you can get to the blending modes under Layers > Layer Style > Blending Options.)

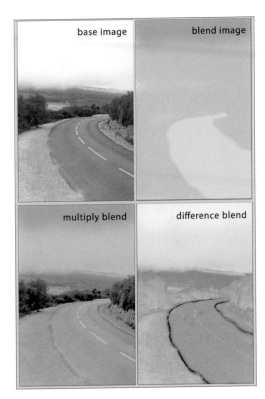

figure | 9-13

The blend image is on a layer above the base image, and contains the specified blending mode, such as a Multiply or Difference blend.

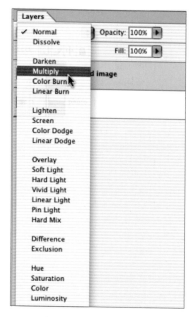

figure 9-14

Multiply blending mode.

3. For an overview of what each blending mode looks like and its description, see *Painting > Setting options for painting* and *Editing Tools > Selecting a blending mode* in the Photoshop Help files.

Layer Styles

A layer style can be applied to items on any selected layer, such as a Drop Shadow, Inner and Outer Glow, Bevel and Emboss effects, and Strokes. Go to Layers > Layer Style to choose a style. A dialog box comes up, where you can modify and add a style or remove styles. To get to the options of any style, click on the style name on the left (not just the check mark, but the actual name) and the options for that style will appear on the right. See Figure 9-15.

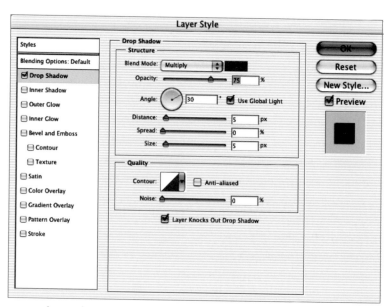

figure 9-15

The Layer Style dialog box—a lot of stuff to tinker with in here!

Filters Effects

One thing Photoshop is famous for is its extensive gallery of filters. Filters directly distort and manipulate the pixels in an image. See Figure 9-16. Keep your image in the RGB Color mode to have the full range of filters available for you to use. (Once the filter is applied, if you need to you can change it to another color mode.) The best way to view all of your filter choices and preview what they will look like on your image is to choose Filter > Filter Gallery from the main menu. See Figure 9-17. A sample file is provided for you to try out filters: *chap9_lessons/samples/filter.psd.*

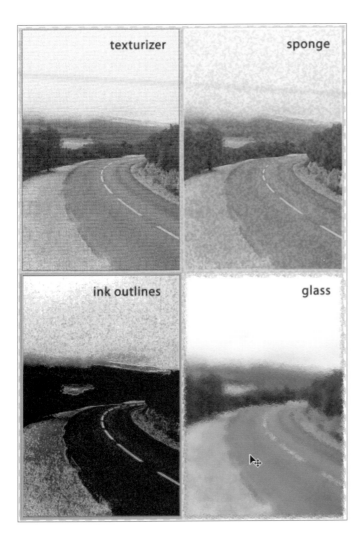

figure | 9-16

Filter examples—
there are a lot to
choose from!

A filter not to be missed and used often by artists and photographers is the Lighting Effects filter, which allows you to create different light styles and properties for your image. Check it out under Filter > Render > Lighting Effects. See Figure 9-18.

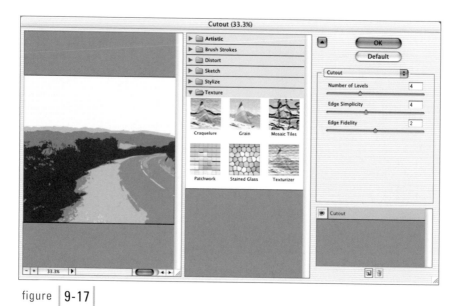

figure | 9-17

The filter gallery. Take your pick and preview.

figure | 9-18

The ever-popular Lighting Effects filter.

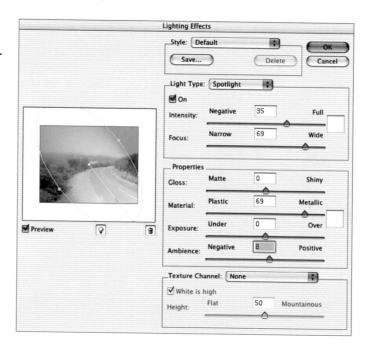

Liquify Effects

Last in our tour of special effects is the Liquify feature—it's sweet. With Liquify you can distort pixels with various Liquify commands, such as Bloat, Pucker, and Warp. Choose Filter > Liquify and from the Liquify menu select tools on the toolbar to the left of the window and adjust options to the right. See Figure 9-19 and the sample file under *chap9_lessons/samples/liquify.psd*.

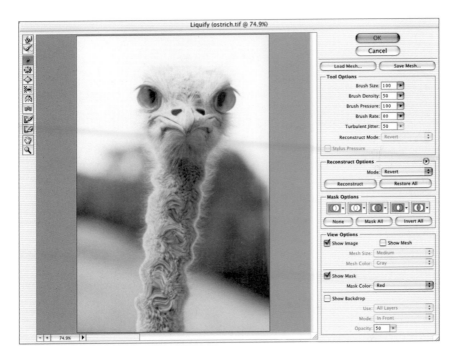

figure | 9-19 |

The Liquify tools in action.

Lesson: CD Jacket Project

Now that you've got a handle on using Photoshop, here's your chance to break from the step-by-step study, explore some of the blending and filter effects, and begin to stretch your artistic muscle.

You have been approached by PaleoExcavators, Inc., to design a CD jacket (a cover, both front and back) for their new comparative collection CD of skeletal remains (see Figure 9-20). The client has provided you with a few guidelines and some content (text and photographs) for the project, but in general they are open to the possibilities of what can be done. They have also provided you with some examples of their previous CD jacket designs (see figures 9-21 and 9-22 and the color insert).

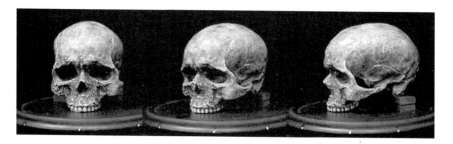

figure | 9-20

Skeletal remains to be composited into a CD jacket design. All photographs are courtesy of Modesto Junior College's graphics design instructor Joel Hagen.

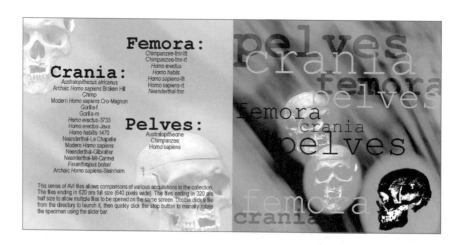

figure | 9-21

CD cover project example 1, designed by Photoshop students at Modesto Junior College, California.

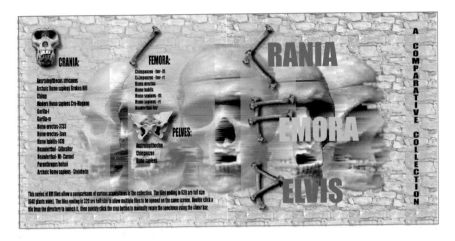

figure | 9-22

CD cover project example 2, designed by Photoshop students at Modesto Junior College, California.

Project Guidelines

1. Required text and a selection of photographs are provided in the *chap9_lessons/assets/CDproject* folder. Photographs are categorized in folders for what each contains: crania, femora, and pelvic skeletal remains. The text for both the front and back of the covers is provided. You need to include and format all of the text. (For text-formatting options in Photoshop, choose a Type tool to bring up its options bar, and make use of the Window > Character and Window > Paragraph palettes.)

NOTE: For your viewing fun, some Flash SWF movies have also been provided in the assets folder as an example of what will be on the mock CD. You will need the Flash Player (free from *www.macromedia.com*) to view the movies on your computer.

2. You may also use a combination of your own acquired raster- and vector-based images.

3. Dimension specifications for the jacket are:

- *Width:* 9.5 inches
- *Height:* 4.6875 inches

- 200 pixels/inch (Resolution)
- *Color mode:* RGB Color (to eventually be converted to CMYK for printing)

4. Before assembling the final designed piece, hone your design ideas by sketching them out by hand or mocking them up digitally. Provide an overall potential "look and feel" for the jacket, including font and color possibilities and a general layout of text and images.

5. Save your final work in both the PSD and TIFF formats.

SUMMARY

This chapter offered a big-picture view of the image compositing and design composition processes. Additionally, it went over often-used organizational and workflow features of the program, and got you hooked (in all hopes!) on Photoshop's unique blending, Liquify, and filter effects. Work out that imagination muscle!

in review

1. Describe image compositing. Describe composition in design.

2. Define five steps in the design process.

3. What question should you ask yourself when deciding whether or not you should use someone else's work in your own?

4. Name at least five features of the Layers palette.

5. How do you change a background layer to a regular layer?

6. To align items on separate layers, what must you do?

7. Most filter effects are only available in what color mode?

↗ EXPLORING ON YOUR OWN

1. Study about copyright online:

   ● U.S. Copyright Office (copyright basics): *www.copyright.gov/circs/circ1.html*

   ● Specifics of the Digital Millennium Copyright Act: *www.copyright.gov/legislation/dmca.pdf*

   ● Copyright web site: *www.benedict.com*

   ● Stanford University Libraries, copyright and fair use: *http://fairuse.stanford.edu/*

2. Design a CD cover or promotional poster for a local band or theater company in your area.

3. Create a home page design for a web site.

ADVENTURES IN DESIGN
FROM THE IMAGINATION

Photoshop can bring out the mad scientist in us all. It's a digital laboratory where instruments are used to piece together pixels, rather than strands of DNA, into new life forms that come alive on screen or paper, tabloid covers, DVD or video game splash screens, or in this book's color insert. Enter an adventure in design for the wild imagination.

Professional Project Example

Our experiment begins with an example brought to you from the digital artist (a.k.a., "Mad Scientist") Jeffrey Moring. Jeffrey reveals the secrets used to bring about his optical vision titled "Yesterday, Today, Forever." See Figure B-1.

"The first step in creating this piece was getting the right digital images to work with," explains Jeffrey. I took some photographs of myself, then photographed many different skulls. (The biology department of your school should have such skulls.) After picking the right digital photos, I brought them into Photoshop [see Figures B-2 and B-3]. The most important techniques for this kind of digital manipulation are selecting

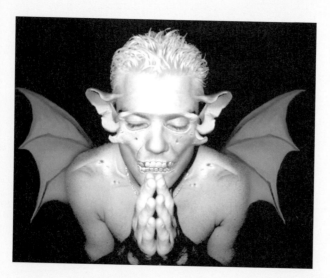

Figure B-1. Artist Jeffrey Moring's altered self in his image "Yesterday, Today, Forever." *(Printed by permission of Jeffrey Moring.)*

areas and your ability to blend two different images together. The tools that I used were the Smudge tool, the Eraser tool, and the Clone Stamp tool [see Figure B-4].

"Getting a good selection of the image you are using is critical. Each picture should be on a different layer when building such images. This is also critical [see Figure B-5]. Being able to change one part at a time is a time saver, and gives great effects. I then scaled down each skull and began placing them over the face layer, changing the opacity and using the blending tools. I left many of my own facial features, but also used the main skull features and blended the two. Feathering the selections can help soften an image, but be careful not to feather a selection too much. The tool I probably used the most is the Eraser tool. After you place one layer on top of the other, you can

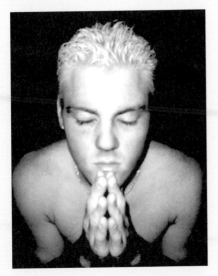

Figure B-2. A self-portrait was taken and imported into Photoshop. A black background was added.

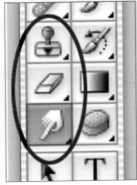

Figure B-4. Tools used to blend the images: the Smudge, Eraser, and Clone Stamp tools.

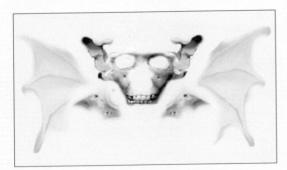

Figure B-3. Photographs of skeletal remains were taken, brought into Photoshop, and their background pixels selected and removed.

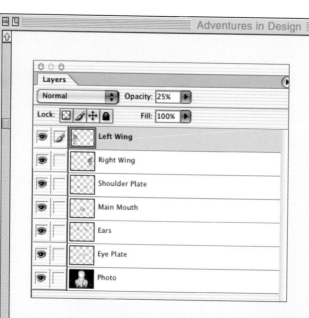

Figure B-5. Each item—including each bone selection—is placed on its own layer.

Figure B-6. Choose the Eraser tool with a soft brush tip to create a seamless blend between layered images.

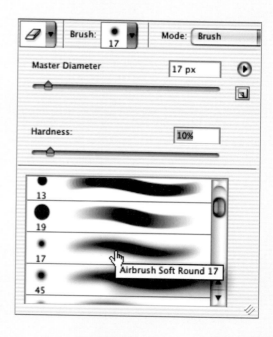

erase (with a soft-tipped brush) what you do not want [see Figure B-6]. The more comfortable you get with the mouse, the better you can blend the images."

Your Turn

Using some of the tools and techniques recommended by Jeffrey, create your own freak of nature or otherworldly vision of yourself.

Self-Project Guidelines

1. Import a photograph of yourself into Photoshop.

2. With the Selection tools or Quick Mask feature, extract the background from the photograph and replace it with a solid color or fantasy-like backdrop.

3. With their backgrounds already removed, bring in other images (with either hard or feathered edges) to composite with the self-portrait. Put each image on its own layer. Duplicate and flip images you might like to use on both sides of the portrait (like the bat wings on Jeffrey's image).

4. Hide and reveal areas of images using Layer Masks or the Eraser tool.

5. Blend images with the layer-blending modes, if needed.

6. Add Liquify or filter effects to individual layers for more distorted and/or textured looks.

Things to Consider

For this Adventure in Design and future experimentations such as this, consider the following:

- For photographs of objects where the background will eventually be removed, shoot the picture against a matte-finished, even-colored backdrop. This, of course, will make it easier to remove the pixels later in Photoshop.

- Take high-resolution digital photos or scan in photos at a high resolution, so that you have plenty of pixels to work with in Photoshop.

- Sketch out on paper some of your creature designs.

- Practice mastering the tools (and their many options) you think you will use—such as the Smudge, Eraser, Dodge, Burn, and Clone Stamp tools—on a separate, blank document.

- Save your work often and back it up.

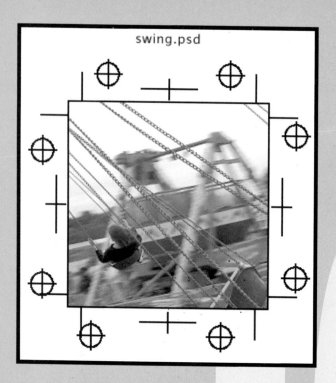
swing.psd

| print publishing |

10

charting your course

Eventually you will want to get your artwork in a format that can be shared, which chapters 10 and 11 prepare you to do. There are many possibilities for where your digital images can appear, including on screen—such as in a web page, an interactive learning environment, a kiosk, or mobile device (see Chapter 11)—and paper, such is in a glossy magazine ad, a flyer, brochure, or poster. These paper media are what we get into in this chapter about print publishing.

 goals

- Learn about the different methods of printing
- Discover why color management can really make a difference
- Understand the halftone and color separation process
- Be able to ask the right questions when consulting a print service bureau
- Get familiar with the Print with Preview command

PRINTING METHODS

There are several ways to get your artwork onto paper: directly from a desktop printer or digital printing press, from a film negative that's used to create a metal plate for a mechanical press, or in the form of a Portable Document File (PDF) or PostScript file.

Let me briefly describe each of these methods for output, and then in the next section show you how you will want to set up your print job in Photoshop's Print with Preview window.

Desktop Printing

Without a doubt, you'll want to print off your work on a desktop printer—if not the final version at least some paper proofs for mock-up and revision purposes. Desktop printers differ, being made by a specific company and having different levels of printing capabilities. A low-end ink jet printer, for example, deposits ink onto a page much differently than a high-end laser printer. It really helps to read up on the specifications for your particular desktop printer, so that you can accurately gauge whether a printer issue is something you can fix on the Photoshop side of things, or is an unavoidable product of your type of printer.

You'll also want to know what resolution your printer will support, and what will give you the best quality, which can vary greatly depending on the type of printer and the paper used. Much of the process of determining this is trial and error (print it off and see what it looks like). In general, laser printers have a resolution of about 600 dpi (dots per inch). For printers, dpi is usually the resolution measurement, whereas for computers the measurement is ppi, pixels per inch. Ink jet printers have a resolution of between 300 and 720 dpi.

NOTE: If you need a refresher on what resolution is all about, or just want to know more about resolution related to Photoshop, go to Help > Photoshop Help and under Index do a search for *resolution*. See Chapter 3 as well.

Digital Printing

A digital printing press is a beefed-up version of your typical desktop computer. As digital printing technologies improve, digital

shaped like a fish bowl, so that you can breath. Just as you must give consideration on how to fit appropriately into the outer space environment, you must assess the printing environment when you finally decide to take your Photoshop work and land it on a piece of paper, so to speak. In general, three areas that need to be considered when going to print are your image's color, resolution (size and quality), and format. This applies if you are directly outputting to a printer device (see the "Printing Methods" section in this chapter) or are importing your image into another program first, such as one that works with layout design. Such programs include Adobe InDesign or Illustrator, Quark Express, and Macromedia Freehand.

NOTE: Programs specifically designed for layout design are also quite savvy for setting up your document properly for print. While Photoshop has the talents to do this, a program such as Adobe Illustrator is even more adept at this kind of translation.

We have discussed each of these areas—color, resolution, and formats—in other chapters, but understanding them is so important that we need to discuss them again here (and again in Chapter 11) as they relate to the printing process.

Color

If you recall from Chapter 5, different devices (whether screen based or print based) have different color gamuts, the range (or limits) of color that can be reproduced. Because of this, it's extra important to prepare your image to match the specific color profile of whatever device or other application you are going to output it to, which is a workflow process appropriately called *color management*. Admittedly, it's impossible to perfectly match colors between a monitor and a printer (one is using light to make colors, the other using ink), but you can get fairly close by creating profiles for your monitor, printer, and printer papers. With these color spaces set, Photoshop's built-in color management system can then correctly transform the color from one working color space to another. The fine points of color management can be explored to a great extent in the Photoshop help files (you can even purchase complete volumes on the subject), but for now a good gist of how to set up color profiles and calibrate your monitor will get you well on your way.

About Color Profiles

A printer's output quality is determined by its color profile (sometimes called destination profile or output profile), which determines how many colors and to what degree of color accuracy it can produce. There are many types of color profiles you can work with, usually identified by the name of the company who designed them or the country who has standardized them, such as Adobe RGB (1998), U.S. Web Coated (SWOP) v2, or Euroscale Uncoated v2. You determine what profile you need by consulting the specifications of your particular printer or, if you are commercially printing, asking your prepress specialist. When you are not sure what to do, stick with Photoshop's default working color space. When working in RGB, and eventually converting to CMYK and going to print, this would be the Adobe RGB (1998) setting. Use this space when you need to print work with a broad range of colors. See Figure 10-3.

figure | 10-3

You can set your specific working space by choosing Edit > Color Settings (Windows) or Photoshop > Color Settings (Mac).

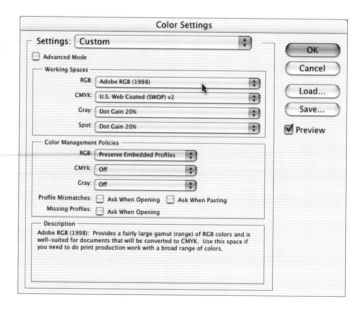

There are several places in Photoshop where you will encounter options for setting color profiles. Let's open up an image and visit each of these places in the order in which you might encounter them.

1. In Photoshop, open the file *swing.psd* in the *chap10_ lessons/assets* folder.

2. Note that the status bar at the top of the image indicates that it is already set in the RGB Color mode. See Figure 10-4.

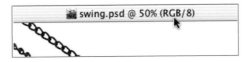
swing.psd @ 50% (RGB/8)

3. Choose View > Print Size to see what dimensions the image will be when printed. You can also get an idea of this size proportionally to an 8.5-x-11-inch sheet of paper by clicking on the status bar in the lower left corner of the program window. See Figure 10-5. And, for exact dimensions and resolution see Image > Image Size > Document Size. See Figure 10-6.

4. Let's indicate global color settings for the current document and any new document you create. Go to Photoshop > Color Settings (Mac) or Edit > Color Settings (Windows). Under the Settings option, choose U.S. Prepress Defaults. Note in this pop-up window the other presets available. See Figure 10-7.

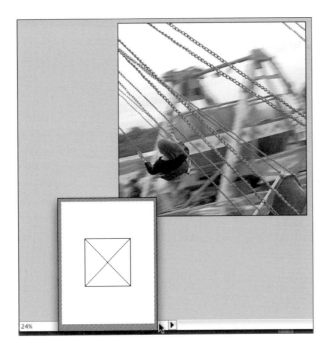
24%

figure | 10-5 |

In the status bar, you can see what an image will look like printed on a piece of paper.

figure | 10-6 |

To get the exact
dimensions of a
document, depend-
ent on its resolution,
go to Image > Image
Size.

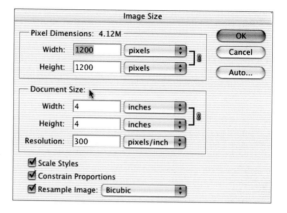

figure | 10-7 |

Indicate a color pro-
file preset in the
Color Settings dialog
box.

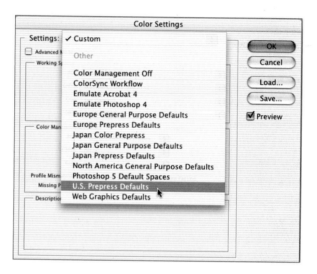

5. Under Working Spaces, note that each color mode (RGB, CMYK, Gray, and Spot) has its own profile. As mentioned previously, when in doubt about where your document will eventually be printed keep your file in RGB Color mode with the Adobe RGB (1998) setting. To read a description of this mode and any other setting in the Color Settings dialog box, move your cursor over the item you want described and view the description at the bottom of the dialog box. Click OK.

6. Now, choose Image > Mode > Assign Profile. Here is where you can choose color management options specific to the selected image. See Figure 10-8. The options include keeping it at the setting you choose in the Color Settings dialog box, using the Don't Color Manage the Document option, or select a specific profile for the particular printer and paper quality

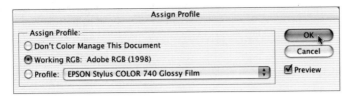

figure | 10-8

Assign a profile for your selected document. Note here that one profile I can choose has been added as part of my EPSON printer software (EPSON Stylus Color 740 Glossy Film). Depending on your brand of desktop printer, there will be different profiles in this list.

you are going to output to. For now, keep the profile the same as what was chosen under Color Settings—Working RGB: Adobe RGB (1998). Click OK.

NOTE: If you choose to embed a different profile in the Assign Profile area than what is indicated in the Color Settings area, be aware that a dialog box will come up next time you open this document reminding you of this setting. See Figure 10-9. If no Color Settings have been indicated you will get another type of dialog box when opening the document. See Figure 10-10.

7. You can also set your document to print a preview of a specific color profile other than the image's assigned profile. Choose File > Print with Preview, select the Show More Options box,

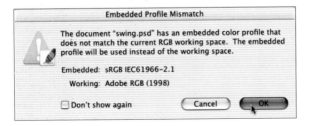

figure | 10-9

Dialog box indicating that a file already has an embedded color profile.

figure | 10-10

If no color settings have been indicated for a document, a dialog box will appear indicating this when you open the file.

and review the options under the Print Space area. (See more about the Print with Preview command later in this chapter.)

8. Close *swing.psd*. Hopefully, now you have a better idea of the color profile settings in Photoshop.

NOTE: I really don't want to add confusion about this color profile stuff, but one thing you should keep in mind is that there are also color profiles for input devices (sometimes called a source profile), such as digital cameras and scanners. Creating an input profile to match your working space can get somewhat complicated, and there's the question of whether or not it's absolutely essential for producing consistent color. For more information on this topic see Producing Consistent Color (Photoshop) > Calibrating and creating profiles in the Photoshop Help files.

About Monitor Calibration

Monitors are the lighted windows in which we view our digital work. Just like printers, they too need to be identified with a particular color profile that, preferably, is consistent with the profiles you have set within Photoshop. While identifying and changing the color profile of your monitor (through calibration) is not the first thing I talked about in the color management process (I wanted to explain what a color profile was first), it should be the first profile you create—even before choosing color settings in Photoshop. You do this using a visual calibrator provided as part of your computer's operating system. Such calibrators include Adobe Gamma (Windows), Monitor Calibrator (Mac OS), and products from other manufacturers. See Figure 10-11.

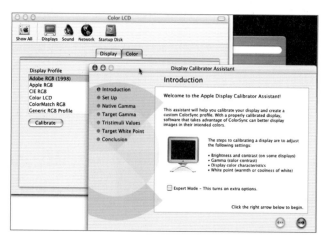

figure | 10-11

Example visual of the calibrating program provided as part of my Mac's operating system. These programs will take you step by step through the calibration process.

Resolution

Argh! Here we are again on the topic of resolution—that illusive concept that pretty much determines everything about your image's final quality and size (both dimensionally and in file weight). For output to printers using halftone dots to render images (see the section "Mechanical Printing"), consideration must be given to the number of dots to be printed within a given area or screen—or in other words, the "resolution." This consideration is like working with the resolution of bitmap images, which, similarly, are made up of a given amount of pixels on a bitmapped grid. In Photoshop, you specify halftone screen attributes before producing a film or a paper output of the image. This particularly applies when you are working with commercial printers. Consult your print specialist for the recommended resolution and screen (frequency, angle, and dot) settings.

Halftone dots are deposited on paper based on a *screen ruling*—the amount of lines or rows within a given screen. Screen rulings for halftones and separations are measured in lines per inch (lpi). The frequency, angle, and size of dots are determined by the screen ruling. High lpi creates smaller and tighter dots, like those seen in a glossy magazine or slick brochure. Low lpi creates larger, rougher-looking dots, but which are easier to print, such as on newspaper. A general rule is that the resolution, pixels per inch (ppi) or dots per inch (dpi) when referring to halftone printing, of a given piece of artwork is about 1.5 times and no more than 2.0 times the screen frequency. Did I just loose you here? Let me clarify. After consulting your print specialist you discover that the screen ruling for the glossy flyer you want to print is 150 lpi and needs to be in the TIFF format (an uncompressed bitmap format). This information gives you some idea of what resolution your TIFF file should be in, which would be somewhere between 225 dpi or ppi and 300 dpi or ppi (hence, 150 lpi x 1.5 = 225). Keep in mind that the resolution of an image and its screen frequency directly relate to what kind of paper it will be printed on and at what quality.

- Newspaper, or similar highly porous, coarse papers use screens of 85 to 100 lpi, and therefore the artwork resolution should be between 128 and 150 dpi or ppi.

- News magazines or company publications with medium coarseness use screens of 133 to 150 lpi, and therefore the artwork resolution should be between 200 and 225 dpi or ppi.

- Fine-quality brochures and magazines with slick paper surfaces use screens of 150 to 300 lpi, and therefore the artwork resolution should be between 225 and 450 dpi or ppi.

NOTE: Photoshop has a nifty little feature that will automatically suggest a resolution for an image based on a screen frequency. Go to Image > Image Size and choose the Auto option. Enter a screen frequency and quality setting (Draft, Good, Best) and the resolution will be updated for the document. This option only specifies a resolution for a suggested screen frequency. To determine the final halftone screen ruling for printing, use the Halftone Screens dialog box, accessible through the Print with Preview command (select Output, then Screen).

Format

Okay, final consideration for output compatibility should be in the format in which the image is saved in. Most likely you've been working on the image in Photoshop's native PSD file format, which maintains all of your layers and effects. Now, you must save a copy of the file in a format specific to its output needs. For bitmapped images, TIFF is the best bet because it uses minimal or no compression on the image (resulting in a higher quality), flattens your layers in a more conveniently sized package, and will preserve alpha channel information. To preserve both vector and bitmapped data that might be in an image, the EPS format is a good choice. This format is especially useful when you plan to import an image into a vector-friendly program, such as Adobe Illustrator or Macromedia Freehand. More recently requested by print specialists is the image saved in the cross-compatible PDF format (see also the section "Portable Document File").

You will quickly find that there are many different formats to save your image into. Each format has specific characteristics, depending on where it's going. As for the web-based formats, that's reserved for the next chapter. An overview of common formats is also provided in Chapter 3. For practice, here are the steps for saving an image in the print-friendly TIFF format:

1. Open the *swing.psd* file from the *chap10_lessons/assets* folder.

2. Choose Image > Mode > CMYK Color to set the image into the CMYK color space. You will set your image to the CMYK

color space if you plan to print this image using the traditional print process. However, if you are simply going to make a quick print off a desktop printer, staying in RGB mode will work just as well.

3. Now, choose File > Save As, name your file, and under Format choose TIFF (take note of all the other formats you can save to). Save the file to your *lessons* folder. Be sure the Embed Color Profile option is selected (if you assigned a profile to the image, this option should be checked automatically). Click Save.

4. A TIFF Options dialog box will appear. Here, you can choose a form of image compression. If the file size of the image is not an issue, stick with a compression setting of NONE to maintain the highest-quality image.

NOTE: Depending on the image attributes, the choice of options in the TIFF Options box will vary. If, for example, your image contains more than one layer, you have the option Layer Compression. If your image has layers, you can choose the RLE or ZIP compression options and preserve the Photoshop layers in the TIFF or reduce the file size of the image and discard the layers (flatten) and save a Copy.

NOTE: Preserving the Photoshop layers in TIFF format will increase the file's size.

5. If you choose to flatten the layers of the image, which is going to happen in any case when you open the file in another program other than Photoshop, be sure you also keep a saved version with the layers. You never know when you're going to need to open the image again in Photoshop and make changes.

6. Select OK to close the TIFF Options box. Out of interest, compare the file size of your PSD version to the TIFF version. To do this, find the saved files in your *lessons* folder (or wherever you saved them), right click (Windows) or Ctrl-click Mac over the file icon and choose Properties (Windows) or Get Info (Mac).

CONSULT THE PROFESSIONALS

If professionally printing your artwork, either via a digital or mechanical press, is a definite "must," alleviate undue headaches and find yourself a reliable print specialist. A good specialist can identify your printing needs, and offer appropriate solutions for getting the best quality print job for your specific situation. That being said, however, don't underestimate the necessity of also knowing something about the printing process and terminology to facilitate print preparation on your end—what was just covered in this chapter. Properly setting up your Photoshop file before handing it off to the printer can save you time and even money. Also, have a clear idea of what kind of paper the print job will be done on. For instance, do you envision your creation on porous newsprint or slick, heavy card stock? Different types of paper produce varying color effects and require different specifications.

NOTE: Your print specialist can provide paper samples and color swatches to aid you in your decision.

During the final output stages of your document, consult your printing service bureau to find out how best to prepare your file for them, such as in what color mode, resolution, and format. Also, be aware that the complexity of your artwork determines a lot about what you need to know to prepare it for print. Transparencies, alpha channels, spot colors, gradients, fonts, vector graphics, and duotones, for example, might require extra attention to print properly.

SETTING UP THE PRINT JOB

The easy way out of the printing process is to choose File > Print and be done with it. Yea, right. If you want your print job to look professional, it can be a bit more complicated than choosing a simple command. (So, if you skipped the rest of this chapter and came directly to here I'm assuming you already know about the quirks and conundrums of printing.) As previously covered, first is knowing where you are going to print your work (desktop printer, commercial printer, PDF), second is understanding output compatibility, and third is to not hesitate to contact a print specialist. With all of that in mind, you can then go to the proper set-up command in Photoshop, recommendation being not simply File > Print but more adequately File > Print with Preview.

The Print with Preview Command

Okay, so you're ready to see your work on some papyrus material. In Photoshop, choose File > Print with Preview and see what's available. See Figure 10-12. (Suggestion: If you want to do this right now, open *swing.psd* in the *chap10_lessons/assets* folder to use as an example.)

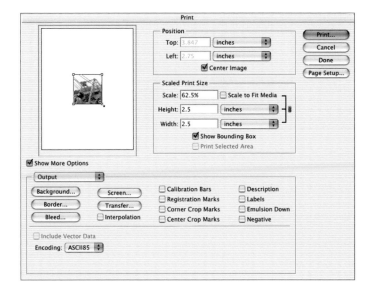

figure | 10-12 |

Output options in the Print with Preview window.

1. The first thing to notice is the option to scale your image to a print size other than what was originally specified under the image size area (Image > Image Size). You might want to do this if your original image is larger than the paper you are printing it on, or if you simply want a smaller, more quickly printable proof for markup purposes.

2. Be sure Show More Options is checked. Right below this option designate Output as your option choice. See Figure 10-12. For output, you can specify numerous goodies (a background color or border treatment, for example). You can also make specifications necessary for a seamless printing endeavor, such as bleed amounts (this is if you have color blending right to the edge of your document), screen and transfer measurements, printer marks for proper registration of an image's color plates (see Figure 10-13), and film output options. For kicks, select the Border option and specify a border width. Also, choose Calibration Bars, Registration Marks, Corner

figure | 10-13 |

An example of a PDF version of the image with file title *swing.psd.* Registration, cropping, border, and bleed specifications were indicated in the Print with Preview's output area.

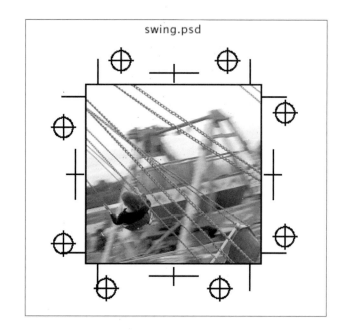

swing.psd

Crop Marks, Center Crop Marks, and Labels (note that each selection is shown on the image in the preview window).

3. Still in the Print with Preview window, switch the Output options selector to Color Management. Here you can choose to keep your document's assigned color profile (normal print) or use the Proof Setup profile. (This is a specification I didn't talk about but which can be indicated under View > Proof Setup for your document. Consult the Help files for more on soft and hard proofs.) In the Color Management area you can also indicate an alternate Print Space for cases where you want to preview the document on a device other than the one in which you have set for the final output (the assigned profile).

4. If you are not quite ready to print but want to preserve your settings, choose Done. However, if you are ready to print, choose Print, and then specify the desktop printer you would like to print from or the Save as PDF option. See Figure 10-14. If your printer doesn't support PostScript data a dialog box will come up indicating that some options chosen might not be available with the printer indicated. See Figure 10-15.

5. If you have managed to print a copy of your image either off a desktop printer or in a PDF document (which you saved somewhere on your computer and can view using the Acrobat

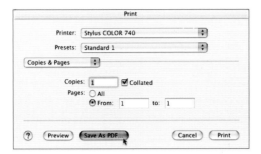

figure | 10-14

Options on my Macintosh for printing to a desktop printer or PDF document.

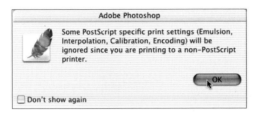

figure | 10-15

Conflict dialog box that could come up if your printer doesn't support PostScript information.

Reader), you will see the specifications set on the image, such as registration and cropping marks. See Figure 10-13 for an example.

As you roam through the various print dialog boxes, you might discover that you can also set scaling options for your image in the print specifications dialog box of your particular desktop printer. See Figure 10-16. The recommendation here is to not set the scaling options in this specific area, but rather in the Print with Preview window as reviewed previously.

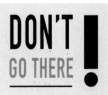

DON'T
GO THERE !

figure | 10-16

Page Setup for printers specifically installed on my Macintosh. To scale to print size, use the options under the Print with Preview command, rather than the Page Setup box for your particular printer.

SUMMARY

With the wave of a wand, I wish I could make the printing process for your digital imagery totally seamless and stress free, but that can't always be the case. As you learned, there are many variables to the printing process, including where a document is being printed, how it's set up, and so on. It's unlikely that your print job will come out perfectly the first time around, so be prepared to waste a few sheets of paper trying to get everything "just right." And of course, it really doesn't hurt to consult the professionals on this procedure, get a proof or two created of your final work, and meticulously edit before running off the full print job.

in review

1. Briefly describe the four printing methods covered in this chapter.

2. What are process colors?

3. Why might you output your image into PDF?

4. What are the three areas that should be considered when preparing an image to go to print?

5. Describe color management and why it's important to understand.

6. What do you do in the Color Settings dialog box (Photoshop > Color Settings for Macintosh users, Edit > Color Settings for Windows users)?

7. Why calibrate your monitor?

8. What does halftone printing refer to? What are halftone dots?

9. Describe what happens when an image is flattened.

10. Where is a good place to set alternate scaling options for a printed image?

↗ EXPLORING ON YOUR OWN

1. Access the Help > Photoshop Help menu option. Read up on the following topics related to printing: "Producing Consistent Color (Photoshop)" and "Printing (Photoshop)." A word of caution: this is a ton of information to wade through— not necessarily bedtime reading, but rather on a "need to know" basis.

2. Find out if your desktop printer supports PostScript, and if you have the ability to specify options for color separations in the Print dialog box. If so, try printing separations for a document that has been saved in the CMYK Color document mode (Image > Mode > CMYK Color).

3. For proofing purposes, make a contact sheet that conveniently creates thumbnail versions of multiple images. To explore this feature, choose File > Automate > Contact Sheet II. See Figure 10-17. With interest you might also discover the other (many automated) features, such as Picture Package, Web Photo Gallery, and Photomerge. When the moment strikes you, explore these cool options.

Contact Sheet II

Source Images
Use: Folder
Choose...   Frankie:Users:anne...0:chap10_images:
☑ Include All Subfolders

OK
Cancel

Document
Units: inches
Width: 8
Height: 10
Resolution: 72   pixels/inch
Mode: RGB Color
☑ Flatten All Layers

Page 1 of 1
9 of 9 Images
W: 1.6 in
H: 1.5 in

ⓘ Press the ESC key to Cancel processing images

Thumbnails
Place: across first   ☑ Use Auto-Spacing
Columns: 5   Vertical: 0.014 in
Rows: 6   Horizontal: 0.014 in
☑ Rotate For Best Fit

☑ Use Filename As Caption
Font: Helvetica   Font Size: 8 pt

figure | 10-17

The Contact Sheet II dialog box. Here you can specify a folder with images that you would like to print and view as smaller, thumbnail versions.

4. Open up the sample file *swing.pdf* in the *chap10_lessons/assets* folder. Take a look at the printer marks that have been specified around the artwork. Using the Help files (under "Setting output options"), investigate what each of the printer marks represents.

5. Awaken the detective inside you. Call up a printing service (or search online) and inquire about what printing services they offer and what file specifications they require. Be specific with your questions, and try out some of the terminology you learned in this chapter.

notes

_____
_____
_____
_____
_____
_____
_____
_____
_____
_____
_____
_____
_____
_____
_____
_____
_____
_____
_____
_____
_____
_____
_____
_____
_____

ADVENTURES IN DESIGN

WINE BOX COMPOSITION

As you learned in Chapter 9, the assembling of artwork pieces (photos, illustrations, and text) together into an aesthetically pleasing whole is the art of composition. An experienced art director or graphic designer can envision the larger scope of attractively arranging elements, while subsequently and just as importantly, narrowing in on each element's minute design details. Moreover, a good handle on current computer graphics software programs and their tool sets is crucial for bringing an inspired vision to actuality. The work of art director Dave Garcez and the graphic artists at Gallo Winery in Modesto, California, is a good example of how composition is not just the bringing together of elements in one program, such as Photoshop, but the coordination of elements among two or more programs (in this case, including Illustrator). See Figure C-1.

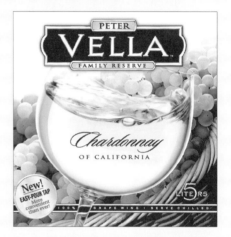

Figure C-1. A 5-liter wine box label was produced using Photoshop and Illustrator. *(Used by permission of E & J Gallo Winery.)*

Professional Project Example

The 5-liter wine box label shown in Figure C-1 was created for Gallo Winery using a combination of both Photoshop and Illustrator. First in Photoshop, photographs of glasses of wine were composited together to achieve the most appetizing look. The final wine glass was then layered together with a basket and some grapes (see figures C-2 and C-3). The logo was created in Illustrator. A hand-drawn sketch was scanned, and placed as a template into Illustrator. The final logo design and photographic images were then composited together in Photoshop, and then saved and imported back into Illustrator, where additional typographic elements were added and the whole file was prepared for print (see Figure C-1).

This same project is used as an Adventures in Design in my *Exploring Illustrator CS* book, but emphasizing the parts of the project (i.e., the logo design) that were done in Illustrator. Here, I want to share with you the techniques used to achieve the perfect look for the wine glass image, all of which you have become familiar with in this book.

Initially, the pixels of two of the wine glass photos were selected, transformed, and blended to produce the most active and realistic looking "swirl" of wine. See the two photos in

Figure C-2 and the final glass in Figure C-3. The glass was then further retouched to produce a more appetizing glow and give the glass more roundness. It was enhanced by first outlining the highlights on an empty glass and then saving each selection into an alpha channel. Using a combination of the Dodge, Burn, and Airbrush tools, the selections (alpha channels) were then used to lighten highlight areas and darken shadow areas. See Figure C-4.

The grapes were also enhanced. The lower right-hand corner was

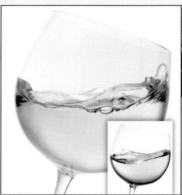
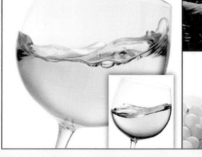
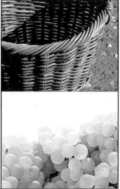

Figure C-2. Photographs were taken and layered together in Photoshop.

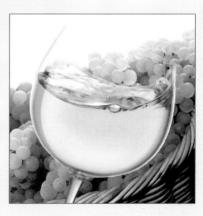

Figure C-3. The photographs were then composited together into a complete image.

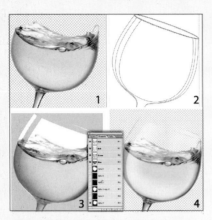

Figure C-4. Alpha channels were used to highlight and darken selections, creating more brightness and roundness to the glass. 1. The original wine glass photo; 2. Highlight outlines are drawn; 3. Alpha channel masks are created; 4. Final retouched photo.

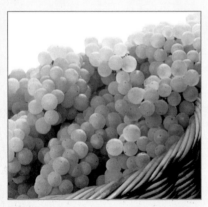

Figure C-5. The grapes are retouched and then the grapes and basket are composited together.

darkened for more light contrast, and many berries were retouched to remove imperfections. They were then placed within the basket. See Figure C-5.

Another subtle improvement was done to the image. In order to have the stem appear in front of the stripe element at the bottom of the final design, another photo of the stem of the glass was taken, and then a color print of the grapes and basket was distorted and placed behind the stem. The areas around the stem were deleted. See Figure C-6.

Your Turn

Putting to practice your image compositing skills, it's your turn to create an attractive image that could be used on a wine box, label, or advertisement. The original photos for the Peter Vella wine box label are provided for your educational use in the *aid_examples* folder *(basket.tif, grapes. tif, chard_glass1.tif,* and *chard_glass2. tif)*, or you can photograph or find your own images.

Self-Project Guidelines

1. Find a selection of images you might like to use in your image composition. They can be photographs you have taken or borrowed for educational purposes, scanned illustrations, or the photos provided in the *aid_examples* folder. Some image ideas could include pictures of wine bottles or barrels, grape vineyards, other styles of wine glasses, or someone enjoying a glass of wine. Try to get the highest quality images possible.

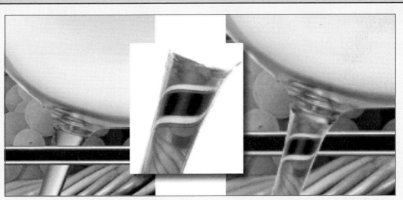

Figure C-6. An effect is created on the stripe element at the bottom of the design. The stripe is reflected through the wine glass stem.

2. On paper, sketch out some ideas of how you see the images assembled together into a completely new image.

3. Determine what techniques you know in Photoshop to design the sketch you like best.

4. On a new document with a resolution of at least 150 pixels, import the photos into Photoshop. Put each image on its own named layer.

5. Work your pixel magic on the images using what you have learned thus far in Photoshop. Adjust tonal levels and color, select and transform pixels, blend layers, and add effects and filters.

6. Save the file in PSD format as well as in a print-ready TIFF format.

Things to Consider

In general, here are some things to consider when working on your image compositions for this lesson, and in your professional work:

● A design is never finished. Leave time to do revisions of your work.

● Save often, and back up your work. I suggest also saving different versions of your work, as in *wine_imagev1, wine_imagev2a, wine_imagev2b, wine_imagev3,* and so on. You never know when you might want to refer back to an earlier version of your work.

● Get your document organized. In other words, use layers and name them intuitively.

● Print your image from a desktop printer (preferably color) to get a good idea of the image size and overall look.

● If you "borrowed" from another's work, or used another's image as a template in the creation of your own composition, resolve any copyright issues.

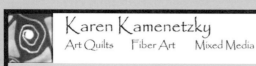

Karen Kamenetzky
Art Quilts   Fiber Art   Mixed Media

Home   Gallery   Artist   Contact

**Recent Juried
Exhibitions:**

**The Art and Soul of
Quilting**
January 18 - March 28,
2004
Anderson Art Center
Kenosha, WI

**Art Quilts at the
Sedgwick**
April 3 - May 2, 2004
Sedgwick Cultural Center
Philadelphia, PA

Art Quilts: Elements
April 30-May 31, 2004
Page-Walker Arts Center
Cary, NC

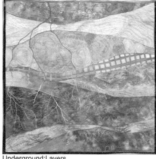

Underground:Layers
Juried into "Art Quilts at the Sedgwick 2004"

| web publishing |

charting your course

Preparing images for the Web or screen-based publication has become such an important task that Adobe created a program—ImageReady—specific for this need. ImageReady, lucky for us, comes packaged with Adobe Photoshop, and it alleviates many of the headaches that occur when trying to find the right balance between an image that looks good but can also quickly download over the Internet for efficient viewing. For the avid web designer there is much to explore in ImageReady, and it's not uncommon to find instructional books specific for using this software. This chapter offers an overview of two of the main features web designers use in the program: the Save for Web command (which is actually executed from Photoshop but powered by ImageReady), and the ability to slice images for fast rendering and creating button and rollover effects so commonly used on web pages.

 goals

- Optimize images like a Pro
- Get a handle on web file formats, including saving files in SWF format
- Understand the interrelationship among image color, format size, and compression in the web publication process
- Get hands-on experience with the Save for Web options
- Slice a web page with ImageReady

ABOUT OPTIMIZATION

In part, Chapter 9 discussed the process of designing a print or web page layout—the integration of many elements (such as text, graphics, and even audio and video) into a pleasing visual display. I want to reiterate here that the layout process usually involves working in more than one graphics program. For web page design and development this most likely includes the use of an image manipulation program to optimize images (i.e., what Photoshop and ImageReady do quite well) and a layout program that assembles web elements and codes them into a web page fit for a browser to read (i.e., Adobe GoLive, or Macromedia's Dreamweaver or Flash).

When it comes to publishing graphics for the Web, it's all about optimization. Optimization, when referring to online artwork, is the process of preparing a functionally optimal graphic, which is an artful balancing act between the visual quality of an image and its quantitative file size. There are three interrelated areas to consider in the web optimization process: image format, image color, and image size. All of these directly relate to *image compression*, which refers to reducing an images file size so that it looks good on screen and downloads quickly over an Internet connection.

About Compression

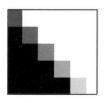

figure | 11-1 |

Antialiasing close-up creates a stair-step effect of color gradation. When viewed at a distance, the edge of the object looks smoother.

An image's file size can be reduced by compression. If you compress a bitmap image too much—make it smaller in file size—you can lose visual quality. For instance, it might lose its *antialiased* effect, which is the smoothing of pixilated edges through a gradation of color. It could *dither*, which is when colors that are lost during the compression are replaced by colors within the reduced palette (see figures 11-1 and 11-2).

There are two basic types of compression: lossy and lossless (sometimes called "nonlossy"). Lossy compression actually discards data to make a file smaller. Let's say you're optimizing a line of pixels into the JPEG format, which uses lossy compression. Ten of the pixels are white, followed by a gray pixel, and then five more white pixels. With lossy compression the computer reads the line as 16 white pixels; the gray pixel, being the odd one in the sampling area, is converted to white.

Lossless compression, on the other hand, does not eliminate detail or information but instead looks for more efficient ways to define the image, such as through the use of customized color tables (more on that later). Ultimately, how compression is applied to an image varies greatly depending on the image's format, color, and size.

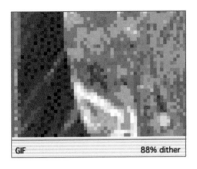

Image Format

figure | 11-2

Traditionally, most web images are saved in the bitmap formats GIF, JPEG, or PNG. Bitmap images, as you probably recall from previous chapters, are reliant on resolution to determine their file size and quality. Because

Dithering attempts to simulate colors that are lost in the compression process.

of this, bitmap images are generally larger in file size than vector graphics, and when it comes to "the Web" that means a much bulkier download. Vector-based file formats (including Macromedia's SWF and Scalable Vector Graphics [SVG] formats) have emerged that allow us to save and view graphics as streamlined paths, shapes, text, and effects in the online environment. Such graphics are scalable in size and easier to download. However, Photoshop doesn't handle these file types, because as we know it's the master of pixels not vectors. Adobe Illustrator does a much better job at creating vector images and can support export of both the SWF and SVG formats.

NOTE: New to ImageReady CS is the ability to export your bitmap images and animations (that you can also create in ImageReady) to the SWF format. In the SWF format, the graphic can go directly to the Web or be imported into Macromedia's Flash. In ImageReady, choose File > Export > Macromedia Flash SWF. For further information on SWF, do a search for SWF in the Photoshop or ImageReady Help files.

The file format you choose for an optimized image has to do with the color, tonal, and graphic characteristics of the original image. In general, continuous-tone bitmap images (images with many shades of color), such as photographs, are best compressed in the JPEG or PNG-24 formats. Illustrations or type with flat color or sharp edges and crisp detail are best as GIF or PNG-8 files. The following lists run down the characteristics of each web-friendly format you can save in Photoshop. Further clarification of these characteristics is presented in the next two sections.

The GIF (Graphic Interchange Format) format

● Supports an 8-bit color depth. Bit depth determines the amount and range of color an image can contain. A 1-bit image supports two colors, black and white; an 8-bit image can support up to 256 colors. A customized 256-color palette is referred to as *indexed* color.

● Works best compressing solid areas of color, such as in line art, logos, or illustrations with type.

● Is supported by the most common web browsers, such as Internet Explorer, Netscape, AOL, and Safari.

● Can be animated.

● Traditionally uses a *lossless* compression method. Lossless compression is when no data is discarded during the file reduction process (see section on compression). You can save a GIF file multiple times without discarding data. However, because GIF files are 8-bit color, optimizing an original 24-bit image as an 8-bit GIF will generally degrade image quality.

NOTE: Illustrator and Photoshop also allow you to create a lossy version of a GIF file. The lossy GIF format includes small compression artifacts (similar to those in JPEG files) but yields significantly smaller files.

● Can be interlaced, so images download in multiple passes, or progressively. The downloading process of interlaced images is visible to the user, ensuring the user that the download is in progress. Keep in mind, however, that interlacing increases file size.

● Includes dithering options (the process of mixing colors to approximate those not present in the image).

● Supports background transparency and background matting, which is the ability to blend the edges of an image with a web page background color.

The JPEG (Joint Photographic Experts Group) format

● Supports 24-bit color (millions of colors) and preserves the broad range and subtle variations in brightness and hue found in photographs and other continuous-tone images (such as gradients).

● Is supported by the most common web browsers.

● Selectively discards data. Because it discards data, JPEG compression is referred to as *lossy* (see section on compression). The compression is set based on a range between 0 and 100% or 1 and 12. A higher percentage setting results in less data being discarded. The JPEG compression method tends to degrade sharp detail in an image, particularly in images containing type or vector art. Because of the nature of JPEG compression, you should always save JPEG files from the original image, not from a previously saved JPEG.

● Can be interlaced, so images download in multiple passes.

● Does not support transparency.

● Does not support animation.

The PNG-8 (Portable Network Graphic) format

● Uses 8-bit color. Like the GIF format, PNG-8 efficiently compresses solid areas of color while preserving sharp detail, such as that in line art, logos, or illustrations with type.

● Has not traditionally been supported by all browsers, but this is changing. It's advisable to test images saved in the PNG format on browser platforms you and your audience might be using to view web pages.

● Uses a *lossless* compression method, in which no data is discarded during compression. However, because PNG-8 files are 8-bit color, optimizing an original 24-bit image as a PNG-8 can degrade image quality. PNG-8 files use more advanced compression schemes than GIF, and can be 10 to 30% smaller than GIF files of the same image, depending on the image's color patterns.

● Can be indexed, like the GIF format, to a specific 256-color palette (such as Adaptive or Restrictive).

- Includes dithering options (the process of mixing colors to approximate those not present in the image).

- Also like the GIF format, supports background transparency and background matting (ability to blend the edges of the image with a web page background color).

The PNG-24 (Portable Network Graphic) format

- Supports 24-bit color. Like the JPEG format, PNG-24 preserves the broad range and subtle variations in brightness and hue found in photographs. Like the GIF and PNG-8 formats, PNG-24 preserves sharp detail, such as that in line art, logos, or illustrations with type.

- Uses the same lossless compression method as the PNG-8 format, in which no data is discarded. For that reason, PNG-24 files are usually larger than JPEG files of the same image.

- Like PNG-8, is not necessarily support by all browsers.

- Supports multilevel transparency, in which you can preserve up to 256 levels of transparency to blend the edges of an image smoothly with any background color. However, multilevel transparency is not supported by all browsers.

The WBMP format

- Supports only 1-bit color, which means images are reduced down to contain only black and white pixels.

- Standard format for optimizing images for mobile devices, such as cell phones and PDAs. Devices that currently do not support viewing complex images in color.

Image Color

First thing, and I've mentioned this before, photographs and artwork to be viewed on-screen, such as on a web page, must be saved in the RGB Color mode. Why? To answer that question, see Chapter 5 and read up on the characteristics of the RGB Color space. To convert your artwork to the RGB Color mode, choose Image > Mode > RGB Color. Next thing on this topic of image color is an understanding of color reduction algorithms, covered in the following section.

Color Reduction Algorithms

"Color reduction algorithms" is the long and geeky name that Adobe calls the methods used to generate a specific color table for an optimized image. You get a better idea of how color tables work in a lesson later in the chapter. Color reduction algorithms only apply to the GIF and PNG-8 formats. Because these two formats support the 8-bit format (i.e., an image with 256 colors or less), the color tables determine how the computer calculates which 256 colors out of the image to keep.

NOTE: If the original image already has less than 256 colors, you can adjust the maximum number of colors that are calculated, further reducing the size of the image.

Each color reduction palette produces slightly different results, so it's a good idea to understand how each type works its magic. The descriptions of the color tables that follow are taken from the Photoshop Help files. (Photoshop categorizes the color tables as dynamic, fixed, or custom.) Just reading descriptions, however, won't give you the full effect of what these color tables do. It's only when you see how they affect an actual image that things begin to click, and you'll get some of that in the lessons.

Dynamic options use a color reduction algorithm to build a palette based on the colors in the image and the number of colors specified in the optimization setting. The colors in the palette are regenerated every time you change or reoptimize the image.

- *Perceptual:* Creates a custom color table by giving priority to colors for which the human eye has greater sensitivity.

- *Selective:* Creates a color table similar to the Perceptual color table, but favoring broad areas of color and the preservation of web colors. This color table usually produces images with the greatest color integrity. Selective is the default option.

- *Adaptive:* Creates a custom color table by sampling colors from the spectrum appearing most commonly in the image. For example, an image with only the colors green and blue produces a color table made primarily of greens and blues. Most images concentrate colors in particular areas of the spectrum.

Fixed options use a set palette of colors. In other words, the set of available colors is constant, but the actual colors in the palette will vary depending on the colors in the image.

- *Restrictive (Web):* Uses the standard 216-color color table common to the Windows and Mac OS 8-bit (256-color) palettes. This option ensures that no browser dither is applied to colors when the image is displayed using 8-bit color. (This palette is also called the Web-safe palette.) If your image has fewer colors than the total number specified in the color palette, unused colors are removed. Using the Restrictive palette can create larger files, and is recommended only when avoiding browser dither is a high priority.

- *Black & White:* Builds a color table of only two colors—black and white.

- *Grayscale:* Creates a custom table of only grayscale pixels.

- *Mac OS and Windows:* Builds an 8-bit palette, capable of displaying 256 colors, using the color table of the system you select. If your image has fewer colors than the total number specified in the color palette, unused colors are removed.

The *Custom* option uses a color palette that is created or modified by the user. If you open an existing GIF or PNG-8 file, it will have a custom color palette. When you choose the Custom color palette it preserves the current perceptual, selective, or adaptive color table as a fixed palette that does not update with changes to the image.

NOTE: For future reference, you can lock, add, sort, delete, and shift colors in the generated color tables. You can also save and load color tables to apply to images.

Image Size

To discuss image size is to mention again the concept of resolution. For online display, an image's resolution need only match a standard monitor's resolution, which is 72 ppi for Mac users and 96 ppi for Window users. This is a welcome relief to what was learned in Chapter 10, where the resolution of artwork going to print varies depending on where it's being printing and on what kind of paper stock.

Please know that none of this resolution stuff applies to vector-based graphics. These types of images are unique in their application to the Web. They are inherently scalable and compact in size. So, keep in mind that much of what we are talking about in regard to file size and compression applies to bitmap (or rasterized) images. Until more web designers advance to using the latest online vector graphic formats, such as SWF and SVG, much of the graphics we see on the Web will continue to be in bitmap format.

A bitmap image's size is directly related to its resolution. Image size can be referred to in two ways, and both impact optimization. First, you have the actual dimensions of an image (e.g., 5 x 5 inches or 400 x 600 pixels). Second, you have an image's file size (its actual amount in digital bits). This is measured in bytes, kilobytes, megabytes, or gigabytes. A byte is 8 bits, a kilobyte (KB) is 1,024 bytes, a megabyte (MB) is 1,024 kilobytes, and . . . you get the idea . . . a gigabyte (GB) is 1,024 megabytes. How big is too big for a web image? Well, it depends on how many images you have on a single web page, whether they are bitmap or vector based, and whether they are dimensionally large or small.

I prefer to keep my web images, especially bulky bitmap ones, to no more than 10 to 20 KB each in file size. In fact, when building web pages it's not uncommon that a client will ask that I keep the total file size of *everything* on a web page under 30 KB for those viewers with slow Internet connections. The ultimate, of course, is to actually post your optimized images to the Web and test how long it takes to download them on different Internet connections.

QUICK TOUR OF IMAGEREADY

It's up to you to delve into the vast array of appealing stuff in ImageReady. However, at the least I feel obligated to show you how to get to the program from Photoshop.

1. Be sure you have a file open in Photoshop (if you need a practice file choose an example image from the *chap11_ lessons/samples* folder).

2. Choose File > Edit in ImageReady. The ImageReady program opens up. See Figure 11-3.

3. Take note that the ImageReady interface is very similar to Photoshop. A few differences include the option to quickly view your image in its Original or Optimized state, or in 2-Up or 4-Up editing windows. See Figure 11-4.

4. Also, many of the tools in the toolbox are different too, designed specifically for manipulation of images going to the

Web, such as the Slice Select and Image Map Select tools. See Figure 11-5.

5. To get back to Photoshop, simply choose File > Edit in Photoshop.

figure | 11-3

The ImageReady interface with the 4-Up window tab selected.

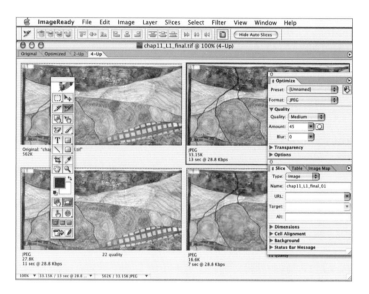

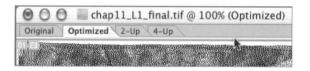

figure | 11-4

Change your window view quickly in ImageReady.

figure | 11-5

The tools in ImageReady are specific for manipulating images for web publication.

Save for Web (Photoshop)

The Save for Web option in Photoshop is actually powered by ImageReady. This option is a compact version of the optimization settings you can also get to in ImageReady. Think of the Save for Web feature as a fitness program for your graphics. Depending on your image's body type (format), you can try out various fitness regimes (compression schemes) to produce the best looking and most lean image possible. A 2-Up or 4-Up window view lets you compare and contrast an image's optimization settings next to the original file. See Figure 11-6.

NOTE: For future reference know that you can also choose File > Edit in ImageReady (or select the Edit in ImageReady icon at the bottom of the toolbox) to open up a similar dialog box within the ImageReady program. To view the optimization settings in the program, choose Window > Optimize. See Figure 11-7.

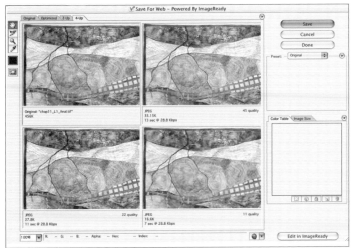

figure | 11-6

The Save For Web window is filled with options for optimizing your artwork, including a 4-Up window view for comparing and contrasting different optimization settings.

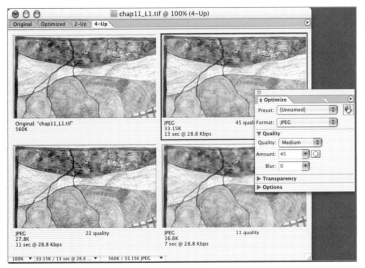

figure | 11-7

The 4-Up window and Optimize palette in ImageReady. Similar to Save For Web in Photoshop.

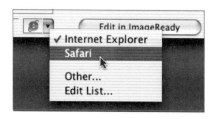

figure | 11-8 |

Select a browser to view your image. If you don't have a browser currently selected, choose the Other option and find the browser of your choice in your *applications* folder.

Another useful feature is the ability to view your image and its selected specifications in a browser window of your choice. In the Save For Web window this option is located in the lower, right-hand corner of the box, next to the Edit in ImageReady button. See Figure 11-8.

As discussed in the section on image formats, there are some general guidelines for what kind of artwork to save as what kind of format—photos as JPEGs, line art as GIFS. However, the finesse to finding just the right size and quality comes from subtly adjusting the options in the Save For Web dialog box. A simple adjustment to the bit depth of a GIF image, for example, can reduce the file size of an image immensely, resulting in a much more efficient Internet download. There are a lot of options to choose from in the Save For Web dialog box, but don't let that overwhelm you. When you are ready to know what each option is all about, I suggest reviewing that information in the Photoshop Help files. For now, I recommend just getting down some of the basics and trusting your visual instincts when you start comparing and contrasting settings in the Save For Web dialog box—something you get the opportunity to do in the next lesson.

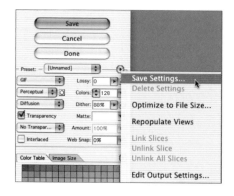

figure | 11-9 |

In the Save For Web panel you can save your optimization settings to use later.

Optimization Workflow Techniques

Understanding how optimization works and how to save an image with proper optimization settings is knowing 90% of the web image publication process. However, for purposes of workflow—producing more efficient ways of doing a task—there are several features related to optimization that might prove beneficial for you sooner rather than later. First, this includes the ability to save and edit optimization settings (see Figure 11-9) and resize the image (pixel size) at export (see Figure 11-10).

Next, for more precise control and higher quality results when optimizing potentially critical areas use *weighted optimization.* From the Photoshop Help files, "Weighted optimization lets you smoothly vary optimization settings across an image using masks from text layers, shape layers, and alpha channels." When creating text or shape layers, masks are created automatically, and as learned in Chapter 8 you can also save your own masks using alpha channels. These masks can be used for weighted optimization. See Figure 11-11.

Finally, when you have many images that need to be saved with the same optimization setting, you can create a clever timesaver called a "droplet." A droplet is a small application that automatically applies specific settings to a batch of images that you drag over a droplet icon. Let's say you just received fifty high-resolution photos that need to be resized and converted to JPEG format, with a 60% compression. Moreover, the project needs to be done fast, because the web developer has to get the photos online (today) as part of the company's new spring catalog. With a droplet action, you record the optimization specifications on one of the photos and then have Photoshop or ImageReady diligently execute the steps on all the other images (while you take a long lunch break, of course).

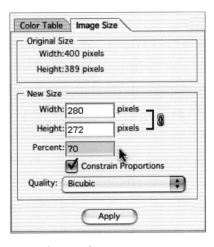

figure | 11-10 |

Create a new size for the optimized image.

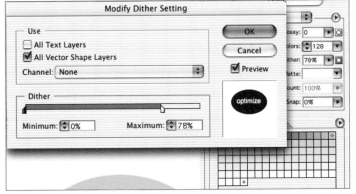

figure | 11-11 |

To find the weighted optimization options for particular color tables, look for the Mask icon and click it to view the masks available for editing.

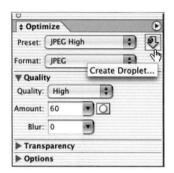

figure | 11-12 |

You can make a droplet directly in the ImageReady's Optimize palette.

There are a couple of ways to make a droplet with specific optimization settings. One way is to go to Photoshop, record your optimization settings into an action, and then execute the action by choosing File > Automate > Create Droplet. Alternatively, you can go to ImageReady, identify your optimizations settings in the Optimize window, choose the Droplet icon, and name the droplet and where the droplet will be saved. See Figure 11-12. When ready to execute the droplet action on images, simply drag a folder of images over the saved droplet.

The difference between the two options is that in Photoshop you need to know how to create an action, whereas in ImageReady you do not. I don't cover the topic much in this book, but Photoshop has an Actions palette (Window > Actions), where you can record a series of individual actions (commands)—like the steps for saving an image to a particular size and format—and then automatically run the action on batches of images. To practice creating a droplet from ImageReady, see the "Exploring on Your Own" section at the end of this chapter.

Lesson 1: Preparing an Image for the Web

In this lesson, you optimally save a colorful photograph of a quilt created by my friend, Karen Kamenetzky. Originally in the TIFF format, you use the settings in Photoshop's Save For Web dialog box to prepare the image for web publication.

Setting Up the File

1. In Photoshop, choose File > Open and open *chap11_L1.tif* in the *chap11_lessons* folder.

2. Press Shift-Tab on the keyboard to hide unneeded windows.

3. Select the Actual Pixels button in the options bar (or View menu) to be sure you're viewing the image at 100%.

4. Familiarize yourself with the file's specifications. Choose Image > Mode and be sure it is saved in the RGB Color mode.

5. Choose Image > Image Size and note the document size and resolution. Right now the image is saved at 150 ppi. When optimized it will be reduced to 72 ppi—the standard resolution for screen-based graphics. Don't make any changes, just select OK.

6. Let's do a little color adjustment to the image. Choose Image > Adjustments > Auto Levels, and then Image > Adjustments > Auto Color. Note the subtle but significant changes in the brightness and contrast (the vibrancy) of the image.

Setting the Save for Web Options

1. Choose File > Save for Web, and select the 4-Up option on the tab in the upper left-hand corner of the window. A four-window view of the image becomes available. See figures 11-13 and 11-14.

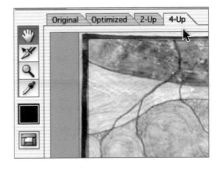

NOTE: As specified earlier, alternatively you can choose File > Edit in ImageReady to open up a similar dialog box within the ImageReady program. To view the optimization settings in ImageReady, choose Window > Optimize. I recommend exploring

figure | **11-13**

Choose the 4-Up option to compare and contrast the image in four different windows.

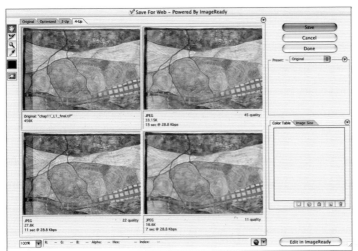

figure | **11-14**

Full view of the 4-Up option under File > Save for Web.

this alternative after you have a clear understanding of the optimization steps in Photoshop.

2. Click on the first window to highlight it. A colored box appears around the image. Note that the first window shows the original image at a file size of 456 K (kilobytes). Also, in the information area to the right of the dialog box note that Preset is set to Original.

3. Click on the window to the right of the first window. A colored frame will appear around the image, and the settings for the image become available.

4. Note the viewing annotations at the bottom of the selected window. These provide valuable information about the optimization settings for that particular window, including format type, size, estimated download time, and Color table specifications.

figure | 11-15 |

Change the Internet connection speed to see how it affects the image's download time.

5. Note also that the download time is determined by a specified Internet connection speed. By default, this is set to the lowest possible modem speed, 28.8 Kbps (kilobytes per second). Adjust this setting to a more standard 56-Kbps modem speed by clicking on the arrow right above the selected window and from the menu choosing Size/Download Time (56.6 Kbps Modem/ISDN). See Figure 11-15.

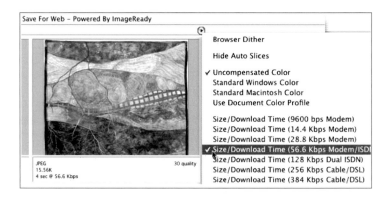

6. Under Preset, leave it [Unnamed]. Then select the following options (see Figure 11-16):

● *Optimized file format:* GIF

● *Color reduction algorithm:* Adaptive

- *Dither algorithm:* No Dither

- *Uncheck:* Transparency

- *Uncheck:* Interlaced

- *Lossy:* 0

- *Colors:* 256 (the maximum number available)

- *Matte:* None

- *Web Snap:* 0%

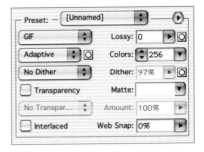

figure | **11-16** |

Set the optimization options.

7. Note the Color Table for the selected window. It indicates all of the colors being used in the image, which is determined by the color reduction algorithm (Adaptive) and the maximum number of colors in the algorithm setting (256). The swatches with a diamond in the middle indicate web-safe colors. (More information on Restrictive [Web] is available in the color reduction algorithm sections in this book.) The others are in the general RGB color space. Roll and hold (don't click) your cursor over a swatch to reveal the color's attributes (see Figure 11-17).

8. Now, select the third window and adjust the settings differently, as follows:

   - *Optimized file format:* GIF

   - *Color reduction algorithm:* Restrictive (Web)

   - *Dither algorithm:* Diffusion

   - *Dither:* 100%

   - *Uncheck:* Transparency

   - Uncheck: Interlaced

   - *Lossy:* 0

   - *Colors:* Auto (the maximum number available)

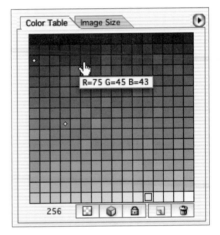

figure | **11-17** |

Roll over a swatch to reveal the color's numeric attributes.

- *Matte:* None

- *Web Snap:* 0%

9. In the Color Table for the selected window, note that each of the swatches has a diamond icon in the middle. These indicate that all of the colors are within the web-safe color palette. Roll and hold (don't click!) your cursor over one of the swatches, and the hexadecimal color number is revealed.

10. Now, select the fourth window and alter its settings, as follows:

- *Optimized file format:* JPEG

- *Color reduction algorithm:* Maximum

- *Quality:* 100

- *Download passes:* Progressive

- *Uncheck:* ICC Profile

- *Blur:* 0

- *Matte:* None

Comparing and Contrasting Settings

1. So, now take a close look at what each optimization setting has done to the image. Magnify each window with the Zoom tool (located to the left of the Save For Web window) and really examine the artifacts of each compression scheme. Use the Hand tool to move the magnified image around in a window.

2. Next, double click on the Zoom tool icon to set the view of each window back to the original image size. Which version looks best to you?

3. Compare and contrast the viewing annotations at the bottom of each window. What are the size differences? Is the one you visually like the best a reasonable size for a quick download from the Internet (under 20 K, for example)?

Getting Picky

1. Okay, let's fine-tune a little bit and try to reduce the file size of the image even more. It definitely needs it. It's a beautifully complex image that could be worth the download wait time, but let's see if we can make a version a user would be able to

view relatively fast, even on a slower connection (e.g., 56 Kbps). Select the second window (top right side).

2. Change the color reduction algorithm to Selective, and reduce the colors to 128. The file size is reduced, but it doesn't look any better. The gradients of color on the rock formations are getting splotchy. This is because gradients are made up of many shades of color, so when the color palette is reduced so is the amount of color that makes the gradient look smooth.

4. Let's look at window 4—the JPEG. The gradient in this looks good, but the file size is way too big. What to do?

5. Select window 4 and change the JPEG compression quality to Medium. Great! The file size is smaller and the image still looks relatively acceptable (compare it to the first window—the original file). It's still pretty big, however. Let's get it under 20 KB.

6. In the Image Size area (below the optimization settings), reduce the scaling to 75% and hit Apply. See Figure 11-18.

7. Now, select the Browser Menu option (bottom of window) and choose a browser to view the optimized image. This is the ultimate test of how good it looks. See figures 11-19 and 11-20.

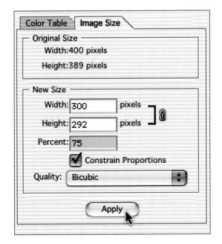

figure | 11-19

From the Browser menu, select the browser you want to view the image in.

figure | 11-18

Scale down your optimized image to lower its file size.

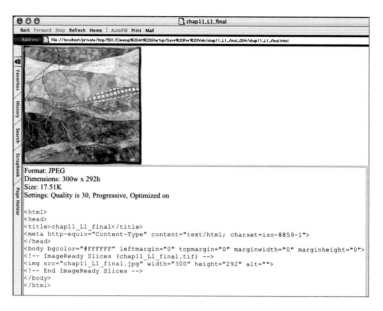

Format: JPEG
Dimensions: 300w x 292h
Size: 17.51K
Settings: Quality is 30, Progressive, Optimized on

```
<html>
<head>
<title>chap11_L1_final</title>
<meta http-equiv="Content-Type" content="text/html; charset=iso-8859-1">
</head>
<body bgcolor="#FFFFFF" leftmargin="0" topmargin="0" marginwidth="0" marginheight="0">
<!-- ImageReady Slices (chap11_L1_final.tif) -->
<img src="chap11_L1_final.jpg" width="300" height="292" alt="">
<!-- End ImageReady Slices -->
</body>
</html>
```

figure | 11-20

Examples of details revealed when an image is viewed in a browser window.

NOTE: You might need to choose Other in the Browser menu to find a browser you have installed on your computer. I like to check my image in several browser types—Internet Explorer, Netscape, and Safari, for example—because you never know which browser a viewer will be using to see the image.

8. Select Save to save this version of the file. Name it *webimage. jpg* and for format choose Images Only. Save the file in your *chap11_lessons* folder.

NOTE: If you don't want to save the file right away, choose Done rather than Save. This will close the Save For Web window but maintain your optimization settings.

IMAGE SLICING

Image slicing is dividing up areas of an image or a complete web page layout into smaller, independent files. If you are familiar with constructing web pages, and working in HTML, you probably have a pretty good understanding of the benefits of slicing. If you are new to web page design and development this might seem like a somewhat crazy thing to do to your artwork, but slicing really is useful for the following reasons:

● Accurate HTML table placement.

● Creating independent files, each containing its own optimization settings.

● Creating smaller, independent files for faster download.

● Creating interactive effects, such as button rollovers.

Lesson 2: Slicing a Web Page Navigation Bar

In this lesson, you prepare a navigation bar that would be placed in a web page. Using the ImageReady's Slice tool, you will slice and optimize areas of the layout for optimal web performance.

Setting Up the File

1. Open *chap11L2.psd* located in the *chap11_lessons* folder.

2. Choose View > Actual Pixels.

3. Press Shift-Tab on the keyboard to hide unneeded palettes, if not already hidden.

4. Choose Window > Layers. Note that there is one layer available, called *nav_bar*.

5. Choose View > Show > Guides, if not already checked, to turn the guides on. Guides have been created for you to indicate where the slices will be made. See Figure 11-21.

figure | 11-21

The guides help to accurately create image slices.

Making slices

1. Choose the Edit in ImageReady icon at the bottom of the toolbar to jump into the ImageReady program. See Figure 11-22.

figure | 11-22

Edit in ImageReady quick link.

2. Press Shift-Tab to hide unneeded palettes.

3. Be sure View > Show > Slices is checked on.

4. Select the Slice tool in the toolbox (see Figure 11-23).

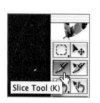

figure | 11-23

Select the Slice tool.

5. Position the point end of the Slice tool in the upper, left-hand corner of the image and click and drag to the right, defining a box around the swirl logo and top header section (do not include the yellow bar of "nav" buttons at the bottom). See Figure 11-24 for clarification. Note that a number for the slice is indicated in the upper, left-hand corner of the defined box. You can choose to unhide/unhide slices by choosing View > Show > Slices.

NOTE: When you make slices you don't actually "cut up" your artwork but create an overlay of divided areas that determines how the individual files will be created when saving the document. Slicing always occurs in a grid-like pattern. Even if you don't define a slice in a particular area, ImageReady automatically creates one to maintain the table structure necessary for exporting into an HTML page.

figure | 11-24

Define a slice with the Slice tool.

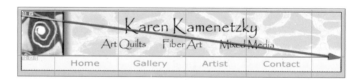

6. Next, with the Slice tool, slice around each button area in the lower part of the navigation bar. There will be six slices across the bottom: a slice defining each of the four buttons and on the two edges. Use the guides to get accurate placement. See Figure 11-25.

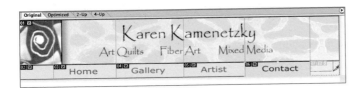

figure | 11-25

Create six more slices, using the guides for accurate placement.

NOTE: Don't worry if you make a mistake. Just Edit > Undo (a few times, if necessary) and try your slice again.

7. Each individual slice can be modified. From the toolbar, choose the Slice Select tool (to the right of the Slice tool, as shown in Figure 11-26), and then click on the slice you want to alter. You can resize it with the handles in each corner of the selection, move it, or delete it.

figure | 11-26

Choose the Slice Select tool to select and modify slices.

8. With the Slice Select tool, select the contact slice area.

9. There are also options for individually selected slices. Choose Window > Slice. In this window, create a name for the sliced area (*contact_button*), make up a link name (such as *contactpage.html*), and an Alt tag (*contact_button*). See Figure 11-27.

10. Choose File > Preview In, and choose a browser to view the sliced image. Roll over the word *Contact* to reveal that the area is now being considered a button link (the little hand icon shows up). This occurs when you add a link name to the slice in the Slice Options window. Close the browser window.

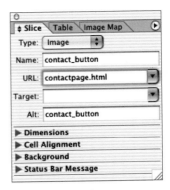

figure | 11-27

11. Choose File > Save As, and save your file in your *lessons* folder.

The Slice window options to modify individual slices.

Optimizing and Saving the Slices

1. There are two places, which I indicated earlier in this chapter, where you can optimize and save out your images. One option is to stay in ImageReady and choose Window > Optimize to set optimization options, and then File > Save Optimized As. Since we are learning about Photoshop, however, let's do this

figure | 11-28

Edit in Photoshop link.

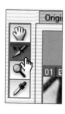

figure | 11-29

Select the Slice Select tool.

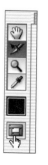

figure | 11-30

Option to turn off the Slice Visibility.

optimization stuff in Photoshop. Select the Edit in Photoshop link at the bottom of the toolbar. See Figure 11-28.

2. Back in Photoshop, choose File > Save For Web.

3. Choose the 2-Up window option.

4. Select the Slice Select tool located on the left side of the window (see Figure 11-29).

5. Select slice number 1 in the second window. It will highlight in yellow. Adjust the optimization settings of this sliced area. I chose JPEG, Medium, Quality 50 because of the many gradations of color in the header and logo graphics.

6. Next, select the first button area (home) and adjust the optimization settings. I chose GIF, Selective, No Dither, and reduced the Colors to 16, producing a very efficient graphic.

7. Select each of the other slices and optimize them to your liking. Balance the image file size with visual appeal.

8. Turn off the Slice Visibility in the tools area to the left of the window to view the final, optimized work (see Figure 11-30).

9. Okay, we are about there. Choose Save in the Save For Web window.

10. In the Save Optimized As box, enter in the following (see Figure 11-27):

● *Save As:* mynavbar.jpg

● *Format:* Images Only

● *Where:* Your *lessons* folder

● *Settings:* Default Setting

● *Slices:* All Slices

11. Wait, before you hit Save I want to show you something. Under Settings, choose Other. In Output Settings, choose the Saving Files option. In the Optimized Files options make sure Put Images in Folder is checked and that *images* is indicated for the folder name (see Figure 11-31). I realize there's a lot of other stuff in this dialog box to distract you, but that's stuff for later, when you really get into web design work using Photoshop and ImageReady. For now, choose OK.

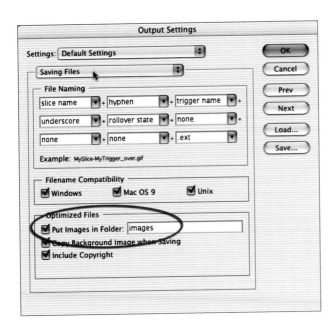

figure | 11-31 |

The Saving Files options in Output Settings.

12. Now, hit Save to save the individually divided files to the *images* folder you indicated previously. The *images* folder will be located in your *lessons* folder. Minimize the Photoshop program and go find this folder. Open it up and amazingly all your sliced images are there, and ready to be placed into an HTML web page. See Figure 11-32.

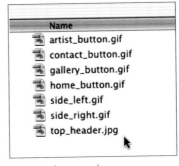

figure | 11-32 |

Find your saved images on your computer.

SUMMARY

Yeah, I know, you are probably all excited now (at least, I hope so) about using Photoshop, not to mention ImageReady. Creating, adjusting, and preparing images for both print and web publication is no longer such a deep dark secret. Now that we are at the end of this book, it's up to you to continue exploring the magic of Photoshop. And as you undertake this graphic design adventure keep in mind the words of the great Harry Houdini, "Don't lose confidence in an effect because it has been presented many times before. An old trick in 'good hands' is always new. Just see to it that yours are 'Good Hands.'"

in review

1. Describe image optimization. What three interrelated areas must be considered in the web optimization process?

2. What's dithering?

3. Photographs are best saved in what format? What about graphics with solid colors and line art?

4. What image formats use color reduction algorithms and why?

5. When would you use the WBMP format?

6. How many bytes are in a kilobyte? Why is that important to know?

7. Name at least two things you can do in ImageReady.

8. Name three useful things about slicing images.

9. Where do sliced images go once you save them?

10. What's so useful about a droplet?

↗ EXPLORING ON YOUR OWN

1. For more information about web graphics with Photoshop and ImageReady, spend some time in the Help files (Help > Photoshop Help > Preparing Graphics for the Web). Relevant information not covered in this chapter that you might also want to read up on is in the content section "Creating Complex Web Graphics (ImageReady)."

2. Using what you've learned thus far about the Save for Web window, decide which optimization settings are best for the example artwork, *fig1.tif,* located in the *chap11_lessons/ samples* folder.

figure | 11-33

An ImageReady droplet icon. Drag a folder of images to this droplet to automatically optimize the images.

3. Automate the optimization process by learning how to make a droplet in ImageReady. Use the batch of images located in the *chap11_ lessons/samples* folder. See Figure 11-33.

4. Using the Automate feature in Photoshop, create a web photo gallery. I admit it, this is a really cool thing! A photo gallery is an ultra quick way to create a working little web site that showcases a series of digital images or photos. You can send the whole gallery package to family, friends, and clients and all they need to do to view it is open the *index.html* in a browser window. Choose File > Automate > Web Photo Gallery. In the options window choose a Style, enter an e-mail you want to display as the contact for the gallery, and under Source Images identify the folder of images you want to transform into the gallery and a destination (for practice purposes you can use the images located in the *chap11_lessons/ samples* folder). See figures 11-34 and 11-35.

figure | 11-34

The Web Photo Gallery options window. Choose File > Automate > Web Photo Gallery in Photoshop.

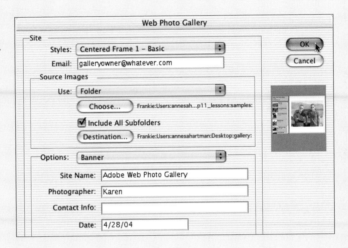

figure | 11-35

Example of a web photo gallery viewed through a browser window.

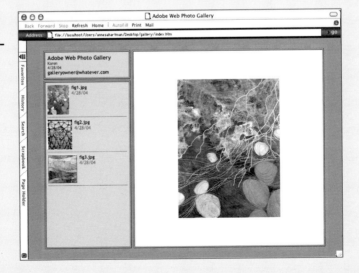

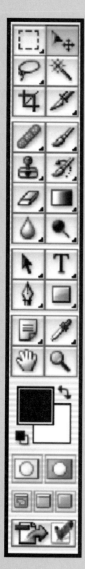

index

index